ANCIENT WISDOM FOR A NEW AGE

ANCIENT WISDOM FOR A NEW AGE

A Practical Guide for Spiritual Growth

Terry Hunt and Paul Benedict

TWINSTAR
nexus

Twin Star Nexus — Las Vegas

Copyright 2012 by Terry Hunt and Paul Benedict

Book design by Paul Rippens
Cover design by Paul Rippens

The Messenger was painted by Nicholas Roerich in 1922
as a tribute to Helena Blavatsky.

ISBN 978-0-9856256-1-0 Hardcover
ISBN 978-0-9856256-0-3 Softcover

CIP data:

Hunt, Terry.
    Ancient wisdom for a new age : a practical guide for spiritual growth / Terry Hunt and Paul Benedict.
        p. cm.
    Includes bibliographical references and index.
    ISBN 978-0-9856256-1-0

1. Spiritual life. 2. Spirituality. 3. Yoga. 4. Consciousness – Religious aspects. I. Title. II. Benedict, Paul.

BL624.H86
204 – dc23

There is a road, steep and thorny,
beset with perils of every kind,
but yet a road,
and it leads to the very heart of the Universe.

I can tell you how to find those
who will show you the secret gateway
that opens inward only, and closes fast
behind the neophyte for evermore.

There is no danger
that dauntless courage cannot conquer;
there is no trial
that spotless purity cannot pass through;
there is no difficulty
that strong intellect cannot surmount.

For those who win onwards
there is reward past all telling—
the power to bless and save humanity;
for those who fail,
there are other lives
in which success may come.

— H.P. Blavatsky

CONTENTS

ACKNOWLEDGMENTS

A book of this nature requires help of various types. We are deeply grateful for all who provided it. To Eugene Godina, we are thankful for his enduring encouragement. His support was critical in the making of this book.

Paul Rippens has been immensely helpful and supportive. We appreciate his talents in graphic arts and his kind and generous endeavors to make the dream a reality.

Janet Kerschner, archivist for the Olcott Library and Research Center, provided much-needed help and expert guidance during the process.

Stephanie and Michael Lamb, Rhonda Hunt-Del Bene, and Brian Armstrong were instrumental throughout the process of writing and revising, providing help from start to finish.

Fred Fernandez-Coll offered to translate the book into Spanish before the first word was written. We are very grateful for his faith in the project and his dedication to the task of translation.

Much help was received from teachers in other realms of consciousness. To those unseen and unnamed individuals we are profoundly grateful.

INTRODUCTION

There is nothing new in this book. In fact, most of the information in it comes from publications that have been available for many years, in some cases more than a hundred. Although the information is not new, there is something different about this book—the approach. Although most of the books that provided information for this one contain an impressive amount, few include many practical suggestions for applying that information in our everyday lives, especially in the twenty-first century.

There is something for everyone in this book, provided the reader has an open mind and is willing to learn a new way of looking at life. If you are searching for the key to happiness, you will not find it here; it doesn't exist. You will find instead the formula for contentment and even the key to eternal life, but be forewarned—the cost is high and it will not bring you fame or fortune.

If you are looking for three easy steps to enlightenment, you will have to look elsewhere. If you are impatient in your desire for spiritual growth, you will meet only with frustration. If, on the other hand, you are willing to take it one step at a time and move steadily and silently forward in your quest for understanding, then you are the type of student who will profit most from this material.

Every creature in the world—whether a morning glory, a hummingbird, a tiger, or a human—has only one goal, to understand how life works. The sorrow and suffering we experience occur because we do not yet understand, and if we understand the concepts, we have not yet applied them in our life.

We do not claim to have all the answers, and we ourselves do not understand perfectly all the concepts presented in this book. However, we have made a concerted effort to be as accurate as possible and to be honest in our presentation. We have built on the foundations of others who have gone before us. New teachers will come along who will bring more accurate and more useful information than we currently have.

Not everyone will understand or agree with everything we teach. That is how it should be. Focus on those things which touch your heart and ring true. Leave aside anything you don't understand or with which you disagree.

Be tolerant of your fellow travelers on the path. It is not an easy path to tread, and it is our responsibility to inspire and assist wherever we can, especially when our brothers fall. Be kind to yourself when you fail to live up to your highest potential. Each time you stumble, pick yourself up and move onward, never wavering in your determination to reach the goal.

Chapter 1

OUR SPIRITUAL JOURNEY

> As a hawk or an eagle, having soared high
> in the air, wings its way back to its resting
> place, being so fatigued, so does the soul,
> having experienced the phenomenal,
> return into itself where it can sleep beyond
> all desires, beyond all dreams.
>
> — *Brihadāranyaka Upanishad*

THE PRODIGAL SON

Once upon a time, in a land far, far away, there lived a
very wealthy family. They owned lots of land and animals,
and storerooms filled with gold, silver, and jewels of great
value. There were many servants to care for the family's
vast holdings.

One day, the youngest son came to his father and said, "Father, I've been thinking. I've spent my entire life here at home. I have everything I could possibly want in life, but I feel like something is lacking. There is an entire world out there I have never seen. I would like to go on a journey to see what's there and what I've been missing. But I will need some money to pay for it. Would you be willing to give me enough so I can set out on this adventure?

The father, being very wise, knew the experience his son would gain by going out into the world would be something he could never get at home.

"My son, I will do what you have asked," he said. "I will give you your share of the family fortune to help you in your adventure. Go and experience all that is out there. It will make you a stronger and wiser person. We will miss you greatly and will think about you every day. If you decide to come back, you will be welcomed with open arms."

So the son set out with his share of the family fortune. Each time he came to a new town or village, he made new friends and entertained them by financing wild and lavish parties. He experienced the best things life had to offer and reveled in newfound pleasures and desires. Each time he became bored with one set of friends, he would set out again, meet new friends, and have new experiences until he was far from home and his former life was only a distant memory.

One day he reached into his pocket for money to pay for his dinner and discovered there was nothing. He had spent his entire fortune and was now destitute.

"What shall I do?" he thought, "I've never had to work a day in my life. I don't even know how to work."

Everywhere he went, he offered to work in exchange for food, but no one wanted to hire someone of his age who had never worked before. Finally, he managed to get a job feeding a herd of pigs. It was stinky work, but he had no other choice, so he learned to tolerate the hard labor and awful smells. There were days when he had no food and his belly grumbled; he would gladly have eaten the swill he was doling out to the pigs.

One night he had a dream. In this dream, he saw his family home, his parents and brothers, and saw how much they missed him. He had almost forgotten about them, it had been so long since he went away. When he awoke, his eyes were wet with tears. Then and there, he made up his mind to return home, regardless of the reception he might receive.

Slowly he retraced his steps, often passing through the same villages and towns he had seen before. At times he encountered the same people who had been his friends, but they did not seem to recognize him. He was no longer the handsome, rich young man they had known, and they had no time for someone who was poor.

At times he slept in the woods, surrounded by howling wolves and other creatures in the night. But he wasn't afraid. He had plenty of experience in the ways of the world and knew how to protect himself from wild animals.

One day, after many months of traveling, he finally recognized the border of the family property. His heart pounded with anticipation and fear as he walked toward the home he had left so many years before. Someone was coming to meet him and he recognized his father whom he hadn't seen in many years. His father embraced him for a long time and, turning to one of the servants, said, "Go and kill the fattest calf we have, and prepare a feast for my son."

Upon hearing this, the older son became angry. "I can't believe this," he said. This good-for-nothing son of yours squandered his share of our family's fortune and has returned with nothing to show for it. I stayed here all the time and you never made a feast like that for me. This is so unfair."

His father turned to him without the slightest sign of irritation and said, "I have always appreciated what you have done and you are very precious to me, but my son, who was gone, has returned; it is fitting and proper that we should rejoice and welcome him."

Which of these sons was best suited to manage his father's estate when the time came to turn it over to a family member? The father, being wise, recognized the immense value of the experience his younger son had gained. Here was someone who understood the problems of life and could appreciate the difficulties of people who were not as wealthy as they were. He could relate to and appreciate the animals which were a large part of the family fortune. He had overcome serious difficulties and learned valuable life lessons while away from home. This was someone he could trust to govern his estate with care and consideration for all involved, both humans and animals, and who would be his trusted successor.

MIGRATIONS

There are some amazing facts with regard to animal migration. The monarch butterfly lives in northern latitudes during the summer but must migrate to warmer climates in the southwestern United States or Mexico when winter comes. What is unusual about this creature is that no individual butterfly makes the entire migratory journey. The lifespan of a monarch butterfly is so short that multiple generations are born and die during the trip. How does a flock of butterflies, none of which has ever completed the entire journey, find the way unerringly? This is one of the great mysteries of nature. Perhaps the consciousness in a dying butterfly transfers into the grub that will become a new monarch caterpillar.

The Arctic tern holds the world record for long distance migration. Each year, the terns complete a round-trip journey from the Arctic to the Antarctic and back. Each little bird flies more than 44,000 miles each year, and he doesn't even receive frequent flier miles. Since the Arctic tern can live more than 30 years, it flies over 1.3 million miles in its lifetime, more than the equivalent of three trips to the moon and back.

We too are on a great migration. We too left our ancestral home long, long ago to gain experience in the world. We too are making our way back home, in many cases with only a faint memory of where it is we are going and how to get there.

OUR SPIRITUAL JOURNEY

Our migration is even more incredible than those mentioned above. We started out eons ago from our ancestral spiritual home. Since that time, the consciousness which currently uses our human body has passed through innumerable transformations, experiencing untold levels of consciousness. On the outbound portion of the journey, we experienced not only various levels of existence between the highest spiritual and the densest physical, but we also experienced consciousness in various forms— mineral, vegetable, animal, and now human. Keep in mind that when we talk of forms, they are not necessarily physical forms. Forms can also exist in matter that is less dense than the physical, as we will see later.

During millions of years in the mineral kingdom, this consciousness experienced mostly a sense of pressure. The minerals that exist on our planet currently endure not only tremendous pressure, but also extremely high temperatures, in many cases so intense that the chemical bonds are changed. Carbon atoms, through great pressure and heat, are transformed into diamonds. This amazing transformation is symbolic of an even greater transformation that takes place over eons of time. The consciousness that currently is experiencing life through human physical bodies on earth experienced the equivalent of the mineral stage eons ago, in a form that may have been very different from the current mineral kingdom.

The experience gained in the mineral kingdom is small in comparison to other kingdoms. Besides heat and pressure, minerals can experience sunlight, wind, and rain when they happen to be at the surface of the planet. This is the beginning of our experience with physical sensation, feeling. The experience of our consciousness in the mineral kingdom was mostly a vague sense of existence and a feeling of pressure. The finest examples of our mineral kingdom are in the form of precious and semi-precious stones—diamonds, rubies, sapphires, and emeralds, among others.

The next stage of consciousness carried us through various experiences in the vegetable kingdom. In terms of earth time, the period we are referring to as the mineral and plant stages are so many ages ago as to be meaningless in our system of time measurement. At any rate, time cannot be measured on other levels of existence the way it is measured in the physical world.

Early plants on this physical earth were single-celled plants similar to algae. These in turn began to develop into more complicated versions and finally migrated to live on land. The first land plants, which appeared about 480 million years ago, were similar to modern liverworts and mosses. They had no system for conducting water and still had to remain close to water sources.

Once vascular systems developed in plants, they could live farther from a water source. They developed spores as a method of propagation. Woody branching plants later appeared, and small shrub-like trees developed. Over long periods of time, these developed into the magnificent deciduous and evergreen forests we know. Eventually, plants began to produce seeds, and true flowering plants were among the last to develop, as a result of the appearance of bees and other insects that help with the pollination process. Flowers, together with large magnificent trees, represent the culmination of the plant kingdom. The most advanced members of the plant kingdom have a close relationship with members of the animal kingdom, providing nesting sites and food for many birds, mammals, and insects. Plants are able to absorb minerals directly from the earth through the root systems they have developed.

What is the current experience in the plant kingdom? Plants have learned survival techniques, reproduction methods, and adaptation to weather conditions, climate changes, and seasonal variations. Plants produce chemical pheromones to attract pollinating insects and even use them as a means of communicating with each other. They have learned a sense of community and connectedness. The plant kingdom experiences birth, growth, reproduction, decay, and death. It has been said that the plant kingdom is the most successful of the kingdoms on earth. We depend on plants' ability to transform the energy of the sun into food through photosynthesis. No animal or human life could exist in physical form without plants.

Once the indwelling life had reached the maximum level of consciousness in the plant kingdom, it began the transition into the animal kingdom. New incoming life took up the bottom ranks of the plant kingdom, and the others shifted upward to inhabit the more complex life forms constantly being created. This is one of the laws of nature—as growth and spiritual development take place, the one that initiated the growth moves up in the scale and automatically brings up others behind it. As Jesus said, "I, if I be lifted up, shall draw all men unto me." Nature never reinvents the wheel. This is the same method that has been used for eons in other systems besides our own. While the process seems incredibly slow, requiring billions or trillions of years, we know that the concepts of time and space are really illusions. They seem real to us here on earth, but in other realms of consciousness they are unknown.

The animal kingdom created even more complex forms for the indwelling life to use in experiencing the outside world. Our consciousness exists not only on the physical plane but on other planes of experience as well, with subtler vibrational rates than we experience in the physical world. As we gain a stronger hold on the coarser vibrations of the physical plane, we lose awareness of the higher frequencies. This should not be a cause of concern, however. It is the way nature works. We will regain awareness at those higher levels once we have achieved the experience we need at this lower level of consciousness. Then we begin the conscious re-entry process of returning to the Source.

It is easy to marvel at the intricacies of the animal kingdom. The varieties of forms and their instincts and habits seem miraculous to us. How did creatures that developed from reptiles gain the ability to fly? How do animals migrate unerringly each year over thousands of miles? Considering the variety of animals, both extinct and still in existence, which developed over millions of years, nature is stunning in its abilities. The giant dinosaurs and enormous sea creatures that inhabited the earth at one time still inspire wonder and admiration in children and adults alike.

THE SPIRITUAL HIERARCHY

The question of whether this development proceeds on its own through natural selection and random chance, or whether there is divine intervention, has been a debate for many years. Although nature is marvelous in its own abilities, it also includes a Spiritual Hierarchy which oversees the process. This Spiritual Hierarchy consists of a large variety of individuals, most of them far in advance of us. Every member of this Hierarchy has passed through, or will pass through, the stage of human consciousness. The Hierarchy has no need to resort to "miraculous" methods of creation in the various realms. The "miracles" they use consist of using the laws of nature, which they follow scrupulously. This is the meaning of the saying "God geometrizes." Everything develops according to natural law, with the caring oversight of those who are creating it.

What is learned during the sojourn in the animal kingdom? Animals have learned a lot, it turns out. They learned about locomotion—the ability to swim, walk or fly, and to move about voluntarily. They experience sex and the pleasure associated with it. They also have learned jealousy and the determination to fend off others whose intention is to take away one's mate or mates. One of the things learned is a strong sense of self-identity, the ego. The personal ego is fairly weak in animals that function as a cohesive group, such as a school of fish or a flock of birds, but as the consciousness moves up the scale of animal evolution, the ego becomes stronger. The alpha male and alpha female come into being and the famous "pecking order" is established. This developed naturally as a means of ensuring that the strongest animals would have the greatest chance of survival and of reproducing. By this means, the group as a whole would have a better chance of survival. We too will regain this sense of "group consciousness," where each member of the group has access to all the knowledge and experience of other group members. For some advanced individuals, this is already beginning to occur. For others, it will be in the far distant future.

How does a gazelle born on the African savanna learn within a few hours not only how to walk, but to run? Obviously, this ability is crucial to the survival of the species, but that doesn't explain how it can happen. Whether we are talking about a geranium, a monarch butterfly, a gazelle or a human, we are all connected on various levels to all creatures, but especially to those of our own species, and particularly to that distinct group which is traveling together with us in our spiritual journey. The members of this latter group are all at approximately the same level of advancement.

Animals have learned to nurture and care for their offspring, often for long periods of time. They form families and communities, sometimes enormous in size. They have a strong sense of belonging to a group, and that forms a major part of their identity. Separation from the group, resulting in a sense of isolation, is often the worst fate an animal can experience.

They have also learned the fight-or-flight instinct, as well as many other emotions: fear, anger, jealousy, revenge, affection, and contentment. They have learned to fight for their own survival, to protect the family members carrying their genes, and look out for the welfare of the flock or herd to which they belong. Each member has to work in conjunction with the rest of the community. Insubordination and any activities that work against the welfare of the community are not tolerated. Those who engage in this behavior are punished and sometimes killed. The welfare of the group is far more important than the desires of any one individual.

Did we actually go through all the levels of consciousness you described?

You as an individual did not. However, the consciousness which currently is operating in your human body, and more importantly in your human soul, has traversed all these various levels of consciousness. Although it may be somewhat difficult to comprehend, they were not always in the physical realm. There are other levels of consciousness which we will discuss in chapter 2. The nature of Spirit is growth and that occurs through expansion of consciousness. As an ancient Kabalistic maxim says, "The breath (ātma) becomes a stone; the stone, a plant; the plant, an animal; the animal, a man; the man, a spirit; and the spirit, a god."

It is almost impossible to conceive of something existing only on the plane of emotions or of thought, with no corresponding physical form, but that is what occurs. The difficulty arises because of our identification with things in their physical forms. Once we re-train ourselves to see everything as energy fields and patterns of interconnecting energy, it makes far more sense. We can, however, simply recognize that each unit of spiritual energy must experience all levels of consciousness, beginning at the ground floor. This transformation, as stated before, requires eons of time, but there is no need to worry. We have all the time necessary, and besides, there is no past or future, only the Eternal Now.

It behooves us to examine carefully the nature of the animal kingdom. Why? Because the bodies we currently inhabit were developed from that kingdom and carry within them many of the instincts that were developed during the animal phase of development. We still have a lot of animal nature within us. We have only to observe the herd instinct of many people and the way ethnic and religious groups try to force their members to comply with their group standards of conduct. There are cultures even today where certain activities not in compliance with their group standards are punishable by death.

I know a lot of people who have retained a lot of animal characteristics, like aggression, mistrust, and greed.

In some ways we have not progressed far from our animal roots, but in other ways we have. The one great difference between animal consciousness and human consciousness is that our mind is developed far beyond that of the animal. In fact, that is the most important feature that sets us apart from them—the ability to think in complex patterns, to plan and execute those plans, to scheme and build. We have free will, the ability to make choices and to affect our own destiny, something that does not exist in any of the lower kingdoms. This free will brings with it an added responsibility. Since we no longer rely simply on natural instinct, but have a hand in determining how we live and what we do with this marvelous ability to think, we are now responsible for our choices. We have entered the realm of karma, something which does not affect the animal kingdom, the plant kingdom, or the mineral kingdom, at least not in the same way it affects the human kingdom. We are now responsible for all our thoughts, emotions, and actions.

Karma is the result of having acquired the status of co-creator. We now have the ability to create by using our thinking abilities. An artist conceives the image in his mind before it appears on canvas or in stone. The writer creates the phrase or concept in his mind before it is ever set down in writing. With added ability comes added responsibility. Karma is the natural law that connects every creative action with the result it produces. The cause produces an effect. We, the creators of the cause, have also created the effect, even when we do not see it immediately. Karma, seen from one perspective, keeps a gentle, and sometimes not so gentle, pressure on us, guiding us always in the same direction that natural law works. The farther we get out of line with natural law, the more intense the pressure to turn us back in the right direction.

PHYSICAL EVOLUTION vs. EVOLUTION OF CONSCIOUSNESS

The evolutionary theories of science focus on a very limited aspect of evolution, the physical. In fact, there are two different types of evolution going on at all times—evolution of consciousness and evolution of form. These two together comprise the evolution of the indwelling spirit. The forms that are continually evolving are nothing more than instruments to provide vehicles of experience for the indwelling spirit and for the constantly evolving consciousness. At this stage of our spiritual evolution, we are so deeply immersed in the physical condition—due to the stage of mind development we have achieved—that we are barely in touch with the higher aspects of our being. It is our attachment to form and the fact that we have lost the connection to our spiritual nature that cause pain and suffering in life.

What animals represent the culmination of animal consciousness? Elephants, horses, dogs, cats, certain parrots, apes, dolphins, and whales. Many of these, through domestication, have come into very close contact with humans. This is an important phase of their development, and we have a tremendous responsibility toward the evolving consciousness within these forms.

Does that mean some of these more developed animals will become humans in a future incarnation?

It does, but not right away. At the current stage of the evolutionary process, it would cause problems to have more individuals coming in at the lowest levels of human development. The necessary conditions do not currently exist for them to have a meaningful existence, and their presence would present difficulties to those who are already somewhat advanced in human experience. We have our hands full as it is, without additional difficulties to deal with.

Karma, as such, does not affect members of the mineral, plant, and animal kingdoms. They are simply following the laws of nature by responding to instinct. All minerals are perfect minerals. They are naturally developing over billions of years through the effect of natural law. Plants too are perfect plants. They follow obediently the natural flow of the universe and fulfill their role perfectly. Most animals also are perfect animals. Even activities which may make us squeamish, such as watching an animal of prey select, kill, and eat other animals, are all part of the natural process. Very few animals stray from this process; most of those who do have been influenced by their contact with humans and are imitating human behavior. We are all familiar with tales of rogue elephants who go on a rampage after years of being mistreated, and pets who "punish" their owners when they feel they are neglected or treated unfairly.

The human kingdom is the most advanced that the average person is aware of on this planet, and because of that, we have for long ages considered that all the other kingdoms—mineral, plant, and animal—are there for us to use in any way we desire. Through lack of understanding, we are sadly unaware of the spirit which dwells in all life forms, even the mineral. It is time for humans to recognize the responsibility we have for other life forms by honoring the spiritual life in all of nature.

Once the indwelling consciousness takes up residence in human form, a tremendous change takes place. The Ancient Wisdom teaches us that, upon reaching the level of human consciousness, there is an additional outpouring of Spirit which creates the human soul. We humans are special because of this guiding principle in our lives. For long ages we have barely been aware of its existence. One of the purposes of this book is to learn more about the human soul and how we can increase contact with it, opening up new realms of spiritual development.

What is the nature of this great migration we are on? What is our current role, and what can we expect in future stages of spiritual development? The purpose of this book is to explain as clearly as possible where we are currently in the scheme of spiritual development, what our state of consciousness will be in the future, and what steps we can take now to accelerate the process.

Chapter 2

THE HUMAN EXPERIENCE

Lead us, O Lord, from darkness to
light; from the unreal to the real;
from death to immortality.

—*Brihadāranyaka Upanishad I*

THE MAGIC TOY

Once upon a time, there was a little child. He had learned
how to crawl, and spent each day exploring and investi-
gating his surroundings, learning something new with
each adventure. Sometimes he would laugh in delight at
the slightest new discovery. At other times he was cranky

and fretful, bored with what he already had and antici-
pating his next adventure.

One day, a god appeared before him, dangling a glittering
object from a string. It was nothing more than a carved
piece of wood covered with tiny bits of mirrored glass, but
when twirled in the sunlight by the god, it appeared to
this child to be the most exciting object he had ever seen.
Reflected light from the many mirrored surfaces danced
on the walls and ceiling in a sparkling, enchanting display.
The child was mesmerized. Intrigued by this magical object, he knew he could not live without it. Surely this was
the most precious thing that had ever existed, and he
must obtain it at any cost.

But how could he get it? It was dangling just beyond the
grasp of his chubby little hand. Time and again he tried to
grab it, but the elusive object of his desire remained out of
reach, resulting in even more determination to get it.

"I know," he thought in his little mind, "I will cry and
show how unhappy I am. Surely the owner of this precious object will have compassion, take pity on me, and
give it to me when he sees how much I want it."

He let out the most pitiful cry he had ever sent out in his
life, certain this would touch the heart of this god and he
would get his wish. But no, the heartless god was un-
moved by his sad lament and the child displayed his dis-
pleasure at having failed to get his way by turning his back
and sulking.

"There must be some way," he thought, and he began to
scheme, trying to plan a way to get his wish. "I know there

are people who can stand up and walk," he thought, "and that always makes them taller." He had tried to do it himself, but it was an impossible task, and he had given up on his previous tentative efforts to learn this skill. Now, prodded by the need to own this magical object, he was determined to learn how to walk or die in the attempt.

Again and again, he pushed himself up with his arms and tried to balance on his wobbly legs. Again and again he fell, sometimes so hard it made him cry out in pain. But this only strengthened his resolve to learn this new skill. Each attempt brought a little more confidence. Each time he tried, he made note of what seemed to work and at what point in the process he was failing. Each time he tried, he came a little closer to mastering this ability to stand up and walk.

One day when he awoke, he somehow knew this would be the day. Throughout the many failed attempts, his little legs had become stronger, and his sense of balance had improved. Each failed attempt had added a little bit to his storehouse of knowledge and experience.

Focusing all his willpower on his legs, he pushed himself up with his little arms. Lo and behold, he was tottering on two legs. At first he was surprised, and smiled, pleased with himself. Tentatively, he took one tiny step. His body began to sway, but he quickly called on his experience from other attempts in order to regain his balance. Once the trembling stopped, he took another step, and another. A cry of joy and pride escaped his lips. He could walk!

All this time, his eyes had never left the glittering object. Now there was nothing that could stop him from getting

The Human
Experience

23

it. Soon it would be his, and he would be the happiest child in the world.

Step by step, he advanced toward his goal, and with great confidence reached up to grasp the elusive prize. Now it was his, and no one could take it away from him. He clasped it firmly in his hands, intent on protecting it with his very life.

His first thought upon awakening each day was to assure himself the precious possession was still there. For hours, he delighted in playing with it in the sunlight and laughed with glee, knowing he had earned this incredible prize.

As days passed, and his knowledge of worldly things increased, he was stunned one day to realize he had been tricked. He was shocked to realize that this, the object of his greatest desires, was nothing more than bits of broken mirror glued to a piece of wood. This magical object, which he had been sure was the most precious object in the world, was nothing more than a worthless trinket. In a fit of anger, he threw it on the floor and smashed it to bits.

THE MAGIC TOYS IN OUR LIVES

Do we have any magic toys in our own lives? We do. They are called money, power, trophy spouses, relationships, cars, boats, businesses, houses, titles and many other names. Anything that includes a sense of desire when we don't have it is a magic toy for us. Whenever there is a sense of pride in "possessing" something or someone, it is a matter of wanting to enhance our ego. When desire is part of a personal wish for something, there is an element of emotion involved. Emotion is the controlling factor in the lives of most people, and we will examine it later in greater detail. In many cases, our desire for things is based on a wish to flaunt them before others and brag about what we have attained. These magical toys are our ego enhancers.

The universe is very clever. From the vantage point of our original spiritual home, there was not much of interest here on the physical plane that would entice us to leave our comfortable surroundings and jump into something we at least suspected would be more difficult than where we were. So the universe dangled shiny, glittering objects before us, tempting us to experience the "underworld." In Greek mythology, the gods are sometimes enticed to leave their heavenly abode and descend to the underworld of the physical realm because they have fallen in love with a human. This human is the magic toy that enticed them to leave their world for ours.

Over vast periods of time, the magic toys of the physical world seem to be all that we have. Each time we obtain one of our desires, there is a period of happiness, and we are anxious to show others how delighted we are. But after a time, the happiness subsides, and we are left in a state of boredom or unhappiness. We now look for a new object. Surely this will be the one that brings us eternal happiness.

There is no such thing as eternal happiness as long as it involves emotion. The allure in the process is the drama involved—the setting of a goal, planning and scheming to obtain it, and then announcing to the world that we have achieved our goal. We bask in the warmth of the attention we attract and the envy and jealousy we incite in others. We are dismayed when the attention fades, and we then set about to find another object to fulfill our desires.

THE NATURE OF THE SOUL

Most people believe they have a soul. Ancient teachings often refer to our being composed of spirit and body. The apostle Paul says we are comprised of body, soul, and spirit. This is an accurate statement, but the concept can be further divided into more categories which help us better analyze what we are made of. Understanding the human constitution is necessary in learning how to achieve the goal of returning to the Source.

"Nosce te ipsum" or "Know thyself," is a phrase few people understand. Without knowledge of human psychology, we can't expect to go far in our spiritual quest. We are not talking only about modern psychology, which has a long way to go in understanding humans. There is much more information available about human nature, but it is not something that can be proved to the academic community. Some of its members recognize the value of these teachings, but academia has its standards and cannot accept anything that is not widely accepted among its most prestigious members.

We cannot hope to know ourselves until we have learned to be scrupulously honest. Few people are honest, even with themselves. You may be shocked to realize that you are not only dishonest with others, but with yourself as well. This is not to say that there are no honest people in the world, but the saying "An honest man is hard to find" is not an idle phrase.

What do we mean by being honest with ourselves? We often are tempted to "put a spin on things," to twist the truth to suit the needs of our ego in order to make us look good. This is dishonest. We learn to do it as little children, lying to our parents to save face. "Did you break that vase?" "No Mommy, it fell off the table." As children, we are convinced our parents won't see through the lies. It is childish, but worse than that, most people continue the pattern of lying into their adult years. "Did you have an affair with that woman?" "No, I did not."

The ego insists on looking good and is embarrassed if it doesn't look good or is caught in a lie. When it is obvious we are lying, we become angry and adamantly insist on our innocence. "How dare you accuse me of that? I can't believe you think I would do something like that!" Anger is a common method of making people back off when we want to protect our ego. It is like brandishing a flame thrower, and saying, "You had better back off if you don't want to get hurt!"

It is very difficult to work effectively with people who lie and use intense anger as a method of manipulating others. The person who lies, even in little things, cannot make much spiritual progress. How can you see clearly when you purposely try to keep things muddled and unclear in order to camouflage the lying?

Take the brightest flashlight you can find, metaphorically speaking, and shine it in all the dark corners of your being. Don't be afraid of what it might bring out into the light of day. Regardless of how "bad" or how embarrassing the thing that is brought out, accept it as it is, with no reaction, without trying to make it look different. It is far better to say, "Wow, I never realized how much anger and resentment I have been harboring," than to continue ignoring it, pretending it doesn't exist. Only then can you really begin to work on your character.

We often speak about spirit and matter as if they were two different things. They are not. All matter is part of spirit. There is not one atom in our world, either physical or in other realms, that can be considered separate from spirit. The concept of matter originates when spirit first manifests by creating new levels through which consciousness can gain experience. It involves creating many different levels, each with a different vibrational frequency. This concept is an important factor in understanding the principles we present in this book. There is no point along this continuum where you can say "At this point matter ceases and spirit begins." It is just that, an uninterrupted continuum. We call anything that is manifested by spirit "matter," but matter is still a form of spirit. It is true that we are divine beings, not because we have Divinity within us, but because we are an integral part of Divine Spirit. We are Divinity itself.

Science is correct in stating that everything is energy or waveforms. The book in front of us which seems completely solid is, in fact, an illusion. It is a specific type of energy frequency which other forms manifesting the same frequency perceive as being solid. Our physical body is an illusion interacting with another illusion, the book in front of us. If you don't believe this, think about your dreams. Have you ever dreamed about driving a car or walking? We are convinced that we experience a solid world in our dreams, but there is nothing solid about it. There is a clue in this to the nature of our "physical" existence.

THE LEVELS OF CONSCIOUSNESS

The most spiritual part of the human being can be divided into ātma and buddhi. These two Sanskrit terms describe the very highest vibrational frequencies within us. Ātma is Spirit itself in manifestation. From our point of view, where we currently operate, it appears to be our spiritual self. At its own level, it does not perceive individuality at all, but oneness with all things in manifestation.

Buddha means "awake" or "enlightened." Gautama Buddha was the first of our human evolution to attain Buddhahood, an advanced level of consciousness. It is the spiritual goal of all humans to become enlightened, to awaken spiritually to new levels of consciousness. When we recognize that, the path before us becomes clear. Once we are clear about our goal, our future progress is certain because there is nothing to cloud our vision.

It is far better to apply in our lives what we have already learned before accumulating more information. We think that all we need to do is read the right book, attend the right class or workshop, and we will have everything we need to know. But understanding life doesn't work that way. Knowledge is only a small part of what is required. The other part is wisdom, that intuitive understanding that comes through contemplation and "sorting things out." It seems a simple concept, and it is, but we are inclined to follow old patterns even when they don't produce results. Einstein's definition of insanity is this—"doing the same thing over and over again and expecting different results."

Lower in the scale of vibrational frequency is the realm of mental activity. In Sanskrit, the word for mind is "manas," and it is from this word that we get the English word "man," the being with a mind. The mind is what sets us apart from animals, this and the fact that we have a human soul. In fact, the human soul exists on the very highest levels of the mental realm.

We often speak of "planes" of existence, and this sometimes causes confusion. We tend to visualize them as different levels in a bookcase, one above the other. This concept works to some extent, but we must keep in mind that they are not locations, but states of consciousness. For this reason, we will often use the word "realm" when referring to these states of consciousness instead of "plane." These realms interpenetrate each other to a certain extent, and each realm has a different range of vibratory rates.

We can make use of all information on human psychology available through academic means, but we can also learn from those who have wisdom, and we ourselves can learn to observe carefully, thus learning from our own observations. The key to this type of knowledge is to see clearly, without the distractions the mind, impelled by desire, is constantly parading before us. We can learn how to do this, and many of the concepts and practices necessary to reach this state of enlightenment are contained in this book.

THE HUMAN CONSTITUTION

The diagrams on the following two pages provide a visual aid to understanding the levels of consciousness we have discussed. The first one graphically indicates the fact that spirit and matter are a continuum and that there is no point along this gradient where one could say that spirit ends and matter begins. Matter *is* spirit. In the second diagram we see that we can indicate intermediate steps in this vast continuum. Thus, St. Paul speaks of body, soul, and spirit as three aspects of the nature of man.

The third diagram shows the human constitution in its various levels of consciousness, with the physical as the most dense and ātma as the most spiritual of the human constitution. This is only one variation of a number of different presentations, and not all teachers use the same delineations, although the general concepts remain consistent.

The final diagram shows the various planes or realms of consciousness in our solar system. All these realms taken together represent only a small portion of the levels of consciousness in the cosmos. The upper realms of our own solar system are inconceivable to humans, and it is useless to speculate on those which lie beyond.

SPIRIT – MATTER
CONTINUUM

BODY – SOUL – SPIRIT

Spirit

Matter

Spirit

Soul

Body

THE HUMAN CONSTITUTION		THE PLANES OF OUR SOLAR SYSTEM
Ātma		Divine
Buddhi	Buddhi-Manas	Monadic
Higher Manas (Higher Mental)		Ātmic
Lower Manas (Lower Mental)	Kāma-Manas	Buddhic
Astral (Emotional)		Mental
Prāna (Life Force)		Astral
Physical		Physical

Chapter 3

THE HUMAN SOUL

To believe without knowing is
weakness. To believe because one
knows is power.

— Eliphas Lévi

FAITH

"Can anyone in the class tell us what faith is?" the Sunday
school teacher asked.

"I can!" shouted Tommy. "It's the ability to believe in
something you know ain't true."

Unfortunately, this definition is often accurate. We believe in something because someone told us it was true or that we would be punished if we didn't believe it. It is repeated thousands of times and becomes tradition. Because we have no reason to disbelieve it, it is easier to go along with the crowd and "believe in things we know ain't true."

Is there any place for faith in our lives, or must we rely only on things that can be scientifically proven?

There is room for faith, provided we have a better understanding of what faith is. Every word has a different meaning for each person who uses it. The beauty is that we get to define the meaning we want to associate with a word. Sometimes we have to explain to others what we mean, and this is the case with faith.

Faith, to our way of thinking, is belief in the concepts or teachings of someone in whom we have great trust, or something that "sounds true." It seems plausible. We may choose to adopt this teaching temporarily on faith and apply it in our lives until such time as we have sufficient experience to prove it to ourselves. At that point, it is no longer a belief, but knowledge, because we have personal experience and proof that the concept or principle works.

Of course, there may come a time when we find that what we previously accepted on faith is not true, or perhaps only partially true. Then, we must be willing to discard the concept or revise our understanding to conform to our experience. If we continue to believe in something without having proved its worth, it is a superstition. For too many people, their beliefs are firmly entrenched; they are an integral part of their self-identity, their ego. Egos are extremely fragile and must constantly be reinforced. One way we do this is by associating with others who have the same beliefs we do. Surely if ten million people have the same belief, it must be true.

For some of us, our beliefs are cast in concrete, never to be changed. This attitude is necessary and serves a useful function in the earlier stages of spiritual transformation, but there comes a time when the old ways cease to be effective and we are forced, often against our will, to adopt a new system of beliefs, one which is more useful at our current level of spiritual understanding.

Don't we have to be able to prove it to others before we can switch from believing to knowing? That's what the scientific method requires.

It makes no difference whether or not you can prove it to others. There are principles or laws of nature which are understood only by relatively few people, and you may be one of them. Why must you prove it to everyone else? If it is a principle that works, you adopt it in your everyday interactions with people. When they see there is something different about you, something they want to have in their own lives, they may ask about it. Then you can explain the principle, how you proved it for yourself, and allow them the opportunity to adopt a new belief because of their respect for you and the way you interact with others.

The result will depend on whether or not they take the trouble to prove it for themselves. We are practicing non-judgment when we allow each individual to progress at his own rate and experience no irritability if he doesn't meet our expectations.

Once he has used the principle long enough to prove it for himself, it is no longer a belief, but a truth. This is how new understanding of natural law is transmitted from one person to another until it becomes an integral part of human understanding.

Of utmost importance is being open-minded. We must constantly refine our concepts of what is true. If, at any time, we are convinced we know all that is true and are unwilling to expand or revise our conception of truth, we have closed ourselves off to further spiritual progress and to gaining new levels of consciousness.

TRUTH AND ABSOLUTE TRUTH

Is there such a thing as Absolute Truth?

There is. It is at the level of the Absolute, or Sat in Sanskrit. Sat simply means "that" because the Absolute has no qualities.

What is Sat, or the Absolute?

It cannot be defined. We can only say what it is not. It is incomprehensible, indefinable, immeasurable, inconceivable, and indivisible. We cannot even say that it exists. We might say it is the potential for existence, but even that would not be completely accurate. It is what "was" before anything existed. You can only conceive of something you can observe. How can you observe something when there is no duality, no polarity?

Remember that the Absolute cannot be understood. The best we can do is recognize there is such a thing and that Absolute Truth is at that level. At our level of consciousness and for a long time to come, we can understand only relative truths. We are "ascending toward" Absolute Truth. We do this by a long, continuous series of awakenings, expansions of consciousness. Once we merge again with the Absolute, we cease to exist as anything separate from it until such time as another period of manifestation takes place. This act of merging again with the Absolute has been poetically referred to by Sir Edwin Arnold as the dewdrop slipping into the shining sea. The dewdrop does not lose its identity. Instead, it is now one with the Absolute. It *is* the Absolute.

ENLIGHTENMENT

It is important to realize we do not have complete understanding. With each awakening, we see things differently, and there must be a period of assimilation. We apply the understanding that comes with that awakening by observing with new eyes and by acting in a different manner in our everyday lives.

You speak of enlightenment and "awakenings." Can you expand a little on this?

Our spiritual progress consists of a series of expansions into new realms of consciousness. It is a very slow and gradual process. Billions of years were required to attain our current state of consciousness. For the most part, this process occurs without our realizing it. In a sense, nature drags us through the experiences we need in life, and we learn our life lessons one by one, whether we want to or not. There comes, however, a point in our spiritual development when we understand what is happening and we make a conscious effort toward speeding up that progress. Then we become co-creators with the Divine. Of course, some people purposely retard their spiritual progress by focusing on the personal ego.

Whether we choose to go with the flow of spiritual evolution or choose to swim against the stream, the final result will be the same. In the end, nature will prevail. As we gain clarity of vision, all excuses for going against the flow fall away one by one. You make life easy or difficult by the choices you make. Choose to work with the forces of nature instead of against them if you would have an easy life.

Some humans have had an experience of so-called "instantaneous enlightenment." This does occur, although it is rare. It happens because that individual has reached a point where he can make rapid progress if he chooses to. The universe "touches" this person and temporarily allows him to see things he couldn't see before. The heightened consciousness generally lasts for a period of months, but gradually it subsides. However, the individual will never completely return to the level of consciousness he had before, and if he makes a concerted effort, he will regain and retain that higher level of consciousness on a permanent basis.

I would love to experience that. How can I do it?

There is no guarantee that a particular individual will experience it in a given lifetime. You can work on developing your own positive character traits like altruism, compassion, unconditional love and the desire to be of service to others. Work on transferring your mental focus from the lower levels of vibrational frequency to the higher levels, where the human soul dwells. It is by learning to control our lower nature, and by learning how to work at the level of our Higher Self, that we can be used as an instrument for helping humanity.

In human evolution, the age of the physical body is not an indicator of our spiritual age. A young child may be far more advanced spiritually than a man of 80 or 90 years. We did not all begin the journey at the same time, so it is only fair to allow others to operate at their own level of spiritual development. There must be no sense of feeling superior to someone else, even if we have progressed farther along the spiritual path. A sophomore in college is not "better than" a child in third grade. Each is at his proper level of learning based on his experience. Those who are more advanced have the added responsibility of using their experience to help others. "Of those to whom much is given, much is required."

"When I was a child, I spoke as a child, I felt as a child, I thought as a child. Now that I have become a man, I have put away childish things." This quote from First Corinthians describes spiritual growth. Few are ready to give up "childish things." What are these childish things? The magic toys—the ego enhancers. To grow up spiritually means we begin developing will power and cease to be led by emotional desires.

Will exists at the level of ātma and buddhi, working through the higher mind. Buddhi-manas is the most spiritual part of our nature expressing through the highest part of our mind. Kāma-manas is our emotions and desires, our ego, working through the lower part of the mind. When we "grow up" spiritually, we begin operating less through kāma-manas and more through buddhi-manas, until that becomes our standard way of operating in life.

It sounds impossible. I don't know anyone who has achieved that yet.

It is impossible currently for most humans because they are not at that stage of development yet. However, there *are* individuals who have attained that level, and many others are arduously working toward it. Everyone, regardless of his stage of spiritual development, can be working toward it. Your goals should not be just for the immediate future or even for this lifetime. They should stretch far into the future and to future lifetimes; otherwise, you are limiting your possibilities.

You have talked about ātma, buddhi, and manas, and said that manas means "mind." Can you explain a little about the human mind?

Don't confuse the mind with the brain. The brain is the instrument through which the mind operates in the physical world. It can only partially transmit what the mind perceives. The mind exists apart from the brain, and without the mind, the brain can function only on a primitive level. The brain exists in the physical realm where the vibratory rate is quite slow. The mind, on the other hand, has a range of vibrations, all of which are higher and more refined than those of the brain.

Manas has two parts, the higher and the lower. The lower part of the mind is the part we are most familiar with. It is also called the concrete mind. Rupa manas in Sanskrit means the mind of form. It is here that the majority of our mind activity takes place. Thoughts at this level can be expressed in "forms"—in words, pictures, or other graphic representations. When our consciousness operates at this level, it must use some sort of "language" in order to communicate with others. By language, we mean an actual spoken or written language, music, art, or any other form by which we communicate concepts, ideas, and emotions to others.

The higher part of the mind is "formless," arupa manas in Sanskrit. At this level of consciousness, the ideas are so lofty in vibrational frequency that they cannot be expressed in any language. When attempting to convey at the level of the lower mind an idea that exists at the level of the higher mind, the best we can do is hint at it. Symbols—whether abstract, concrete, or even words used as symbols—are a poor representation of what one is trying to communicate, but it is all we have available.

Remember that the realm of the higher mind is where the soul dwells. When you are operating in the realm of the lower mind, you cannot appreciate the consciousness which exists at the higher level, and when you are operating at the emotional level, you are even further removed from any comprehension. Only by ascending in consciousness to the higher level, through meditation and contemplation, can you achieve any degree of awareness of what transpires at that lofty level.

To comprehend something in a realm beyond that of the lower mind, you must raise your consciousness to that level. The only way two people can communicate at the level of the higher mind is if both have developed their consciousness at that level. If one has developed a degree of consciousness in the higher realm and the other has not, the one with the greater degree of consciousness can try to inspire the other to make an effort to raise his own consciousness or communicate at the lower, distinctly in-ferior, level.

J. Krishnamurti spent most of his life teaching people about raising their consciousness. Many of his followers listened to him and read his teachings for years. Yet, few of them could adequately explain what he was teaching. Most of them agreed on this—when they were in his presence, they felt something special, a spiritual vibration they did not experience in their everyday lives. While they listened to him in person, it was as if they understood everything he taught, and it made sense. But when com-paring notes later, they found their comprehension was not at all what it was when they were in his presence, and they seldom agreed on what he had said.

Their consciousness was temporarily raised by the power of his vibrational frequency. We all have an energy field of vibrations which accompanies us wherever we go. It is our aura, and it has vibrations at all the different levels of con-sciousness. When we are in the proximity of a person with a very pure and highly developed energy field, we are affected by it. When we leave that influence, we return to our "natural" state of being, but it has now been changed to some extent by interacting with that person. On the other hand, when we are in the presence of someone with a low level of vibrations, we feel a heaviness or negativity, and our first thought is to get away from the influence.

A highly evolved individual has vibrations composed only of the highest vibrations on each level of consciousness. The vibrations of the soul are far more powerful than those of the personality.

THE NATURE OF THE SOUL

Is it at this higher level of the mind, or arupa manas, that the human soul exists, and if so, what can I do to expand my consciousness to that level?

It *is* at this level that the human soul exists, and there are things you can do to expand your consciousness, resulting in contact with your soul. The remainder of this book includes information and practices you can use to make that happen.

Can you enlighten me as to what the soul is like?

The soul is the intermediary between this physical experience and your higher spiritual nature. It is the soul that leads you back home; it consistently re-directs you, pointing out the way of return. Few people are ready to return just yet. They are still "having fun" in this world and don't care to leave their magic toys behind just yet. Spiritually speaking, they have not yet grown up.

What are the qualities of the soul?

The concept of vibrational frequency is of utmost importance. The soul operates at a level where currently only the most advanced human beings can operate consciously. There is nothing mean or coarse or negative in the realm of the soul. Anger, hatred, resentment, and vindictiveness cannot be perceived at that level. Instead, the qualities possessed by the soul are: unconditional love of mankind and all other creatures, compassion, kindness, and an intense desire to help others in their spiritual growth. There is also indescribable bliss, something far beyond the feeling of "happiness" we experience. The life of the soul is filled with tranquility and the perfect assurance that all is well in the world. The quote on page 333 describes these qualities. "Those who live in the Eternal" refers to those whose soul is the driving force in their life, not the ego. The Self, with a capital S, is often used as a synonym for soul.

Currently, there are few individuals who have achieved this level of soul consciousness. There is a great need in the world for more people with personal experience in contacting the soul. The only way to gain this experience is through disciplined, diligent effort. Only those aspirants who possess dauntless courage, spotless purity, and strong intellect can hope to make the effort, and even that is no guarantee of success.

I've heard that the soul is eternal. Is that true?

No, it isn't. Once we achieve perfection as humans, the soul ceases to exist.

I can't imagine not having a soul.

Once we graduate from the human kingdom, there is no need for the human soul. The soul is what inspires us during the human portion of our journey. It is our beacon showing the direction we should follow. Once you have mastered the highest level of human consciousness, you need a new beacon at a higher level. The previous one, the soul, has served its purpose and disintegrates. The new beacon has been there all along, but it now takes on a more prominent role than before. It is referred to as the monad and it operates through ātma and buddhi.

When does our journey end? When do we reach the final goal?

It never ends. That's why it is called eternal progression. The following quote from Pranava-Vada refers to this concept:

> "Atoms make up molecules; molecules compounds; compounds cells; cells tissues; tissues organs; organs bodies; bodies communities; communities classes and races; classes and races kingdoms; kingdoms of many grades and varied linkings make up a planet; planets make up a solar system, solar systems a vaster system, and so on, unending; nowhere is found indivisible simplicity; nowhere, final complexity. All is relative."

Is this spiritual journey really as difficult as you make it sound?

The average human will not achieve this higher level of consciousness until millions of years and hundreds of incarnations have been passed. Periodically, a special effort is made by the Spiritual Hierarchy, and an opportunity for very rapid progress is offered. But if you haven't developed the three qualities mentioned before—dauntless courage, spotless purity, and strong intellect—you must work on those first. This is not an endeavor for the faint of heart, and it is not without danger. The time for that opportunity is now.

Earlier you mentioned character development. What do you mean exactly by that term?

Character development means contacting our soul and then, through a long and steady process, transferring control of our personality to the soul. The ego is no longer in charge, but rather a more spiritual part of our being. The personality then is simply an instrument through which the soul can operate in the everyday world. It can only become a vessel if there is space inside. You may have a piece of bamboo, but until you remove the pith to provide a passageway for the breath, it cannot be used as an instrument. So it is with the human personality; as long as it is filled with ego, personal desires, and unresolved emotional baggage, it is useless as an instrument for the soul.

It doesn't sound very easy.

It's not easy at all. In fact, it takes tremendous discipline and will power. Even if we're not ready to make the effort now, we can learn what the future holds for us, and we can begin to change our attitudes so that, in the future, we *will* be ready to start the process.

So far you have mentioned the different levels of human consciousness as ātma, buddhi, higher manas and lower manas. Are there more levels of consciousness?

The other levels we are very familiar with. They are the emotions we feel and the physical sensations we experience by having a physical body.

Do animals have souls?

Everything in nature has a soul because it is Divine. The soul is what motivates us to make the journey home. It "shows us the way." However, the human soul is different. It is individualized, unlike the soul in other conscious beings. It is said that the human is "part animal, part god." In the early stages of our human development, we are much more like animals in that our desires, passions and emotions motivate us to think and act. As we continue to grow, there comes a time when we see the writing on the wall. The things of the world no longer are as attractive as they were; however, we do not yet have anything with which to replace them. We are beginning to perceive our spiritual potential, but it is not yet clear.

This is when an intense struggle takes place, the struggle between immersion in the material world, one we know well, and the call of the spiritual realms, something about which we know very little. Only when the struggle is resolved in favor of our spiritual nature can we proceed toward completion of the human phase of evolution, permitting us to rise to a higher level of consciousness. Then we become co-creators with the universe. We have adequately understood the Plan of Spiritual Progress and take our place among those who work for the cause with no thought of self. We have earned our place in the Spiritual Hierarchy, among those who are no longer centered in personal self-consciousness, but in the consciousness of the One Life.

This powerful struggle between the personality and the Higher Self is beautifully told in the allegories of the Bhagavad Gītā and many of the parables of Jesus in the New Testament.

The story of the magic toy shows us how the universe uses emotions to teach us life lessons. Is that correct?

Exactly. If we had no emotions or desires, we would never learn the lessons we were intended to learn. There would be no reason to descend to this level of existence or to make the effort necessary to return home. We are pilgrims on a quest for knowledge and experience. Desires are the motivational factors, enticing us to learn what we need in order to make spiritual progress. These lower desires and emotions will not always be necessary. As you notice, they are among the lowest of the human levels of consciousness, and they are used only for the early stages of advancement. There comes a time when they are no longer needed. Will supersedes emotional desire as our motivator, and buddhi-manas replaces kāma-manas as our means of operation.

Desire exists at all levels, not just the physical or emotional. No statue, building, planet, solar system, or universe was ever made without desire. Desire is the motivating element that impels us to act, to do something. Desire can be of a lower quality, such as the desire for attention or for possessions, or it can be the desire of an exalted spiritual being to manifest a solar system. In humans, there is a large range of desires, some motivated by our emotions—desires which are selfishly motivated—and some motivated by our higher nature and the desire to help others in their spiritual progress. This latter type of desire is unselfishly motivated and altruistic in nature.

When a builder wants to create a foundation for a building, he doesn't just pour concrete on the ground. He first builds a form in the shape of the finished product. Then, when he pours the material into the form, it assumes that shape. The form is a temporary object and is useful only for a limited time. In the same way, the Divine Builder builds forms and pours the material, otherwise known as Spirit, into them. Unfortunately, we develop emotional attachments to these forms and are upset when they are destroyed. They were never meant to be permanent. They exist temporarily for the indwelling Spirit to gain experience. The forms continue to change over time, but a form can only grow so much before it is no longer useful. It is then destroyed and the same indwelling Spirit is poured into a new form, one more appropriate for the level of consciousness attained.

When we become aware of the process we are experiencing and embrace it, we are in a position to develop and use will power. We learn to overcome the hold that emotions and personal desires have over us. We begin to see the illusory and ephemeral nature of physical life, and are anxious to become co-creators with the Divine Builder.

Chapter 4

REINCARNATION

THE RECURRING DREAM

A young man lives in a magnificent palace on a moun-
taintop with the rest of his family. Everything in this
home is of exquisite quality and beauty. They enjoy un-
dreamed of music and art. It is an atmosphere of unconditional love, caring, compassion, and bliss.

Every morning the young man leaves his home and goes down into the neighboring village. But something strange occurs. Each time he leaves home, he completely forgets what his home is like. Try as he might, he cannot recall except very vaguely that he even has a home.

Each day he meets new people, finds new friends, engages in passionate desires, attends lavish banquets, and has a variety of experiences. Some of these are pleasant, but others are distinctly unpleasant. At times he gets into quarrels, and fights with those he disagrees with.

While he is out during the day, he is completely immersed in the emotional drama of the village life. One day he may find a young woman he falls in love with, and he spends the better part of the day with her, until she leaves him for someone else or he becomes bored and finds another woman who is more attractive. At times, he experiences an immediate attraction to someone, whether a love partner or a friend he enjoys spending time with, and he has a vague sense of having known this person before.

The early part of the day is always exciting. He is filled with energy and the desire to explore and experience all the town has to offer. He visits the market place and buys items that appeal to him. He partakes of the food and drink that are offered, often eating and drinking to excess. Sometimes this causes him to feel sick and out of sorts, and the happiness turns into pain and regret.

He also experiences carnal desires and engages in relationships of many kinds. Each one is an alluring enticement in the beginning, and he and his lover delight in discovering new and different ways of making love. But after a while, even this loses its appeal and he realizes that the excitement does not bring lasting happiness.

As it gets late in the day, his energy fades. By this time, he is so tired and sick from his activities throughout the day that his only desire is to get away from it all. Even though he has almost no memory of his home, he longs to return there, regardless of what it might be like. The attraction of the village has lost its glamor and he just wants to rest.

He finally recalls a vague memory of his home, and at the end of the day, his weary feet somehow find the way. He makes the return trip, retracing his steps from the early part of the day. Finally he arrives, exhausted, and the memory of the day's events are already fading away. As he reaches the courtyard of the palace, he sees his loved ones awaiting him, but he can't join them just yet. First he must be cleansed of the dirt that has accumulated during his sojourn. He is bathed and dressed in new clothes. All traces of his journey are washed away and his traveling clothes are discarded. All of the trinkets he acquired during the day must be left behind. Only that which is pure can return to his ancestral home.

The same applies to his thoughts and emotions. No selfish desire can return with him, no desires for carnal pleasures, nothing that is in discord with the harmony that prevails in this loveliest of places. All the lower thoughts and emotions vanish. All that remains of his day's experience are his loftiest thoughts, his most unselfish desires, the kindness and compassion he has felt for others. All the rest is laid aside for him to take up again the following day when he returns again to the village. The details of what happened that day vanish like a mist.

For the time being, he experiences much needed rest and bliss throughout the night, having completely forgotten all but the most exquisite qualities gained from the previous day's events. After a period of rest, he hears the call of the siren again, beckoning him to return to the village.

Imagine a rover, a vehicle transported through space to land on a far distant planet. It only comes to life when it arrives at its destination after a long and precarious journey. A signal from the command center activates it. The rover has known no other existence until it "comes to life" in this alien environment.

If it performs as expected, it explores the surrounding area, sampling and testing various materials in its environment and faithfully transmitting the raw data to the command center millions of miles away. It knows nothing about this command center except that it receives instructions from it from time to time and is expected to respond, sending back the data it has collected.

At the end of its allotted time, the rover is not brought back, but dies slowly as its life forces wear down, until it is no longer a functioning vehicle. Its life experience now no longer exists within its own structure, but has been carefully recorded at home.

The data collected now goes through a long process. Billions of bits of information are sifted through and only the most pertinent are retained. The remainder goes to long-term storage where it can be reviewed at some future date if necessary.

At some point in the future, the command center will send a new and improved vehicle to the same or a different planet to again collect information, to experience life in another alien environment. The command center is the real life of all the vehicles, not the individual vehicles that gather information. But without the various vehicles and the information they supply, there would be no reason for the command center to exist. It would be useless.

The problem? We associate our sense of self with the temporary vehicle, not with the more permanent command center, otherwise known as our Higher Self.

Is it really that simple? Is it simply a matter of identifying with our Higher Self instead of the personality?

It is that simple, but only if you know how to do it. Few people have taken the trouble to learn the process. Just like anything else in life, that which you know how to do is easy. That which you have not yet learned to do is impossible at this time.

The soul, the Higher Self, *is* the human being. We generally consider our personality to be the human being and the soul as something unknowable, a spiritual part of our self that is beyond comprehension. The soul is not the same as ātma, or Spirit. That which we experience in our everyday life is the personality, the temporary vehicle created by the soul on the lower levels of consciousness in order to gain experience. Each form, or vehicle, lasts a certain number of years, and then dies and fades away— ashes to ashes and dust to dust.

Are you saying nothing remains of this lifetime except the experience gained?

What else is there to retain? The physical body dies, and despite the best efforts of mortuary science, it decomposes until it finally disintegrates. There is no reason to preserve the physical body.

But what about those of us who believe in resurrection?

What is it that can be resurrected? The old, worn out, diseased body that finally lets go of its desire for physical existence?

No. We are taught that it will be a perfected body.

Think about what you are saying. If it is a perfected body, then it is not physical. It is a vehicle that has existence in a more exalted realm of being. When you spend some time in contemplation of this subject, you will realize that the only reason for having a physical body is to gain experience in this lower realm of consciousness. Our true level of consciousness as spiritual human beings is at the level of the soul, not at the level of the personality.

So once a person dies he will never exist again as that same personality?

That is exactly what happens. This personality exists for a specific period of time for the purpose of gaining experience. Once that phase is over, it is over.

That sounds awfully fatalistic, and would be disturbing to a lot of people.

We become attached to what we know. Letting go of our personal attachment to people is not easy, and yet in the end we must do so whether we want to or not. Why not learn non-attachment early in life. It makes life much easier to do it now.

Then if I understand what you are saying, the key is to tune in to the higher consciousness at the level of the soul, because it is eternal, is that right?

Even that which we call the soul is not eternal. As we said earlier, it exists only until we have become perfected human beings. Then, our sojourn in the human realm comes to an end, the soul ceases to exist, and our consciousness enters a new phase of developing consciousness, far higher than most of us can conceive of right now. We will discuss this in greater detail in the next chapter.

I think I understand a little of what you are saying. After my mother died, I felt sad for a long time. I often thought about her and the special memories we shared. Now there are days when I don't think about her at all, but when I do, I no longer dwell on the memories and how much I miss her, but on her essential qualities and the great love she had for me. In a sense, she is not gone at all because I still feel her love for me whenever I turn my thoughts in that direction.

That's how life is. Everything assumes its proper perspective through the passage of time and the gaining of further experience.

As we grow wiser in spiritual things, the great emotional desires and anxieties that ruled our life in the past fade away and are replaced by a calm assurance that all is well in the world. Everything is exactly as it should be.

You can never lose your connection with someone who is dear to you. You are both part of the same spiritual being, and that connection can never be broken. The more we raise our consciousness through contemplation and meditation, the more we become aware of this unbreakable connection.

I'm intrigued by the idea of reincarnation. I have to admit it does seem to make sense.

It *does* make sense. All natural laws are perfectly logical in their functioning. The universe does not act in an erratic and unpredictable manner. It also does not re-invent the wheel each time it creates a new realm of experience.

Take the example of a musical genius who composes complicated pieces at five years of age. Where did that genius come from?

Some would say it was a gift from God.

Fortunately, life is a hard taskmaster. We have to work for everything we get. Otherwise, not only would we not appreciate it, but we would still not have acquired the experience we gain during the struggle of learning how to do it. If you do your daughter's homework for her because you feel bad about seeing her work so hard, how will she ever learn? We do not do our children any favors by trying to make life easy for them. In fact, doing that is really for the benefit of our own ego at the expense of the life experience our children might have gained.

A wealthy person could hire a musician to be on call and play a live performance whenever he wanted, but this is not the same joy and sense of accomplishment as being a master of a particular instrument. There are no shortcuts in life. We keep repeating the lessons until they have been learned, and only then can we move forward.

Many people do not believe in reincarnation, and yet they believe in an existence after death. It makes no difference whether or not you believe in reincarnation. The fact is, death is not the end of the real human being, but only of the vehicle he was using temporarily. No one can learn in a single lifetime all that is required to become perfect. There are so many lessons to learn, it makes sense that the soul would send out new vehicles, new rovers, until all necessary experience has been gained before moving on to the next realm of existence.

A student in the 6th grade does not move to the 7th grade until he has gained a certain minimum level of competence in 6th grade matters. Moving on too quickly would be a mistake; incapable of working at the higher level of expectation, he would drop out in frustration.

THE PERIOD AFTER DEATH

Can you tell me a little more about how reincarnation works and what happens after a person dies?

An entire book would be necessary to adequately discuss what takes place after death, but we can point out some of the most important aspects of the process. The period between the death of the physical body and the next physical incarnation is called "bardo" in Tibetan. A person who dies is not aware of the moment of passing from physical existence any more than you are aware of the moment you fall asleep.

When a person is born, a certain amount of time is allotted for the experience to be gained in that particular lifetime. It may be only a few minutes or hours, or ninety-seven years. For most people, it is somewhere in between.

Then the exact moment of my death is predetermined?

The exact moment, no, not even necessarily the exact month or year. In fact, we can extend or shorten our allotted time by what we do, the food we eat, how much exercise we engage in, the amount of stress in our life, and so forth.

When we are born, the natural period of time we will live is already determined by our past karma. This is beautifully stated in the phrase from Ecclesiastes, "a time to be born and a time to die." That time can be lengthened or shortened, based on the decisions we make during this life. If we eat poorly, get little or no exercise, and create stress on our bodies through unrestrained emotions, worry and anxiety, the length of our life will be shortened. If we treat our bodies well and provide the best nutrition, exercise without overstraining, and learn to diminish the amount of stress in our lives by controlling emotions, we can extend the amount of time we live.

There are two times in a person's life when angels are invariably present to help. One is at the moment of birth and the other is at the moment of death. During the death process, they often work as a team of two angels.

ACCIDENTAL AND VIOLENT DEATHS

Students often ask what happens in the event of accidental or violent deaths. There are times when these deaths are not accidental at all, whether caused by an auto accident, a murder, or an act of war. In some cases, the karma of the person foreordains that he will die suddenly, so it can hardly be said to be accidental if this is the case.

In other cases, the person's life comes to an end because of his own carelessness or that of someone else. It can also end prematurely because of premeditated murder or suicide. In that case, the normal lifespan has not been reached, and this can affect the person's experience on the astral plane after death.

At the end of a person's life, the physical body is discarded and is, at that point, simply a collection of atoms and molecules which deteriorate, either rapidly through cremation, or over a long period of time through burial.

The physical body, including the brain, is now gone, and what remains of the earthly personality consists of emotions and thoughts. Remember that the mind is not the same as the brain. The first period after death is a period of unconsciousness. The length of time varies between individuals, but it makes no difference, because there is no sense of time. Slowly, the remaining portion of the personality begins to re-awaken in what is very similar to a normal dream state. This phase is called kāma-loka in Sanskrit, the realm of desires. If the person is somewhat evolved spiritually and has resolved all or almost all lower emotions—such as anger, resentment, and anxiety—this phase will be fairly short, sometimes only a few days or even hours. For others, those who died with a large buildup of emotional energy, it can extend to many years.

Accumulated emotional or mental energy does not simply disappear at any point in time. A battery must be discharged over a period of time in a controlled manner. Otherwise, a dangerous explosion results. So it is with all the accumulated but unresolved emotional energy in one's lifetime.

The best course of action is to resolve this emotional energy as we go through life so there is no appreciable accumulation at any given time. The next best course of action is to actively work on resolving, or discharging, this energy when we feel the end of life approaching. In fact, a fairly large number of people do this naturally. As their energy wanes and the cost of each negative emotion is felt more strongly by the weakened physical body, they begin to realize that such emotions are not worth the pain and suffering they cause. It is a wise person who realizes this early in life and takes steps to control his emotions. Control of the emotions is so important that it will be covered in chapters 12 and 13.

The last course of action is no action at all, just the continuation of emotional reaction to everything in life—anger, upset, denial, frustration, resentment, and fear. Unfortunately, the majority of people still fall into this category. Their physical transition is often difficult, both for them and those caring for them.

The enlightened person experiences nothing of the sort. He is fully prepared to leave his physical existence behind, having carefully thought through the process and, more importantly, having let go of all attachments, emotional and otherwise. Any last bits of emotional energy are resolved so the death process is easy and natural, regardless of the external circumstances.

It is important to be clear on what not to expect after the death of the physical body. Once the physical world is left behind, there is no food, sports, television, alcohol or drugs, no drama, sex, or shopping, not even computers or video games. All these things account for tension and stress of varying degrees in your life. This is your chance to rest from all the cares of the world. It is amazing how many people are incapable of relaxing while in the physical world. When we wish for someone to "Rest in peace," it means exactly that. For most, this is the first time in decades that they really are able to rest in peace and practice non-attachment, even if it is forced non-attachment.

So there is a period of unconsciousness, followed by a gradual "awakening" in the kāma-loka. What happens once any remaining unresolved emotions are worked out?

Kāma-loka, by the way, is not a location but a state of existence, a realm of consciousness rather than a place. Everything transpires in cycles. You will notice the same patterns repeating over and over in nature. As we said, this period is similar to a dream state, the quality of which is determined by these unresolved emotions. For some people it may be more like a nightmare if their emotions are of a lower nature.

Toward the end of the kāma-loka period, as the amount of emotional energy diminishes to the vanishing point, there is again a period of unconsciousness, just as there was at the beginning of it.

Sometime during this part of the after-death period, an assessment is made as to whether or not the lifetime resulted in enough useful experience for the soul's growth or whether it was a wasted experience. If there is anything that could be called a final judgment, it is this decision process. If the lifetime is retained, as is most common, the essence of the lifetime of experience is absorbed by the Higher Self, but not the details. The soul cares not at all about the personal drama, the emotional reactions, or the success or failure of personal desires. What is important to the soul is very different from what is important to the personality.

If the decision goes the other direction, and this only happens if the personality truly can be characterized as evil, this life experience is discarded, and the soul begins almost immediately with preparations for a new incarnation. The lifetime becomes "a torn out page" in the series of lives, and it is as if it never occurred, from the perspective of the Higher Self.

So, in a very real sense, it is possible to "lose one's soul," though it is very uncommon; even those who seem horrible to us often have just enough goodness in them to make that lifetime of value. And to be clear, it is not a matter of the personality "losing" the soul, but of the soul discarding the personality.

Let's assume I have lived a lifetime good enough to pass this "final judgment." What comes next?

Most people now pass a longer or shorter period in a state of complete bliss and joy. This corresponds, at least to some extent, to some people's concept of heaven. In Sanskrit it is called devachan, the realm of the shining ones.

It is somewhat difficult to describe devachan. It is not the city with streets of gold, bejeweled trees, and celestial music imagined by some. In fact, that would be extremely boring for most people. Instead, it corresponds more closely to the most peaceful and blissful dreams you can imagine.

Is it a dream state or a real experience?

What is real and what is not real? Have you ever replayed an event in your mind so many times you are no longer sure what part of it actually happened and what part is a product of your imagination?

I have more than once realized that I was not certain whether an event had actually happened or whether I imagined it.

Is it any less real if you imagined it, as long as you are convinced it occurred?

No, I suppose not.

This is important to understand. In our development as conscious beings, it is not important what events occur during our life experience, but rather how we perceive them and what our reactions are. That is what constitutes our life experience.

Are you saying that if I simply imagined my life experience as if it were all a dream, it would be just as significant as if it actually happened?

Yes. This entire universe exists because an exalted being created it, first as a thought, and then in matter. Everything in existence is māyā, an illusion.

If you believe something exists, it is very real to you. If you dream you are falling from a high cliff, your body and your emotions react just as if you were falling in the physical world.

But can't we say that the physical world is real and the dream state is not?

No, it would be more accurate to say that any level of existence other than the Absolute is unreal and that the farther we get from the Absolute, the more unreal it is. The physical world is not more real than the astral or emotional world, nor is it more real than the mental realms.

I can knock on the table in front of me and it seems completely solid. But is it? Physicists tell us that atoms are almost entirely composed of space and most would even say that our "physical world" is nothing but a collection of focal points of energy interacting with each other. I am an illusion knocking on another illusion. When you are dreaming and you "knock" on a door or "drive" a car, doesn't it seem just as real as when you are awake?

It certainly seems real while I'm dreaming, but then I wake up and realize it was just a dream.

You will also wake up one day and realize that all of life is a dream.

That makes me think my entire life is useless if it is unreal and only an illusion.

Not at all. You can think of it as real if you like or unreal if you prefer, and neither point of view would be incorrect. What is important is relative reality. The only absolute reality is at the level of the Absolute. It would not be inaccurate to say that soul consciousness is more real than physical consciousness or that the consciousness at the level of the monad is more real than that of the soul.

I think I preferred it when everything was black and white and I didn't think about these things. Life was certainly easier then.

Was it really? As adults we may bemoan the difficulties and responsibilities in our lives, thinking things were far easier when we were children. There is a price to pay for greater awareness and consciousness, but would anyone really be willing to give up the experience he gained by learning to deal with life's difficulties?

It may be disconcerting to realize that life is not so simple a child can readily understand it, but would you rather stick with simplistic ideas that are no longer useful, or grow in consciousness?

I guess I would prefer to expand my consciousness, but it seems very difficult.

Life is only as difficult as we make it. If we choose to hold on to outdated concepts that are no longer useful, and if we resist change, which is going to happen whether we accept it or not, then life seems terribly difficult and unfair. If, on the other hand, we cheerfully accept whatever happens with equanimity, and if we are willing to give up old ideas for new ones that are more accurate, then life is extremely simple. Attachment, resistance, and emotional reactions are the things that make life difficult.

Do you see how your attitude is the determining factor in how you interact with life?

I'm beginning to realize that now. But are there some things I can do to learn non-attachment and learn to control emotional reactions?

The purpose of this book is to give you the necessary background of information and some helpful practices to do just that.

DEVACHAN

You were discussing devachan earlier. Can you tell me more about it?

Devachan is not a place, but a state of being, one of intense selfishness, during which the individual reaps the reward of his most unselfish acts while on earth. All the energy accumulated through his most noble acts of kindness, compassion and unconditional love can only be recompensed at this elevated level. During this period, which can last from a few hours to several centuries, he is completely enveloped in blissful dreams of all his earthly affections of a higher nature. If he was musician, his period in devachan will include the enjoyment of unimaginable works of music, impossible to reproduce in the physical world. However, many living artists who are spiritually advanced are unknowingly inspired by these masterful works on the inner planes, and we see something of the divine nature in their physical works.

In devachan there is no pain, no grief, and no sorrow. A mother in devachan spends her time dreaming dreams of immense joy where her children are the principal players.

Is that mother aware of what is going on in the lives of her children on earth, and if so, can she help them with the problems they encounter?

If she were aware of their problems, it would be no heaven world. Her immense joy would be exchanged for sorrow and anxiety for her children, and it would not be the period of blissful rest she has earned. Devachan is at the very level of the soul. Nothing the least bit coarse can ever be experienced at that level. The soul in devachan cannot come down to your level of existence, but in rare instances, you may be able to ascend to its level.

How is that possible?

During sleep or deep meditation, you may sometimes get a glimpse into the world of the person in devachan. The most likely result will be a sense of indescribable joy and peace upon awakening or returning to normal consciousness. It is not an emotional experience in itself, but you may have an emotional reaction to it.

If the devachan experience is just a dream, why does it even exist? It seems like a waste of time.

It is the result of the law of karma. Every action, every thought, and every emotion must have its effect. The effects of our most elevated and unselfish acts can only exist at this exalted level. They accumulate during our lifetime, and we enjoy our well-deserved period of bliss after the lower energies have been discharged in the earlier stages of bardo.

It sounds like the most spiritual members of humanity spend long periods of time in devachan. Wouldn't they want to forego it and come back more quickly to help their struggling brothers?

Normally this is not permitted, but the current conditions in the world are such that exceptions are sometimes made. It *is* possible, under very strict conditions, to postpone the devachan period and return almost immediately, but it happens only in rare cases. We will see a few of these in the coming decades, although it will seldom be recognized except by those who are quite enlightened.

Chapter 5

BEYOND THE HUMAN KINGDOM

The path of the just is as the shining
light that shineth more and more
unto the perfect day.

— *Proverbs* 4:18

OUR GOAL AS HUMAN BEINGS

What is our goal as human beings? To become perfect.
The Bible refers many times to the "perfect man," or "just
men made perfect." Can we really become perfect? Yes, we
can; otherwise, what is the purpose of going through the
human experience? When consciousness was gaining experience in the vegetable kingdom, it began in the simplest

of forms, like mosses and lichens. It does not begin as a giant sequoia tree or a bristlecone pine. Instead, it passes through eons of experience in different forms, increasing in complexity of form and in consciousness until it reaches the apex of the plant kingdom. Only then does that consciousness "graduate" and continue its journey in the animal kingdom. It is not only physical plane consciousness that is being developed, but emotional, intellectual, and intuitional as well.

The consciousness did not have to experience every species of plant, but its experience was well rounded. The goal was not to learn everything that can be learned in that kingdom, but to increase sufficiently in consciousness to be ready for the next level of experience in a higher kingdom.

After spending millions of years in the animal kingdom, the same divine spark, growing ever more in consciousness, began its journey through the human kingdom. Upon entering this human realm of experience, it gained a human soul. It is this human soul that sets us apart from all other creatures on earth. The mind we have earned is the tool that will enable us to become co-creators with the Divine.

It is important to realize our mind is evolving also. We started our journey in the human realm with the same level of consciousness we had at the apex of the animal kingdom. Nature does not work in fits and starts. It follows a slow, steady expansion and growth, both in complexity of form and of the indwelling consciousness. This is not to say that everything it tries is a success. In fact, failure is something we have in common with nature. We learn by trying something, assessing whether or not we have succeeded in our goal, and re-commencing if it did not work out. Nature proceeds in the same manner. A plan is put in place, and at various stages of its development, is evaluated. If something is not right, a correction can sometimes be made, but it may also become apparent that it cannot be saved. Then the project must be scrapped and either begun anew, or a different plan is started.

Are you saying that our entire universe develops through intelligent design?

That is how everything develops. It is not by chance that evolution of forms and consciousness takes place.

But if this intelligent design is from the Divine, why doesn't it work out perfectly the first time?

With a little reflection, it will be clear why it cannot work out perfectly every time. If a master architect designs a house and builds it himself brick by brick, it will be perfect. But why would he want to build it himself? If he is motivated to help teach others, wouldn't he use artisans and craftsmen to do the work so they can learn from the process and in turn become masters in their own right?

I guess that does make more sense. So you're saying this world is a school of learning?

Of course it is. We are all here to gain experience. Unfortunately, some people in this world have the same attitude as certain college students. They think only about the weekend parties, the socializing, the football games and the possibilities for sexual encounters. The serious student in college and the serious student in life have the same goal—to gain as much as they can in each phase of their learning experience.

If your goal in life is to find perpetual pleasure and happiness, you are doomed to encounter disappointment. It is not possible to find eternal happiness in this physical world. "Store up your treasures in heaven, where moths and rust cannot destroy, and thieves do not break in and steal."

Are you saying we should not enjoy life?

We are not saying that at all. The enlightened person enjoys life, but in a very different way from the less enlightened person. The more enlightened you are, as long as you have put into practice what you have learned, the more content you are and the more you have a sense of fulfillment.

The person who understands the least how life works is the one who experiences the greatest swings of happiness, if this happiness is based on the desire for emotional fulfillment. That person has great highs and lows, and many are addicted to the rollercoaster ride of emotions. It is what makes them feel alive. The person who is more enlightened will remain outside the maelstrom of emotions that others find so attractive. He observes and interacts with others, but from a different level of consciousness. Just because others are not addicted to the same emotional desires you are does not mean they are less happy. In fact, they are probably much happier than you are.

But I get a lot of enjoyment by sharing my happiness with others. We all love a good party, don't we?

No, not everyone finds a party atmosphere enjoyable. A person who is more sensitive to vibrations than the average person would find the vibrations at a party excruciating. It would be equivalent to a room full of noisy equipment with no protective gear to avoid damage to your hearing. As you progress in consciousness, your sensitivity to all vibrations becomes more acute. You become aware of vibrations that others do not perceive at all.

Most of us have encountered people so drunk they can barely stand up. Yet they are convinced they are having a "good time" and want you to join in their enjoyment. From a point of view outside their alcohol haze, we can clearly see that their "good time" will turn into a head-splitting hangover and that there is a high cost to their experience of a "good time." In the same way, those who are more enlightened look from a distance on those who are immersed in the ego and in the emotional roller coaster ride. They do not envy them in any way, preferring their own quiet life of spiritual development and contact with the soul.

So during this human phase of our development, we go from the lower forms of human consciousness and gradually work our way up. Who are the higher forms of humans, and how do they differ from the average?

There is a great variety of human beings sharing space on this planet, and each one is at his particular level of development. As humans, we tend to judge others based on appearances—the clothes they wear, who they socialize with, the kind of cars they drive and the number of university degrees or titles they have. None of these are valid indicators of a person's spiritual development. That can only be seen with the inner vision. Something that exists at a particular level of consciousness can best be perceived at that level. From the level of the personality we cannot properly appreciate the qualities of the soul. We may have a vague understanding of it and feel its influence on us to some extent, but to appreciate it fully, we must lift our consciousness to that level of vibration.

Some of the more spiritually advanced beings on our planet may not even think of themselves as having made appreciable spiritual development. Many are immersed in something of great interest to them to such a point that the rest of the world fades into the background. The great thinkers and scientists, like Einstein and others, who are completely devoted to their work and care little for the things most people find essential in their lives, are examples of some of these more advanced human beings. They may also be great artists, musicians, writers, or builders. The one thing they have in common is that their motivation is not fame or money, but love of their art or their craft and appreciation for the wonders of the universe.

Wouldn't this also include many of the mystics and contemplatives, those who live in a convent or monastery?

Some of those who choose the cloister life are among the most advanced of our humanity, but it is no guarantee of spiritual advancement. There are numerous reasons for entering a monastery or convent. It could be an escape from responsibilities and difficulties in the outer world. It may also be that they recognize their attachment to material things and choose the monastic life as a way to overcome it. But this is no better. It just means substituting spiritual pride for pride in material things. It is still ego. It is still indicative of an unenlightened being.

What about St. Francis, St. Teresa of Avila, and others like them? Shouldn't we emulate them and adopt their way of life?

It is true that in past centuries the monastic life was well suited for spiritual development, but the time has come for humans to remain in the world and develop spiritually at the same time, to be in the world but not of the world, as Jesus taught.

Why has that changed?

Humanity is at a stage where there are many on the verge of taking a giant step in their spiritual growth. The arena for this growth has shifted from the cloister to the everyday world. We can touch the lives of more people by working with them, by having families, and by raising children in homes where these qualities are an everyday experience. The time has come to be more active in our work, not just contemplative. It is not at all easy to balance the two aspects of our being, but this is where we currently are in our evolutionary path.

Many people have reached a stage in human development where they are very much aware of the limitations of this physical world. They are beginning to look for something more meaningful than the magic toys still so attractive to the majority. The number of these people is quite large, but there is a severe lack of teachers advanced enough to be shining examples and an inspiration to those who are ready for something else. There is no lack of preachers and gurus and "slightly enlightened" persons, but to find a teacher who is genuinely enlightened is rare.

What happens when we reach the end of our human journey? Do we cease to exist?

Not at all. There are still many stages of our spiritual advancement. Once a human being has learned all that is required as a human, he "graduates" and moves on to a new level of spiritual work. There are several paths that open before the human who has reached his goal in humanity.

Can you tell us what they are?

We will mention two of them. One option is to transfer into the angelic kingdom, to become a deva or "shining one." Another is to serve as a teacher of humanity, to remain on the planet in human form and help in the spiritual evolution of the world. This involves a tremendous sacrifice on the part of those who choose this path; it means they must remain in an environment that is distinctly different from their own level of vibrations.

Does that mean these advanced beings are living in the world among us?

Not usually. The vibrations in the world, and especially in our large cities, are such that they would have to expend too much energy to counteract this distinctly lower energy. Instead, they live in areas remote from civilization where they can work quietly. The majority of their work is accomplished during a state of meditation.

I would love to meet and talk to one of these beings. How can I do that?

You can't, unless you yourself are a highly advanced spiritual being. They are the busiest people in the world. Even when their bodies are asleep they are working on higher levels of consciousness. There is no such thing as a vacation for them.

How can they have physical bodies if they have graduated from the human kingdom?

Not all of them choose to use a physical body, but some do. In that case, the human body is the best available to them. However, their physical bodies are very different from ours. For one thing, they do not have illnesses like we do. Their bodies are as perfect as they possibly can be. They know more about their bodies and how to care for them than any human being.

But aren't they also human if they have a human body?

It is not the possession of a human body that makes one human. To be human means you have achieved a specific level of consciousness. When you die, you lose your physical body, but does that mean you cease to be human?

I see what you mean. It is the level of consciousness that makes me human. So what are these advanced beings if they are not human?

81

THE ADEPTS

They are sometimes referred to as the fifth kingdom in nature, as Adepts or Mahātmas. Mahātma is a Sanskrit word meaning great soul or great spirit. Science recognizes only three kingdoms of nature—mineral, plant and animal. We humans are considered by scientists to be animals because of the physical bodies we occupy. In esoteric science, we make a distinction based on consciousness, not on form. Thus, we claim that humans constitute a fourth kingdom and the Adepts an even higher kingdom because of their level of consciousness.

I've heard of Ascended Masters and channeled messages that people receive from them. Is that who these beings are?

There are many people in the world who are convinced they receive messages from Archangels, "Ascended Masters," and high members of the Spiritual Hierarchy. In most cases, even if the person is sincere, he is deluding himself and others. There are entities in the astral-emotional realm who love to impersonate well known individuals. It isn't hard to do. There are thousands of people who have some degree of clairvoyance, but it is limited to the emotional realm. The entities appeal to the ego in these clairvoyants, telling them they have been specially chosen to deliver important messages to the world. Of course the message would not seem important unless it came from a highly revered source. This makes the clairvoyant very proud to have thus been chosen.

"Ascended" seems to have various interpretations. To some, it describes someone who has been taken up to a higher level of consciousness but has retained his physical body. It is true that some Adepts retain a physical body, but for them the body is simply a tool to function in the physical world. Other advanced beings do not have a physical body. If one is necessary in their work, they create a temporary body through kriyāśakti. This is not done often, however, because it requires an expenditure of energy; they are scrupulously efficient in their use of available energy. In any case, there is no attachment to the personality like we experience.

How can we know whether messages are coming from one of these advanced beings or if they are simply from an entity in the astral realm?

"By their fruits ye shall know them" refers exactly to this situation. Almost every "communication" of the type mentioned above is attributed to a well-known member of the Spiritual Hierarchy, or at least well-known among those who study these things. Take away the name and look at the message itself. If it is full of platitudes and flowery phrases, if it appeals to the emotions and the ego of the receiver of the message, you can be reasonably sure it is *not* from a spiritually advanced being.

The Adepts have no desire to have their names known and have no reason to appeal to the ego of the recipient. Any real messages from them are sent into the world as they are, with no need to include the author's name. One of the tests of a person's level of spiritual advancement is in whether or not he can discern these real messages from false ones.

The first qualification for spiritual growth is discernment, or viveka in Sanskrit. Viveka means the ability to tell the real from the unreal. A test for all aspirants is to learn to separate truth from fiction. One who has not yet learned to do it will spend several lifetimes wandering about, wasting time on things that are not useful.

How does one distinguish the real from the unreal?

In one sense, anything that exists at a higher frequency of vibration is more "real" than something at a lower level of vibration. Thus, as we increase in consciousness, we are attaining to a more "real" level of existence. There is only one reality, at the level of the Absolute. From that point of view, everything else is "unreal," but we can also say there are varying degrees of "reality" as we come closer to the Absolute. Truth is relative.

Channeling and the receiving of spirit messages are very much in vogue. It is true some people receive communications from other realms, but few are very spiritual in nature. Of those that come from something other than the astral-emotional realm, the vast majority are from one's Higher Self, from the soul. A few messages may come infrequently from an advanced chela or pupil of one of the Adepts, and very, very rarely from an Adept himself. This latter is extremely rare, and it is important for us to be wary of anyone claiming to receive messages from an Adept or any member of the Spiritual Hierarchy. If the message is robed in flowery language and appeals to the emotions, it is *not* from a member of the Hierarchy. Wariness is essential for the spiritual student wanting to avoid the numerous pitfalls along the path.

There is another aspect of viveka which might seem a little less abstract, and that is in determining whether something is useful or not useful, helpful or not helpful in your spiritual growth. This means that we must constantly be evaluating things and making a determination. "Does this help in my spiritual development, or does it hinder?"

As Socrates said, "The unexamined life is not worth living."

What does that mean?

It means that if we simply blunder through life, always allowing our desires and passions to control and lead us, we are not acting like the divine beings we really are. Instead, we are more like animals that act from instinct and desire and make no effort to improve their situation. Of course animals are incapable of acting any other way. We, on the other hand, have a human mind and a human soul. Much more is expected of us, yet for long eons of time, we plod along and fail to perceive our true potential.

At some point, however, we begin to see a faint glimmer of what our spiritual possibilities are. At first it is as though we are "seeing through a glass darkly," but if we persist and put forth some effort, that effort is rewarded by seeing more and more clearly. This can only happen when we begin to take charge of our life, when we stop thinking life is unfair and that we can do nothing to change our fate.

If we wish to make rapid spiritual growth, we must examine everything about our life—our motives, our desires, our thoughts and emotions—everything. Only by doing this are we accepting responsibility for our life and our future spiritual growth.

I know a lot of people who are self-centered and introspective, but they don't show much spiritual growth.

This is not the type of self-examination we are talking about. Many people's universe is very tiny, about the size of a motorcycle helmet. Everything they encounter, every person they meet, every event in their life comes back to one idea. "How does that affect me? What do I get out of it? What's in it for me?" The kind of introspection we are talking about is more like, "Am I being the best person I can possibly be? Are my motives pure and unselfish? What can I do to make the world a better place?"

DISCIPLESHIP IN THE NEW AGE

Is it possible to become a student of one of the Adepts you were talking about?

If you are talking about a student in frequent communication with a teacher and a situation where the teacher hovers over the student, correcting him and offering suggestions, then the answer is no. They have no time for that, and anyone who thinks they do is delusional.

I thought you said their purpose was to help in the spiritual growth of humanity. I'm trying to work on my own spiritual growth. Why wouldn't they help me?

They do help, when the motive is pure, when it is for the benefit of all humanity and not because of a personal desire for spiritual growth. When that help comes, it is extremely subtle. There is no burning bush, no fervent message to be delivered to the world with great fanfare. It is in the form of a "still, small voice," the "voice of the silence."

But isn't that "still, small voice" the voice of my own soul?

It can be. If you receive a message from an Adept or one of their pupils, it is transmitted to your soul. Whether or not you as a personality receive it will depend on your connection to your soul.

So they do have pupils!

None of their pupils are trained directly under them through a sort of on-the-job training, at least not any more. In the distant past it was possible, but in the world today, it is no longer feasible. The pupil must train himself, pull himself up by the bootstraps, so to speak. If you are hoping for someone to teach you every step of the way, you're out of luck. In the not-too-distant future, that will be a possibility, because there will be schools of learning similar to the mystery schools of old. Unfortunately, that is not the case right now.

If you are sincerely motivated to help humanity's spiritual evolution, your goal really should be to become an Adept.

I'm not sure I want to become an Adept.

Why not?

Because that implies I would no longer be involved in the everyday world. I'm not sure I'm ready for that.

That alone indicates that you are not ready to sacrifice all that is necessary. There is no reason to become a pupil if your ultimate goal is not to go all the way. In fact, once you begin making any real progress in that direction, the door slams shut behind you and there is no turning back.

Why aren't there such schools in existence now?

The reason is simple. There are millions of potential students and only a few humans who have reached the stage where they can teach others in a formal situation. Those students are given some behind-the-scenes hints and suggestions, and then they are observed to see whether or not they respond to them. Self-motivation, discipline, and will power are vitally important to the process. Anyone who is standing around, waiting for someone to come along and take him by the hand to show him the way, will continue to do just that, stand and wait. In the meantime, he is likely to become enthralled with the illusions and glamor of the astral realm, receiving messages from entities posing as great spiritual beings. This is a drastic setback to his spiritual progress and shows that the personal ego still is very much in control.

If there are millions of people ready to be trained, why wouldn't it be better to spend the time training at least some of them so they can help others?

That is exactly what is happening. But instead of being trained by someone who takes them in hand and spoon feeds them, they must train themselves by developing their intuition and vision. Only those who have the wherewithal to drive themselves forward with nothing but the slightest bit of help are qualified at this point to be the avant-garde of the movement. The Hierarchy is looking for CEOs and generals, not foot soldiers, clerks, and secretaries. "For many are called, but few are chosen."

How can I set about to be one of these CEOs or generals?

What is your motive? Is it to be recognized as a powerful figure in the spiritual movement? Then you may as well forget about it. That is not a pure motive and will only lead to sorrow and disappointment. Is your motive 100% altruistic, to help struggling humanity in its quest for growth? Are you certain there is not so much as a hint of ego or desire for personal enhancement? If there is even a tiny amount of ego in your desire, you will fail. Work on development of character first before desiring anything else, and the rest will fall into place. There is no chance you will be overlooked if you have the qualities of character required.

How is it not possible to be overlooked?

Because the Adepts are always searching for those who can help in the work. They look out over the world and see at a glance anyone who is even approaching the qualifications necessary to help.

How do they do that?

Have you ever met people who have something very special about them? It's as if they have a bright light shining through them that touches everyone they meet, a light that inspires and brings a sense of calmness and peace.

I have met a few people like that.

That's exactly what the Adepts see, except that their vision is far more advanced than ours, and they can't possibly miss a single individual. There is a saying in the East, "When the pupil is ready, the Master appears." The truth is, the Master is aware of the aspirant who is making progress long before the pupil is aware of the Master's presence. The moment the pupil is ready for the next stage of advancement, opportunities open up automatically. Nothing special is required to make it happen except to recognize and take advantage of that opportunity. Failure to recognize and to act on it means a lost opportunity.

Let's say I'm willing to start the process of becoming one of these more advanced beings. How would I begin?

It is sometimes said, only half in jest, that a good sense of humor is the first requirement. Although it is not an actual requirement, it certainly helps. If you take yourself too seriously, always see the difficulties in life, or seldom laugh, then you would have a difficult time of it. On the other hand, if you can laugh at your own foibles, not react to the criticism of others, and lighten up an otherwise difficult situation by injecting some humor into it, this attitude will make a very difficult road more bearable.

There are three primary requirements before even attempting to begin this perilous journey. These are mentioned in the quote at the front of this book—dauntless courage, spotless purity, and strong intellect.

DAUNTLESS COURAGE

This path is not for the faint of heart. It requires courage far beyond that of the average person. If you are afraid of the dark, of being alone, of heights or enclosed spaces, or have other fears and phobias, you do not have dauntless courage. Examine your own life and determine whether or not there are any fears you would be unable to overcome with some effort, and then work to eliminate them. If you shrink from the task, then you are not ready.

Why would this be a requirement? Surely living a spiritual life is not physically dangerous.

It is extremely dangerous—physically, emotionally and mentally. Those who ignore the qualifications and try to press forward without them set themselves up for disastrous results, including emotional and mental imbalance, and even death. It is not our role to frighten, but the risks are great, and the number of aspirants who fail, retarding instead of hastening their spiritual development, is large.

There are many fears that assail the ordinary individual. As described by Thoreau, most men lead lives of "quiet desperation." The fearful person lives in perpetual torment, in fear of the unknown and of what *might* happen.

Many are afraid they will fail, whether in passing an exam or in the success of a business enterprise. Fear is the greatest impediment in this case, and it must be overcome. In the phrase "I'm afraid I'm going to fail," the only part that life respects is, "I'm going to fail." It is an affirmation, and life says, "Your wish is my command." The very fear of failure almost assures that you will fail.

There is no reason you should fail in anything if you have done your homework. If you know what is required to succeed, if you have done all the preparatory work, and if you have done proper due diligence, then you will succeed. Watch those who are successful and emulate them. By following the same methods, you also will succeed, whether it involves a business goal or a spiritual goal. There are no shortcuts. Make sure the goal is clearly defined, that it is attainable, and then take all the necessary steps to make it happen.

SPOTLESS PURITY

Spotless purity is another requirement that eliminates a lot of would-be applicants. It sounds impossible for many aspirants, and quite often it is. The majority gloss over this requirement, hoping it will not apply to their situation. Most people assume that spotless purity involves following a set of rules. This is not the case at all. It is not whether or not you act in a certain way. This is how most people judge things, from external appearances. Instead, the purity in this case is measured by the types and qualities of vibrations within you. This applies to the physical body, your emotional nature, and your mental nature.

Earlier in the book we studied the human constitution. Each level of our consciousness has a number of sub-levels as well. For example, the lowest types of emotions we feel, such as anger, greed, and revenge, can only exist on the lower sub-levels of the emotional realm. Others, such as kindness, contentment, and peacefulness, vibrate at a frequency in harmony with those of the highest sub-levels. This is true at all levels of existence. The vibrations at any given level are confined to that level. They cannot also manifest on a higher or lower level of vibration.

In order for the personality—consisting of physical, emotional, and mental vibrations—to attract the attention of the soul, it must be refined, that is, purified. This means that all of the coarser vibrations in each of the three realms must be eliminated, and the vibrations of the upper sub-levels must be energized and brought into full expression. Only then is the soul willing to work with the personality, because it now has vibrations it can work with.

So you're saying I must attract the attention of my soul by becoming more pure? Why wouldn't it already be interested in my well-being?

It *is* interested in your well-being, your spiritual well-being. There is nothing whatever in the makeup of the soul that would allow it to be interested in the football games you like to watch, the tabloids you like to read, or the movies you are so enthralled with. Not even video games or surfing the internet have the slightest appeal to your soul. Instead of waiting for the soul to descend to your level, you must raise your consciousness to its level. Then you can function from the soul level instead of the personality level.

It sounds very boring.

It is only boring because you have little or no experience with operating at that level.

But surely the soul has experience with operating at its own level.

The only reason for the existence of the soul is to bridge the gap between the animal man and the spiritual man. It is that part of your being that sends out the clarion call and then waits to see if there is a response. If there is no response, it knows you are not yet ready for the return journey. On the other hand, if you are one of those who have reached that point in the life experience where you are ready to take a giant step forward, you will respond to the call.

Then, over the period of several lifetimes, you, the personality, work at achieving the qualifications necessary to raise your vibrations to harmonize with those of your soul. There generally is one lifetime where a tremendous tug-of-war takes place. The soul continues to call out from time to time, but the personality is reluctant to respond because of attachment to the material world and the desires of the ego. A great struggle ensues to determine whether the soul will be in command or the ego, which exists primarily in the realm of emotional desires. Which one wins will determine the future of your spiritual progress. It determines whether you will graduate from the human kingdom in a relatively short period of time or whether you will graduate with the rest of the class in the far distant future.

This struggle between the soul and the personality is the subject of the story in the Bhagavad Gītā. The story takes place on the battlefield between two opposing armies, who happen to be different branches of the same family.

STRONG INTELLECT

You mentioned strong intellect also as being a requirement for spiritual advancement. I must admit I've never considered that to be a primary factor.

And yet it is. Survival of the fittest is certainly important in the case of plants and animals, but by the time we reach the level of more advanced animals, and certainly in the case of humans, intellect becomes more important. The more advanced we become, the more we value intelligence. We cannot hope to figure out how life works without a high degree of intelligence.

I'm afraid that won't sit well with people who expect to make progress because they follow all the rules.

Their reaction will not change the facts. When we first became humans, our intellect was practically non-existent. Over long eons of time, it has developed to what it is today, but even our most advanced intellectuals will appear primitive in comparison to the human intellect that will develop in the coming millenniums.

Just because someone is a "good" person or "follows all the rules" does not mean he is in a position to become a leader in spiritual matters. In fact, sometimes it is the "bad" person who is a better candidate.

Why do you say that?

There is a passage in the *Book of Revelation* that is often misunderstood. "I know your works; you are neither cold nor hot. I wish you *were* cold or hot. But because you are only lukewarm, and neither cold nor hot, I will spit you out of my mouth."

The very intelligent but selfish person is potentially far more useful to the Spiritual Hierarchy than the "good" person who follows all the rules in hopes that he will gain a prime position in the hereafter. In the latter case, the selfishness is still there, but it is spiritual selfishness instead of material.

The person who uses his intellect for nefarious purposes can sometimes switch gears almost overnight and redirect his energy toward helping others instead of himself. We are not talking about "clever" people who are cunning and manipulative, but rather those who really *are* intelligent, who can figure things out like few others can. If their motive becomes pure, they are extremely valuable. The less intelligent person is far less useful, regardless of how pure his motives are.

What if I'm not someone who has great intellect? How can I develop it?

Don't expect to develop great intellect overnight. You already have some degree of intelligence. Keep a constant pressure in the direction of expanding it. This, as with all spiritual goals, is a long-term effort spanning several lifetimes, not just several years.

Should I read more books, get a university degree, or what?

There is no one solution that works for everyone. The number of degrees and titles you hold is not an indicator of your intellect. It only means you were willing to jump through the hoops required to get them. It *may* indicate persistence and perseverance, both of which are important. Do you know what they call the person who graduates at the very bottom of the class in medical school?

No.

Doctor. When you consult a doctor, you have no idea how well he did in school, and it doesn't matter. He was persistent enough to pass the tests and earn the title of doctor, but what really counts is what he learned *after* medical school. There is a reason we say someone "practices" law or "practices" medicine. It is a never-ending process of learning and honing the intellect. The best doctor is not the one who graduated at the top of his class, but the one who is intuitive and able to interpret subtle clues that others often miss.

There is a method of gaining knowledge that is even more advanced than the intellectual process we know. It was referred to by one of the Adepts in a letter written in 1881: "Believe me, there comes a moment in the life of an Adept, when the hardships he has passed through are a thousandfold rewarded. In order to acquire further knowledge, he has no more to go through a minute and slow process of investigation and comparison of various objects, but is accorded an instantaneous, implicit insight into every first truth. ... the Adept sees and feels and lives in the very source of all fundamental truths ..." (*The Mahatma Letters to A.P. Sinnett,* 55)

The good news is that you do not have to read and understand every book that was ever written. The one thing you can't avoid, however, is developing great intellect. Without it, you are not in a position to acquire the ability mentioned above. You must be able to prove the truth of everything you learn to yourself. Nothing can be accepted on faith except temporarily.

The student who wants to become a chemist does not simply take several classes in chemistry and then call himself a chemist. He spends long hours in the lab reproducing the same experiments that have been done millions of times before. Only after he has learned all that others have learned is he in a position to begin adding more information to the universal store of knowledge about chemistry.

The spiritual scientist does the same thing. He must learn and *put into practice* all he can that has been written about by others. His job is much more difficult than that of the physical scientist though. There are no legitimate universities that offer degrees in spiritual science. There are a few that profess to do that, but they generally appeal to the ego and have little to offer of any real worth.

The spiritual scientist must sort through thousands of pages of "teachings" and "revelations" and determine what is useful and what is a waste of time. The student who has not developed a high degree of discernment can spend lifetimes pursuing spiritual studies that, in the end, yield no gain in wisdom. It is much wiser to spend your time developing discernment instead of chasing every new theory that is popular for the moment.

How can I develop that instantaneous method of learning the Adept was referring to?

You can't just decide you want to do it and then make it happen. Some people have experienced a sort of preview of this method when, during meditation or contemplation, concepts that were previously unclear suddenly become comprehensible. This is not to say you can necessarily explain them in words to another person, but still the concept is integrated in your own ability to understand life, and eventually it will show up more and more in your work.

The higher you climb in your understanding of life, the fewer the number of people who can share what you understand, and the more difficult it is to explain to those who do not share in that understanding. It is a fallacy to think that any concept can be expressed in words. You can only really share your understanding with someone at the same or a higher level of consciousness than that which you have achieved, and most of the communication takes place telepathically, not in the form of spoken or written words. Many highly intelligent people refuse to believe that anyone could possibly understand things they are not able to comprehend. Although great intellect is a requirement for spiritual growth, that alone is not enough; it must be combined with spotless purity and dauntless courage.

What the Adept was referring to only occurs to any great degree to one who is very advanced. However, it is nice to know that we will not have to become an expert in every field of study in the world.

Just how much do we need to know? I can see that it's important to have intellect, and to know some things, but I don't know how far that goes.

You need to have some knowledge of many different subjects, like the proverbial Renaissance man. At the same time, you should become an authority on some things, whether it is art, psychology, physics, music, medicine, archeology, history, or any other of numerous subjects that are important to human evolution. You must have something to offer besides enthusiasm.

Most important of all is to develop character. At the same time, work on increasing your intellect. It may be helpful to take some college courses, regardless of your age, just to keep the pressure on to learn more. Instead of watching television or playing video games, learn a foreign language or take an art class, anything to stretch your intellect and expand your knowledge.

Your education will never end. A solar logos is still learning, so be clear about the fact that you will never know everything. What *is* important is to have the right attitude toward learning. Learn something new every day, not some useless piece of trivia, but something that will make you a better person and will help you become an instrument for raising the consciousness of the world we live in.

Those who make an effort to expand their intellect early in life, generally under pressure from their parents, often slow down when the outside pressure is removed, learning only the bare minimum to get by in the everyday world. This is the person who always struggles in life, is often unhappy, and is convinced that life is unfair. He spends long hours watching television and telling stories with friends and colleagues, but spends almost no time or effort improving his intellect.

The person who is always alert to the possibility of learning something new is like the excited kid who goes to school each day knowing he's going to learn something amazing. Be careful though about where you invest your energy. Invest your time and effort in learning things that help you understand how life works. Be the leader among your friends and family in being the "expert" on life. Be the one they come to when faced with difficult situations, not the one they come to because they want a good laugh and an ego boost.

At some point we humans must become the intelligent factor in intelligent design. The statement in Genesis that Adam was given "dominion" over all living things is a poor translation of the original concept. It is more accurate to say that humans have been given "stewardship" over our earth, including all life-forms that inhabit it.

It is a responsibility and opportunity for growth that we inherited, not divine license to pillage, exploit, and take advantage of our position. We have so far done a rather poor job as stewards of our planet. It has definitely suffered under our guardianship, especially in the past five hundred years as we have become more clever and cunning. Let us be the generation to wake up and resolve to change the situation. It can only happen under the leadership of enlightened people.

Some scientists have made progress in using their intellect to influence nature. Horticulturists create new hybrids of plants with very specific properties, usually to make them more marketable or to increase the crop yield. Unforeseen side effects sometimes occur, at times with disastrous results. All experiments in cloning and gene manipulation must be done under strict guidelines set down by people with the highest ethics. We could easily destroy our planet if certain technologies fall into the wrong hands. The development of morals and ethics must always precede intellectual development. Otherwise, we risk annihilation of all physical life on our planet.

KRIYĀŚAKTI

The most advanced of future civilizations, those who are motivated only by the good of all, will work in conjunction with the Hierarchy for the advancement of all consciousness, whether it dwells in minerals, plants, animals, humans, nature spirits, or devas. A few advanced pupils are beginning to learn how to use kriyāśakti.

That's a word I'm not familiar with.

Kriyāśakti is the ability to create through the use of the mind. Every solar system and every planet first begins as a thought, an energy pattern. "In the beginning was the Word, and the Word was with God, and the Word *was* God." The "Word," or Logos, is the intelligent creative principle in the cosmos.

When we humans want to create something, it starts with a thought, an idea in our mind. We analyze it, examine it, and test the various possibilities and potential methods in our mind before anything physical ever happens. Once we are reasonably certain the idea will work, we create it in physical form, either through our own efforts, the efforts of others, or a combination of both. Regardless of how it is constructed, we are the architect, the intelligent designer. Modifications in the plan almost always are made during construction as new ideas occur to us or it becomes clear that an idea we thought would work is not really feasible. There is always the possibility the project must be scrapped entirely for the time being, either due to external circumstances we cannot control or because of a flaw in our original plan.

Planets, stars, and solar systems are constructed in the same way. A very advanced being conceives the idea in his divine mind, it is carefully thought through, and then construction begins, but in this case the construction phase is billions or trillions of years. And most importantly, the architect does not do the labor himself. Through the use of his mind, he collects the workers, who are beings at a lower level of consciousness, and they are guided in the work.

We human beings are part of the labor force, whether or not we are aware of it. Because we have intellect, we just as often cause delays and problems with the work instead of working hand in hand with the architect, but it is not our fault. We do the best we can, based on our level of expertise which, in most cases, is not great. As we gain in intelligence and intuition, we become much better at working with the plan and at being a help to the architect instead of a hindrance. It is all part of our education. Although we cannot possibly know all the details of how this work takes place, this is the general outline of the process called kriyāśakti.

As a more concrete example, a yogi who has developed the power of kriyāśakti could take the teacup in front of you and, using the power of his will, keeping clearly in his mind the form of the original, create in physical matter a duplicate of the cup. The physical matter comes from the surrounding atmosphere.

Would the result be exactly like the original?

The degree of accuracy would depend on his ability to hold the picture clearly in his mind. Any distraction or lack of focus would result in some deformity.

Why haven't I heard of this before, and why isn't it common knowledge?

The expenditure of energy is enormous and far outweighs the value of the product. Scientists have the ability to transform common elements into gold, but the cost of producing an ounce of gold in the laboratory far exceeds the cost of mining it. More importantly, the ethics of members of the Hierarchy forbids them to use their abilities to entertain and titillate, and the knowledge in the wrong hands would be a disaster, so they are wise enough to use kriyāśakti when their own work warrants it and teach the ability to others only when there is no possibility the power will be misused.

The educational goal of every human being is to become a future Logos, a divine creator of solar systems. Do you see now why strong intellect is one of the first requirements toward becoming a member of our own Spiritual Hierarchy?

I do.

Chapter 6

THE NATURE OF GOD

> Ignorance is preferable to error; and
> he is less remote from the truth who
> believes nothing, than he who
> believes what is wrong.
>
> — Thomas Jefferson

OUR CONCEPT OF GOD

I notice you never mention God. Why is that?

Let's talk about that subject now. How do you conceive of God?

A Supreme Being who is all-knowing, all-powerful, omnipres-ent—a kind, wise, and compassionate father who created the world and cares deeply about his children.

This raises a question. If God is all-powerful and cares deeply about the children he has created, why is there evil in the world, and why do some of those children suffer dreadfully, apparently through no fault of their own?

That is a question I have struggled with for a long time, and I admit I don't have an answer.

You are not the first to wrestle with this problem. In fact, it has been a concern for so long and for so many people, there is even a word for it—theodicy.

What is theodicy?

The philosophical conundrum that asks the question—if God is all-powerful and all-knowing, why did he create a world filled with evil and suffering? Millions have tried for centuries to come up with an adequate answer. Let us ask you another question. How do you account for the passages in the Bible that describe God as angry and vengeful, punishing severely any of his children who do not revere him and follow his orders?

I've struggled with that one too. I know he was originally a god who required the killing and sacrifice of animals, but I think that all changed when Jesus was born.

Then God sometimes changes his mind about things?

I don't know. Maybe humans have made enough progress that he doesn't have to be quite as strict as he once was. I don't have the answers.

Let's discuss this in more detail. Our goal is not to make people feel bad about their deeply-held beliefs, but to give them more understanding. We are all seeking to understand better how life works, are we not?

I am. I'm always willing to learn something new.

MYTHS AND LEGENDS

We sometimes fail to realize that our traditions and beliefs come from millions of years of evolution. They did not come about just in the past few hundred years. Unfortunately, recorded history is only accurate to any great degree for a few hundred years back. We have some fragments of human history going back about four thousand years or so, but before that, information is very scarce, a few monuments and inscriptions, and not much else. Previous to that, we depend on archeologists and the few human fossil remains that have been found. Even that doesn't help much because of the cataclysmic changes in the earth's surface which have occurred in the past and which continue today. The majority of physical evidence is deeply folded into the earth or under the oceans. In most cases, all we have left of our ancient history are myths and legends that have been handed down through the ages, the stories of our past, often more fantastic than any fairy tale, yet containing gems of information for those who can decipher them.

These legends of gods living among us are not inventions. They describe, in some cases, how things once were. We think it entertaining to read tales of giants and of Cyclopes. The truth is, both have existed. Even modern physiologists teach that the pineal gland is the vestigial remains of what was once a third eye. This primitive eye developed before the two we currently have were fully developed so yes, millions of years ago, there was a race of humans, hardly recognizable as such by our own standards, which had one eye. The pineal gland, or "third eye," is a very important organ when it comes to meditation. René Descartes described the pineal gland as the "seat of the soul."

Why don't we find fossil remains of Cyclopes?

They were not yet dense enough to leave fossil remains. They existed on etheric levels where atoms and molecules do not bind as tightly as they do in denser regions. Future science will depend on the ability to read records that are not physically in existence. We have a long way to go before that occurs, but it will one day be a reality. The *Matrix* movies and *The Minority Report* are not as far-fetched as they might seem. When you compare the science of just 500 years ago with the science of today, there is no comparison. The science of the future will be even more astonishing in its advances. However, physical science will never learn how to solve the problem of suffering in the world, no matter what it invents. Each individual is responsible for the end of his own suffering, and it comes not from something more, but from something less—getting rid of the ego and personal desires.

So these ancient myths and legends depict some very real circumstances. In the early days of human development, when our minds were still developing and we were more innocent, advanced beings were provided to guide us and set an example for us to follow. Some were probably not much more advanced mentally and ethically than the most advanced humans on our planet today, but to a primitive race of humans, they were gods. They were extremely intelligent, seeming to know everything, and we revered them as great heroes and divine beings. They, in turn, were in communication with beings even more advanced than they were. Thus, we have the source of the myths of gods who came to dwell among men. They were truly our divine kings. The office of the Dalai Lama has for centuries been regarded as that of a divine priest-king. The institution of monarchies, of which we have some remaining today, comes from a remote past when there was a race of men far superior to the average. Many of our concepts of God derive from those ancient days when our gods dwelt with us physically on earth.

In an early part of our human evolution, in what are referred to as "Lemurian" times, we were still innocent and had retained much of our divine connection, at least up until the latter part of the Lemurian period. Throughout the earlier stages of that period, we were much more childlike and followed our priest-kings obediently. We were far more spiritual than we are today because we had not yet entered the most dense part of our physical evolution. The veil between the physical and more spiritual realms did not yet exist. At a certain part of the densification process, the veil had to be lowered; otherwise we would not have continued our "descent into the nether world." The Lemurian period lasted for millions of years.

By the end of this period, we had developed the intellect that sets us apart as humans and were beginning to learn how to use it.

THE ATLANTEAN PERIOD

At the beginning of the next period of development, the "Atlantean," we were still relatively spiritual in nature, but as our intellect became stronger, and personal ego came into existence, everything began to change. There came a time in human history where things got rather ugly. As our intellect continued to develop, we reached a stage where we were now accountable for our actions. We had "partaken of the fruit of the tree of knowledge of good and evil." We "fell from grace" and were "cast out of the Garden of Eden." Sin came into the world in a major way.

It did not happen overnight as many suppose. The allegories of the Bible, beautiful as they are, are a succinct way of describing events that took place over eons of time. A few sentences in *Genesis* cover billions of years of earth development and millions of years of human development. It must also not be supposed that it is a great shame that sin came into the world and that we would still live in the Garden of Eden if only the serpent had not beguiled Eve and Eve had not enticed Adam. Why? Because it is all part of the plan of human evolution. In order to become co-creators with our gods, we must be given the chance to start creating something. Mistakes are always made in the beginning, and in this case we made some stupendous ones.

Once free will was introduced in the world, made possible by the stage of intellectual development we had reached, the world became far less predictable than before. Being only slightly developed in all aspects of our human-ness, we also were extremely self-centered and still are to a large degree. So when the mind developed to a point where we could control our environment to some extent, and our emotions had reached a fairly high level of development, the two combined wreaked havoc in the world. Lust, greed, ambition, and the need for power and control all came to the forefront. Our personal ego was operating in full force.

Some humans managed to retain much of their innocence and continued to revere their god-kings, but the majority slipped deeper and deeper into the material side of their nature until they lost virtually all contact with their spiritual self. Eventually, the more spiritual of humanity were concentrated only in smaller groups left to themselves, while the bulk of humanity became more and more depraved. This latter group eventually learned to practice black magic and became quite advanced in knowledge and power. Most of their ceremonials are probably best left to the imagination.

Although they had lost contact with their soul, they retained some clairvoyance and communication on the astral-emotional level where there were, and still are, entities of a loathsome nature, all resulting from their own lascivious thoughts. These entities often gained psychological control over people and could only be propitiated by elaborate rituals involving animal and human sacrifice.

The members of the Spiritual Hierarchy who had the task of guiding young humanity were in a serious predicament. Despite their best efforts, humans had decided to use their intellect for selfish and carnal purposes. Something drastic had to happen, and it did.

Over a period of thousands of years, the bulk of humanity was wiped off the face of the earth. Keep in mind that only their physical bodies were destroyed, meaning the entire personality. The souls of these individuals, which cannot be evil, continued to exist. Do you see now where some of the concepts of an angry and vengeful God came from?

I do, and it makes sense. What kind of catastrophes occurred, and how many people were destroyed in them?

There were four major catastrophes, and innumerable minor ones, mostly in the form of volcanoes, earthquakes, and tidal waves. As many as two billion humans lost their lives over the course of many centuries. People often wonder how reincarnation could be possible, given that the human population a few thousand years ago was so small. As we now know, human civilizations have grown up and declined drastically in the past. The world population has risen and fallen many times as well.

Then who survived? Obviously someone did, or we wouldn't be alive today in physical form.

The ones who survived were, for the most part, the ones who did not succumb to the sinful practices of the majority. They had advance warning through their priest-kings of the impending disasters and were moved to safe locations, either by land or by sea.

Could that be the origin of the story of Noah's ark?

The story of Noah's ark can be interpreted in several different ways, but this is one of the origins of the story. It is interesting to note that similar stories involving survivors of a great flood occur in the legends of many indigenous peoples around the world.

What was the final catastrophe, and how long ago did it happen?

The final catastrophe was the sinking of the island of Poseidonis, the last remnant of a once-powerful continent and civilization. It happened in 9,564 BC, according to one source, and was discussed by Plato in *Timaeus*.

That's not really that long ago.

No, it isn't, and you can perhaps see now why our knowledge of human history is so small. All records of the prior civilization were destroyed along with the inhabitants, and for good reason.

What was that?

Because of their degenerate behavior and traditions, it was important to make a clean break. All of their history, including writings, had to go. Humanity needed a chance for a fresh start, and it required drastic action in order to make that possible.

But didn't the people who perished reincarnate and engage in their evil ways once again?

Good question. Because the world population after the destruction was so small, many had to wait for centuries before they were able to reincarnate, and the world had changed drastically in the meantime. Many of those who lived at that earlier period are living among us today. All have made progress, some more than others. Remember that there are hundreds of millions of rather unenlightened people in many countries around the world.

As you can see, this is not a very pleasant part of our human history, and it has been very rocky since then. We still have a long way to go before regaining that more spiritual and elevated existence we once had, but we are making progress, and some people are making very rapid progress; they have chosen to do everything possible to make it happen.

What about the priest-kings? If there was some remnant of the population that did not succumb to evil practices, why don't we still have these divine leaders with us today?

We do, in the form of certain members of the Spiritual Hierarchy. However, with the state of the world as it exists today, we are still at a crucial period of time, and every possible effort is made to keep things going in a positive direction. If they lived among us in the world, their energy would be dissipated by the energy of the masses who are completely self-absorbed. Look at our leaders in the world today. Their energy and time are occupied with the personal emotional needs of the people, and little time is left to do work of a spiritual nature.

The members of the Hierarchy who deal directly with the billions of people in the world are careful to avoid the emotional turmoil in the outer world. While we may be aware of their existence, the work they do occurs in the background, not in the arena of human drama. At some point, we will have grown enough that they can be among us again, but that time is not yet.

What does all this have to do with my concept of God?

As we said before, our traditions and religious beliefs are the result of our experience in the human race. Our myths, legends, and religious allegories are all intertwined. In some parts of the Bible, God is angry and seeks revenge. No one in the Spiritual Hierarchy was angry or vengeful, but that certainly was the perception of those who were affected by the catastrophes. Our concepts of the righteous being protected and evil ones consigned to the flames of hell all come from this period of history.

The idea of a god who was bloodthirsty, demanding the killing and burning of animals to satisfy his thirst, comes from remnants of the evil religious practices of those days. Obeah, Santería, Voodoo, and other primitive religious practices are carryovers from those unenlightened times.

I can see that our concept of God is a conglomeration of different religious practices of the past, but I still like to think of him as a kind and loving father. There's nothing wrong with that, is there?

There is nothing wrong with it. However, there is a distinct advantage in knowing what is true as opposed to what we would like to believe is true. Scientists would be foolish to work as if their beliefs were laws of nature without bothering to prove that they actually work. There is also a field of scientific study of our spiritual nature, and it too must rely on what has been proven to work, not on fanciful speculation.

Who are these spiritual scientists?

All are members of the Spiritual Hierarchy, those human and super-human beings who have taken the time and effort to prove for themselves some laws of nature not known to most people.

Then why don't they share that information with others? Surely the world would be better if we had more information about how the universe operates.

It is not information about heretofore unknown powers that will make the world a better place. Some of this information *is* shared, but it often appears so fantastic that it is scoffed at and derided as delusional. Much of it is purposely withheld because, if it gets into the wrong hands, it could be disastrous for the world.

As an example, members of this group could force an individual to do their bidding from a distance, simply by using the powers at their command. They could also project their consciousness to any location, peer into anyone's bedroom, and read his most private thoughts. They would never do it because it is not in their nature and is against their code of ethics. They have developed the very highest morals and manifest naturally an abiding love and compassion for all beings. Until a person develops this same moral and ethical nature, and until that person has proven his ethics to the highest degree, it would be foolish to give him these tools, would it not?

I guess you're right. There are many people in the world who would love to have that kind of power, but it would not be used for any good purpose.

Not only is much of the knowledge purposely withheld, but much of it is not even comprehensible at our level of consciousness. It is only understandable and transmissible at a higher level than we have currently attained, but we can always strive to reach higher and one day achieve the moral purity and high level of consciousness required to gain access to that knowledge.

THE NATURE OF EVIL

Why does evil exist in the world?

Nature did not create evil, nor did any spiritual deity. First, it is important to recognize that there *is* evil in the world, if you equate evil with sorrow, suffering, and the emotional and physical harm that some humans perpetrate against fellow human beings, either on purpose or unknowingly. Animals are not capable of creating evil. The bird that eats a butterfly and the cat that eats the bird are simply following their natural instinct. They are in tune with nature and are doing what they are supposed to do.

Evil exists because of humans. We are gods in the making, but we are also great trouble makers. We cannot become co-creators with the Spiritual Hierarchy unless we learn to work with our intellect, and we can't develop our intellect unless we have free will. No one learns without making mistakes.

Evil is quite simply that which goes against the laws of nature. Only man has the intellectual ability to do this, and we do it on a regular basis. Why? Because of ego. Our ego wants to feel superior to others, and we do this by becoming wealthier and more powerful than those around us, ignoring the suffering we cause in the process.

Isn't it possible to be rich without causing harm to others?

Of course it is, and we must never assume that every wealthy person got there by trampling on others along the way. But the temptation to achieve the goal at any cost, even if it harms others, is always a possibility. The truly enlightened individual has no need for more money than necessary to satisfy basic needs. He may become wealthy because of his endeavors in the world, but the accumulation of wealth is never his primary goal.

It is not just the desire for wealth that can tempt someone to disregard the welfare of others. Power is another enormous ego enhancer. If you want to know what a person is made of, give him a little power.

At the very core of the matter, it is ignorance that creates evil in the world, ignorance of natural law. But ignorance of the law is no excuse. Natural law operates invariably, whether we are aware of it or not. As we gain in understanding, and align ourselves with natural law, our contribution to the pain and sorrow in the world ends; from then on, we are an instrument for making the world a better place.

Cease to do evil. Learn to do good. If evil is anything that goes against natural law, good is anything that is in harmony with the laws of nature. We can't stop the evil that is perpetrated in the world on a daily basis, but we can stop contributing to it ourselves and do our part to teach others how life works.

In the long run, evil can never prevail. It is based on ignorance and on selfishness. The person who perpetrates evil is thinking only of himself. There is only a limited amount of power even in a group of people who conspire to perform evil deeds, because each one is really only looking out for himself. In a group of more enlightened people, there is tremendous power because there is no selfishness involved. The very nature of their actions is in tune with nature's plan. Anything that goes along with the laws of nature, instead of against them, has great power. Good will always prevail in the end.

How would you advise me to think of God?

First, be clear about your concept. One of the first things you mentioned was a Supreme Being. Supreme implies that there is nothing higher, nothing beyond what we are describing. The only thing that could satisfy that requirement is the Absolute, which is indefinable, indivisible, indescribable, and unimaginable. There is no being even at that level, because there is no polarity, no manifestation, and no means of comparison. The Absolute is "be-ness" itself, a potential being. This is not the being you describe as a loving father.

The prevalent concept of God as a loving father is quite accurate, when you understand where the concept came from. When there were priest-kings who reigned, we were literally, in many instances, their physical offspring. One of their goals was to improve the quality of humanity, and one way they did that was by having large families; thus, many people carried genes of bodies made as perfect as possible by the priest-kings. This same group lived within the influence of their fathers' and mothers' auras. They also received special training and instructions from them. Thus, we were literally the children of gods who loved us, and the idea still has a powerful emotional effect on us. It is only natural that we should long for a return to those conditions. They will return one day, in the not so distant future.

The Spiritual Hierarchy consists of all beings who have reached a certain level of spiritual development, and even includes a number of humans who have attained a high degree of moral and spiritual development. Above that level there are Adepts or super-humans, Devas, Chohans, Mahāchohans, Manus, Bodhisattvas, Buddhas, Planetary Logoi, Solar Logoi, and so on, ad infinitum.

You can choose, if you like, to think of the Absolute as God, or the Logos of our solar system, or the Planetary Spirit of our earth, known as the Lord of the World. You could even consider your own soul or monad to be God if you like, but none of these fit your idea of a loving father who created you and has a special interest in the emotional needs of your personality.

Many past civilizations revered the sun as a deity. We tend to smile and consider them rather naive in their beliefs, but it actually makes sense. The physical sun is one aspect of the being referred to as the Solar Logos. Of course there are other levels of consciousness included in the consciousness of that being, but the only one we can physically perceive is the sun, the center of our physical solar system. Many people through the ages and even today have chosen to revere this highly advanced being as God, but even his consciousness does not comprehend every aspect of the solar system he created, any more than you can understand and know every aspect of your own child or even your own body.

THE DIVINE ARCHITECT

You just said he created the solar system!

And so he did, in matter, but he did not create the spiritual force which inhabits that matter, and he did not create matter itself. No one can create matter, but you can use it as a building material, and all builders do just that, whether it is a Solar Logos, a Planetary Logos, or a brick mason. Speculation on a god personally interested in your ego is indulgence in a fantasy.

There is one more aspect of the concept of God we have not yet touched on.

What is that?

For most people, our belief in God is very emotional. Any conversation on the subject results in emotional reactions.

As long as this happens, we will not be able to analyze the situation with any degree of clarity. Emotions always cloud our vision and prevent clear analysis. To most people, their belief in God is intimately connected with their own ego. Any difference of opinion on the subject leads to a violent emotional reaction, so violent at times that it results in someone's death. Fanatical religious beliefs have been responsible for the deaths of millions of people in the world, all in the name of their god. More evil has resulted from emotionally-held religious beliefs than from any other cause.

How could that be?

Because some people's beliefs are so tightly held that they are unwilling to change any part of it. They are convinced that their beliefs are true, and nothing will change their minds. Otherwise perfectly good candidates for spiritual development who are quite intelligent, pure of motive, and have dauntless courage, are unable to make spiritual progress because their minds are closed and they will not consider new ways of thinking.

What about the concept of Satan?

It is interesting to note that the percentage of people who believe in God has not changed much over time, but the percentage who believe in Satan, also known as the Devil, has declined. The truth is, there is more evidence of a personal devil than of a personal god.

What do you mean?

Every human has a dual nature. There is the Divine Nature, the indwelling ātma, but there is also a baser, more evil nature. In some people this dichotomy is very apparent—some days they are radiant angels, and other times they are raving devils. Some are completely incapable of repressing their lower nature, and it comes to the surface with the slightest provocation. Most people, however, manage to keep it under control, often for years at a time. In these people, the lower nature has not ceased to exist, but it only comes to the surface in moments of great stress.

The lower nature also surfaces during riots or other events where mob mentality reigns and the basest of our animal nature manifests. Often the worst aspects of human nature are expressed during war and acts of violence. But the opposite may be true for a few individuals, and the atrocities of others may intensify their own divine compassion.

Over many lifetimes, many who have made a certain amount of progress in spiritual development are unaware of a hidden factor, the so-called "Dweller on the Threshold."

What is that?

The term was coined by Edward Bulwer-Lytton in his novel *Zanoni*; it is an apt description of something that comes up at some point for everyone on the path. It may not show up during this particular lifetime, but it will at some point. No personal energy ever dissipates on its own. Unless we have done something to re-train and re-orient it, it remains in the background for years. Then, just when we think we are making great spiritual progress, the increase in positive energy awakens the sleeping negative energy and we find ourselves face to face with an entity of our own making, although unknown to us.

We have no choice but to do battle with this entity, but it is no physical battle. It is entirely psychological in nature, taking place in the astral and lower mental realms, although the effects are often felt on the physical plane as well. If we vanquish this "Dweller on the Threshold," we have taken a major step in our progress. If we shrink back in fear and cower, we have lost the battle. It means we are not yet ready for the difficulties of the higher life and have more work to do before we will have another opportunity to prove ourselves.

The battle is seldom a one-time event but more often a series of battles. The temptation of Jesus in the desert is a good example of the battle between the higher and lower forces within a person on the verge of spiritual advancement. As you see, dauntless courage is not just an idle phrase.

So to your way of thinking, there is no personal god, but there is a sort of personal devil. Is that correct?

Yes, but if you state it that way without also giving the background information, you will probably get a variety of reactions from others, ranging from intrigue to amusement and even anger. We are our own personal god and our own personal devil, the god being our innate spiritual nature and the devil being the agglomeration of negative energy from numerous lifetimes.

Now you see why it is so difficult to discuss this topic with most people and why we do not use the term God casually. If everyone could lay their emotions aside, useful conversations would ensue, but most people are not ready to do that.

You have given me a lot to think about. It will take some time to process it and contemplate some of the ideas you have brought up. I think I have some work to do.

Freedom comes from the knowledge of what is true. "You shall know the truth, and the truth shall set you free." There is no limit to what we can learn, but if we close our minds to further learning, we are at a standstill for the present time and can make no more progress. Anyone who is so egotistical as to think he has a monopoly on the truth is deluding himself and stunting his own spiritual growth. When that happens, nature intervenes and creates a situation where he has no option but to change his point of view. Some of us willingly accept the changes which are the result of expanding consciousness, and some are dragged along kicking and screaming.

Chapter 7

THE LAW OF CAUSE AND EFFECT

Give me understanding, and I shall
keep thy law; yea, I shall observe it
wholeheartedly.

— *Psalms* 119:34

AS YOU SOW, SO SHALL YOU REAP

"What goes around comes around," "As you sow, so shall
you reap," "For every action there is an equal and opposite
reaction." These are all ways of stating a law of nature
sometimes referred to as karma, or the law of cause and
effect.

Even science recognizes that everything in the universe is connected and that the slightest action affects the entire universe. Scientists are also aware of the "observation factor," the fact that merely observing something causes subtle changes in the object under observation. The importance of this is that we can never "know" something as it was before we began to observe it. We have already changed it, simply by focusing our attention on it.

Every thought we think has an effect on the object of that thought, whether it is a person, a physical object, or even an abstract concept. We will look at thought in greater detail in chapter 10.

More people than ever are familiar with the term karma, but there is much confusion as to what it is and how it operates. People often assume it is a system of rewards and punishment for respecting or ignoring a particular law laid down by a divine being. Thus, they speak of "good karma" as something desirable, and "bad karma" as a painful or unpleasant result of past actions.

The word karma simply means action, but it encompasses more than the simple idea of a physical act. It also includes the concept of a reaction, the inherent result of the action, the "cause" and the "effect." It also includes "actions" on all planes of existence, including emotional and mental.

Thus, our emotions, thoughts, and desires, as well as our physical actions, all create karma. "As a man thinketh in his heart, so is he," is not an idle phrase. Jesus understood well that every action begins as a thought and the thought itself creates a result, whether or not the physical body is involved. "Whosoever looks upon a woman to lust after her has committed adultery with her already in his heart." The thought alone creates an energy field, and that energy field affects not only the one who created the thought, but the object of the thought and those nearby.

Near the thinker or the object of the thought?

Both.

Are you saying I'm responsible for every thought I think?

If you created the thought yourself, then yes, you are responsible. However, we are constantly bombarded with thoughts from other people. The closer they are to you physically, the more those thoughts affect you. It is fortunate that most people are quite ineffective in their thinking, so their thoughts have little energy behind them and are therefore little likely to have a great impact on us.

A notable exception to this is when a person is extremely angry or filled with thoughts of revenge directed at another person. It is especially so if he becomes obsessive and spends hours each day adding more energy to the accumulated thoughts of anger and revenge. This energy cannot help but affect the unfortunate object of such angry thoughts.

If someone is angry at me and directing negative energy my way, how do I avoid being affected by these negative thoughts?

The best way is by not having anything in your own character that could vibrate in sympathy with angry thoughts. Every thought and emotion has a specific vibratory rate. If that energy finds a field of like matter in you, it will set it vibrating more strongly, just as a tone causes the corresponding string of a guitar or piano to vibrate. If there is no energy field within you with the same low vibratory rate, it cannot affect you. Unfortunately, few people are so pure in character that these negative thoughts have no effect on them.

At the same time, if you have not developed the higher vibratory rates within you, your Higher Self has no way of communicating with you. This is why purity of thoughts and emotions is so important if you would make spiritual progress. Without this purity, you are at the mercy of the barrage of thought-forms that are always in the surrounding atmosphere.

Wouldn't it be better to live in the mountains, far away from human beings, so as not to be affected by these negative energies?

It would, and in fact, those who are most advanced do exactly that. However, it is also important that someone be available to help lift to some extent the vibratory rate of our fellow beings by interacting in a positive manner with them. You can be an instrument for sending positive energy to your surrounding area if you fit yourself to the task.

To be "in the world but not of the world" is no easy task, and yet that should be our goal if we would do our part in improving life on this planet.

I'm still thinking about the fact that I'm responsible for even my thoughts. I thought it was okay as long as I didn't say or do anything that would hurt someone else.

Most people refuse to believe they are responsible for everything that happens in their life. They are convinced that life is unfair, that some people are just lucky and did nothing special to deserve the good fortune they enjoy. The enlightened person, on the other hand, is quite willing to accept that he or she is responsible for everything experienced in life.

Wait a minute! I don't mind being responsible for what I do in this lifetime, but how is it fair to be born with physical or mental defects? You said yourself that this personality has never lived before and will never live again, so it certainly seems unfair to inherit karma that I personally did not create.

Whether it is "fair" or "unfair" depends on how you choose to view the situation. When the Bible speaks of "punishing the children for the sin of the fathers to the third and fourth generation," the prophet was not speaking of the physical offspring, but of future incarnations of that individual soul. You, this current incarnation, are the result of all previous incarnations created by your Higher Self. You are the child of your "ancestors," or previous incarnations. Just as you inherit the "good" or "bad" karma, you also inherit all the experience gained in previous lifetimes.

Whether you choose to see life as "fair" or "unfair," it is as it is. We do not have the option of deciding how the universe should operate. We can choose to accept it as it is and work in harmony with natural law, or we can choose to believe life is unfair and spend our entire life in opposition to the laws of nature. If you want life to be easy, choose the former attitude. If you want a difficult life, choose the latter.

It still doesn't seem fair that I have to pay the price for someone else's transgressions.

We humans cannot possibly see all the causes and effects that make up our current world situation or personal situation. The Higher Self does not care about the problems that seem so important to the personality. It cares only about one thing—spiritual progress—the continual expansion of consciousness. Karma is the natural law that makes that possible.

How is that so?

Because karma is the natural force that gently, and sometimes not so gently, guides us again and again back to the path of spiritual progress. Without karma, there would be no reason not to engage in any activity that would benefit the personal self, with no regard for anyone else.

Many people "believe" in karma, yet they continue to lie, cheat and steal. Obviously, belief is not enough. Once a person has gained the unshakeable conviction that the law of karma will operate in all circumstances, he will never again be tempted to lie, steal, or even say anything that could be harmful to himself or any other being.

It makes sense when you say it that way.

Everything in nature makes perfect sense when you see it from a high enough perspective. No one ever encounters a difficulty that is not an important learning situation. Once the lesson is learned, you never have to learn it again, not even in a future lifetime. The recapitulation period during the first years of each lifetime is designed to help us remember what was learned in the past and then make additional progress from that point forward.

What happens if I do something that harms someone else but was not intentional? Does that create a karmic response?

Motive is everything. Even our laws recognize that. There is first degree murder, second degree murder, manslaughter, and negligent homicide. Each results in the death of someone, but the punishment is different in each case. Karma is far better than the best judge in the world at determining what the motive was behind a particular action, and that motive determines the resulting karma. Negligence on your part will still result in a karmic effect.

In some cases, the cause for something that occurs in this lifetime did not originate now but is a carryover from a previous lifetime. It is quite possible that the underlying factors go back much farther than anyone might imagine, even thousands of years in some instances. This is precisely why we should not judge others, even in situations that seem egregious. We do not know if the current situation is the result of previous karma or is the beginning of a new karmic situation.

Does that mean we shouldn't punish an individual because what he did might be justified by something that happened in a previous lifetime?

The purpose of the legal system should always be first and foremost to protect the citizens. We often get emotionally involved in court cases we watch on television, and our emotional reaction is an intense desire to see the perpetrator punished. It is your ego that has created this emotional drama wherein you have appointed yourself the judge, jury, and executioner.

Our main concern should be to get dangerous people out of society and give them a chance for rehabilitation if that is possible. If you are one of those individuals who have strong emotional reactions to court cases, take the time to examine yourself and you will find that it has everything to do with your own ego.

Karma is the law that re-balances everything in the universe. "For every action, there is an equal and opposite reaction." The universe is a finely-tuned machine. It may seem imperfect from our imperfect point of view, but it is not. Everything is exactly as it should be because the current state of things is the sum total of all previous actions that have ever occurred. And through the passage of eons of time, it will not be unbalanced by one jot or one tittle.

"The wheels of the gods grind slowly, yet they grind exceedingly fine."

PERFECT JUSTICE RULES THE WORLD

How can you be so certain of that?

Because perfect justice rules the world. It is inherent in the design of nature.

It sounds like you're saying there is no such thing as evil if even evil has its place in the world.

Whether you call something good or evil is based on your own imperfect perspective of things. As you grow in consciousness and perception, things that appeared "awful" in the past assume a different perspective and turn out to be blessings after all.

That is true. I've had some terrible health problems in the past that I wouldn't wish on anyone, but in hindsight I recognize that I have grown tremendously through those difficult experiences and I wouldn't trade them for anything. Still, it's hard to see others suffer, especially children.

The difficulty lies in our limited field of vision. We do not see all the previous causes that have resulted in the current situation. Once we think things through and see the beauty of the laws of nature, we accept everything just as it is, whether it affects us or others. Everything is just as it should be. Would you want it to be different?

No, I guess not.

The best thing we can do is to adopt an attitude of equanimity. Nothing fazes us, nothing upsets us, there is no emotional reaction to the "drama" of life because it is exactly as it should be. The Sanskrit word for this is vairāgya, often translated as desirelessness, although a better definition might be "indifference to pleasure and to pain," in other words, non-reaction.

Wouldn't it be better if everyone lived in peace, if there were no wars, just loving, peaceful coexistence?

The only way to do that currently would to be to impose it on everyone, and you would be taking away people's ability to make choices.

Still, that would be preferable to the awful things that happen in the world every day.

Would it? You would be short-sighted to think that by creating an artificial appearance of peace, it would somehow translate into a real and lasting peace. It cannot be. You would be annihilating all the past causes that have been built up over millions of years. Every energy pattern created must work itself out naturally. It cannot simply be discarded and ignored. Stop looking at life as a snapshot, and learn to see the bigger picture. Then you will have a greater perception of the beauty of the plan which is unfolding exactly on schedule.

VIOLENCE OR WORLD PEACE?

Consider for a moment the existence of violence in the world. All good people throughout the world yearn for peace, for an end to fighting and strife. Ask yourself this, "Have I eliminated all anger, resentment and acrimony from my own life?"

No, I can't honestly say that I have.

Then how do you expect the rest of the world to be ready for peace when it doesn't even exist within your own heart? Even those of us who are somewhat enlightened are often at war with family members, acquaintances, and even with fellow travelers on the path. Do you really think you can help others achieve peace if you have not found it for yourself?

Obviously, we are expected to be aware of and concerned with the outer world, but we also recognize that we have more important work to do than attend to the world's physical and emotional needs. Perhaps we fail to realize just how much we can influence the world around us by our very presence and by the higher frequencies of vibration we have hopefully developed in ourselves through years of contemplation. We place so much emphasis on meditation that we often forget the equally important phase of contemplation. Through pondering on the problems of humanity, whether it be civil rights, poverty, politics, violence, or any of a thousand other problems, we are helping in ways that are subtle, yet extremely powerful.

Our function is to open men's hearts and understanding to charity, justice, and generosity, attributes which belong specifically to the human kingdom and are natural to man when he has developed the higher qualities of a human being. We have available to us the necessary information to transform our animalistic instincts into the highest human qualities, and when people have learned to think and feel as true human beings should, they will act humanely; works of charity, justice and generosity will be done spontaneously by all.

Let us develop fully within ourselves all the qualities we would like the rest of the world to display. Let us practice altruism, compassion, and complete honesty in all things. Let us give up arguments and anger and the need to be right. Let us stop judging others, and look carefully at our personal, selfish motives. Let us eliminate pride and the smugness that characterize so many "spiritual" persons. Let us get rid of our need to feel important. Once we have developed all of the character traits that distinguish the true spiritual aspirant, our influence on the rest of the world is already in effect. We have already made an impact on the world around us.

JUDGMENTS

If we could see the motives behind every situation, we would be in an excellent position to make judgments about them. Instead, we see only appearances, the results of the motives and the previous actions, so we are severely hampered in making an accurate assessment of the situation.

Practice non-judgment. Why should you presume to know everything about a situation when it is impossible to know with any degree of accuracy what has caused something to be as it currently appears?

It's only human nature to make judgments and give our opinions on things. What a boring world this would be if we had no opinions!

Most people would agree with you. We are describing, however, how enlightened people operate. They know the danger of making judgments when it cannot be done with any degree of accuracy. Why judge others?

Because it makes life interesting.

Have you forgotten that every thought you think affects everyone around you, and especially those who are the object of that thought? If you decide a person is "evil," or "mean," or "rude," you automatically know your judgment is based on limited information. Are you willing to create negative karma for yourself because of a habit of passing judgment on other people?

When you put it that way, maybe I should take a closer look at the concept of judging and expressing opinions. But don't we sometimes have to make judgments?

Of course we do. A judge or jury must render a verdict at the end of a trial. If you have ever served on a jury, you know how difficult that task is, aware that your decision could deprive a person of liberty for a number of years. Despite the realization that we can never know with one hundred percent certainty whether or not a person is guilty, our obligation in such a case is to do the best we can in order to protect our fellow citizens. The keyword is obligation. When it is our duty to judge, then we must render a judgment that is as fair as possible.

But in everyday life, if we believe someone is guilty of a crime, it doesn't take away their liberty.

It doesn't? More than likely, you will express that opinion to other people, and even if you don't, you have added your bit of energy to the pool of public opinion created by those who are convinced this person is guilty and should be punished. When hundreds, thousands, or even millions of people are adding to that thought-form that says, "This person is guilty," how are you *not* affecting him?

I never thought of it that way.

That's the problem with most people. They don't think through a situation and come to a logical conclusion. Instead, they indulge in knee-jerk reactions based on emotions and delight in rendering a judgment on someone else. The deliberation time is usually a matter of seconds. Are you so insightful that you can render in seconds a judgment that would take the legal system months, if not years, to accomplish?

No. I guess I need to re-visit my ideas of judging people. But surely it isn't harmful if I express opinions about others that are positive.

GIVING COMPLIMENTS

Imagine that you meet a young girl and say, "What a pretty girl you are!" or to a boy you say, "You are such a smart boy!"

Surely you're not implying that would be inappropriate or even harmful. It's only natural to want to make people feel good, especially children.

Think about it. First of all, by saying a girl is pretty, it implies there are other children who are not pretty and might be downright ugly. If you say a child is smart, it imparts a stamp of superiority, and the child may very well think, "Aha! I knew I was smarter than the other kids. Now I have confirmation from an adult." You are simply appealing to their young egos and reinforcing the idea that it is okay to feel superior to others. We teach children early in life to indulge in the practice of mutual ego enhancement. It can do nothing to help the child become a responsible adult.

I don't see it that way at all. It's just a formality, a way to connect with someone.

People often use ego enhancers as a way of "connecting" with others. I will give you a compliment in hopes that you will compliment me. You enhance my ego and I'll enhance yours.

I'm not expecting any compliments from the children. I'm not complimenting them in hopes of enhancing my ego.

Are you so sure? The fact is, you hope they will like you because you have boosted their egos. Is this not a way to pump up your own ego?

I think this is far too small a thing to even deserve much attention. Surely there are more important things to be concerned about.

There are no small things in life. You ignore the "small" things to your own detriment. In fact, this is precisely why few people make much spiritual progress. You remind them of a very simple lesson and they say, "I learned that a long time ago. Teach me something important." In fact, they did *not* learn it a long time ago. They heard about the concept and it made some sense, but they never bothered to apply it in their life. Why? Because that requires work and they don't want to make the effort. It is much easier to read another book, attend another seminar, take another workshop, or watch another television show that will help them look up their past lives or determine just how advanced they are on the spiritual path. But to actually change the way they operate in life, practice non-judgment, non-reaction, and non-attachment? It's easier to skip over that, pretending those things are not as important as something that is more fun.

Yes, the little things are very important. Until you actually apply those simple concepts and make them a part of your character, you will never make real progress.

Just as an example, how would you suggest I interact with children or anyone else if I shouldn't be giving out compliments?

A compliment is nothing more than your own judgment of the individual. Stop focusing on the individual, whether it is yourself or another person. Every time you offer an opinion, it is a statement that somehow your opinion matters and that others should pay attention to it. After all, not everyone receives compliments from you, so they should feel special, having received a compliment from such an important person as you are.

You can never offer an unsolicited opinion without ego being involved, and even if it is requested, there is still probably ego enhancement attached. To answer your question, focus on something besides personalities. Focus on nature, on life, on something marvelous you just discovered or read about; go for a walk with that person and share a personal experience. Learn to enjoy simply *being* with each other and experiencing the life within instead of the form. Walk together in silence. It may take some practice, especially if you are among those who think there must be constant chatter when in the company of others. You will not change old habits instantly, but you will not change them at all if you think it is unimportant to do so.

The less you talk, the more others will pay attention when you do talk. Have you ever been around someone who talks non-stop with no lack of opinions and judgments?

Every day at work. After a while I stop listening.

Exactly. Spend more time thinking, observing, analyzing.

But isn't that judging?

Not at all. You never want to stop observing. That's how you learn. You can even make comparisons. That does not necessarily involve judgment. Unnecessary judgment always involves ego, a sense of superiority or smugness, regardless of how subtle it may be. Observe and learn. Speak little, but when you do speak, be sure your words are carefully formulated and that they convey precisely and succinctly what you want to convey. Many people talk around a subject, certain they have accurately expressed their thoughts. In fact, they could not have been accurately transmitted, because they were never clearly conceived in their own mind.

By being scrupulously careful in our thoughts and speech, they become very powerful. Then there is tremendous energy behind each thought, and it is far more likely to have an effect on others. Say what you mean, and mean what you say.

How can I avoid some of the thought-forms that pollute our atmosphere?

Whenever you can, maintain a quiet atmosphere around you. Turn off the television. Turn off the radio in your car. Be observant instead. Read and contemplate. Spend time in nature. There is almost nothing on television that will help your spiritual progress, and the noise factor alone is harmful to it.

One of the worst things you can do is fall asleep with the television or radio playing. It is as if you were hypnotized, in an extremely receptive state of mind, and are completely at the mercy of the nonsense we call programming. We will speak of this more when we talk about meditation and contemplation.

If you live in an urban environment, make it a practice to get away on a regular basis. Even if you live in San Francisco, or Mumbai, or any other major metropolis, you can go to a public park and find a quiet spot where you can commune with nature. Marvel at the trees and flowers, the birds, and other wild creatures. You will lose all track of time as you gaze into the sky and leave behind your identification with the physical body.

The more often you get out of your body and out of your mind—that is to say your thoughts—and experience the one-ness with all that exists, the more you will know that *you* are not the body. Once you know this and have experienced it enough to enter that state of consciousness at will, you will never again feel alone or experience a fear of death. After all, what is the fear of death but the fear that you will cease to exist? This can never happen because you are life itself. There is nothing in the universe that is not you. This one simple realization would eliminate forever one of the most negative emotions in the world, the one known as fear.

Can you tell me a little more about how thought works? I must admit I had never thought much about thoughts before.

As humans, since few of us personally know other beings much more advanced than we are, we automatically assume we are the apotheosis of evolution and that our human mind is one of the most powerful things in the universe. The mind *is* powerful, in potential, but it is far from having achieved its maximum level of perfection, and it is far from being the highest level of conscious awareness. The vast majority of humans are controlled more by their emotions than by their minds. The mind becomes a tool of our emotional nature. Use of the mind by our emotions in order to achieve our personal goals is called kāma-manas in Sanskrit. Kāma (desire) and manas (mind) work together, but it is emotional desire that is the motivating factor.

For the time being, our goal as humans is to gain control over the mind. As a great teacher once said, "Strictly speaking, you don't think; thinking happens to you." We believe we are using our ability to think in order to make things happen, and that is true. However, we have not

The Law of
Cause and Effect

even begun to discover the true power of thought and what it can produce.

We are still at the kindergarten level where thought is concerned, and it will be many thousands of years before we as a group make significant progress in developing the power of the mind.

Is there something I can do to speed up the process? I don't think I want to wait that long if it really is as powerful as you say it is.

What is your motive for wanting to develop your mind more rapidly than the normal rate?

I suppose so I can achieve my goals more easily. It certainly would make my life much easier. I wouldn't have to work so hard at everything.

It sounds like your motive is still focused on you and making *your* life easier. That is not really a proper motivation. Do you remember the three prerequisites for rapid spiritual progress?

Strong intellect, spotless purity, and dauntless courage.

Precisely, and purity of motive is paramount in this process. Without it, your results will be mediocre at best. When your motives are pure—meaning impersonal and based on a profound desire to help humanity—then the power of the universe is behind you. You are one with nature, and you will consistently be led in the right direction to achieve the goal. If there is one iota of selfishness in your motive, if pride and ego enter into the equation, you will fail in your quest of obtaining the Holy Grail of Wisdom.

But if there were no ego and no pride in accomplishment, humans would not make any progress.

That is true at the current point in human evolution, and we will examine this later in chapter 12. However, that is the normal path of development, the one that average humanity is following. If you do this, you are simply going along with the crowd and will achieve at the same rate as the rest of humanity. If you hope to advance more rapidly, it must be on very specific conditions.

What are those conditions?

Just what we have stated before. You must be motivated only by a desire to be of service. Any desire for personal gain will inevitably result in failure.

GROUP KARMA

Most people who have heard the term karma associate it with personal karma, but there is also group karma. Group karma is just what it implies—more than one individual shares in the responsibility of the karma, sometimes millions of individuals.

Can you give me some examples of group karma?

We all belong to various groups, whether of our own choice or by "accident." There is no accident though with regard to the circumstances in which we find ourselves, or the groups of which we are a part. Your individual karma determines when you will be born, in what family, under what conditions, in what country, and so forth.

Isn't it true that we choose our parents?

Not in the way you might imagine. You, as a new personality, do not look out over the world and say, "I think I want to be born in this family." Otherwise, we would all choose to be born in families with some degree of wealth so as to have the best opportunities in life, would we not?

I guess it does sound a little simplistic when I think about it. How does it work then?

The karma generated by the various personalities of different lifetimes is connected to the soul. Ultimately, it is the soul that is responsible, although it does not at all feel the effects of your physical, emotional, and mental karma, other than by the fact that it cannot make progress until you make progress.

So the soul's growth depends on me, the personality?

It does. For millions of years your soul has been biding its time, waiting for the lifetime when the personality has achieved enough enlightenment that it, the soul, can now use the personality as an instrument for helping the world in its spiritual progress. Up until then, the personality has been concerned only with itself and its personal needs.

Then the soul selects my parents?

Karma really determines who your parents will be and the circumstances of the coming lifetime. Your soul is completely in tune with your karma and with the laws of nature. It works in conjunction with these factors to select the most appropriate environment for the life lessons you need to learn this time. In a very real sense, these circumstances are the result of all the actions—karmic causes—of previous lifetimes. Thus, in a sense, you *do* choose your parents, but not in the way most would imagine.

In the same way, not only your family, but your nationality, socio-economic group, ethnic heritage, and religion (or lack thereof) are determined by past karmic causes.

Shouldn't we feel fortunate then if we are born in a great country where we have freedom and plenty of opportunities?

Not necessarily. There are plenty of people in powerful democratic countries who are born under dire circumstances, whether economic, physical, or mental. Part of your karma may be that you are born in circumstances that aren't so bad in themselves, but you are surrounded by people who have much more than you do. If you had been born in a more impoverished country under the same circumstances, you would be among the average or even above average. Everything is relative, even karmic circumstances.

In the very best of countries you may be born in a minority or with limitations that set you apart from the rest. You are just as apt to be ridiculed and despised in a progressive country as in a backward one.

Still, I would choose to be born in a progressive country if possible.

You are born exactly where you need to be. All is well in the world. It is not our place to try to make the world uniform. Countries have made serious mistakes by invading other countries under the pretext of improving the lives of its citizens. During colonial times, this reasoning appeared even altruistic, but the underlying motives were far more selfish. When we try to impose our way of life on others, we are not only interfering with their current karma, but we are creating new karma for ourselves as a nation.

It is not by chance that there are different conditions in different countries. These are necessary for the great diversity of life experiences needed by our fellow human beings.

Does that mean we shouldn't try to improve conditions in other countries?

When we do it by force, it creates disasters, for us and for the country we invade. The proper way to do it is through education. It takes a little longer, but it is far safer. The karma created by physically and violently invading a country is tremendous and will require decades, if not centuries, to re-balance. The karma of creating educational and social programs to help under-developed countries is far more positive.

As a nation, we must elect leaders with vision, not just for the economic well-being of our own citizens, but for the spiritual well-being of the world. This does not mean we impose our religious beliefs on others, but that we share with everyone the understanding we have gained of how universal law works. Some of the countries we believe to be seriously disadvantaged actually know far more than we do about these universal laws, or at least certain individuals in them do. There is a national ego just as there is a personal ego.

Shouldn't I be proud of my country and the fact that we have freedom?

What is there to be proud of?

I don't know. I guess the fact that it's a powerful country with great economic advantages, one that is admired and respected by the rest of the world.

Do you see what you are saying? You are using your nationality as an excuse for pumping up your personal ego. There is a certain smugness and sense of superiority when you announce to others that you are a citizen of such and such a country. It is just one more way of feeling more important than others. If you are secure in yourself, then it matters not whether you are a citizen of Uzbekistan, Panama, or France. Anything else is simply your own ego.

The karma of each country is made up of the accumulated karma of its citizens with regard to national issues and interactions with other nations. The same is true of all other groups, religious, ethnic, and so on. All males in the world share in male karma, all females in female karma, all Catholics in Catholic karma, and all Boy Scouts in Boy Scout karma.

But I as an individual didn't create this karma. Do you mean that when I'm born I inherit the karma of perhaps hundreds of years of actions in which I was not a participant?

As a part of that group, yes, you will experience a share of that enormous karma, pleasant or unpleasant as it may be. Personally, you did not create all the enjoyable and pleasurable things that are a part of your country's karma, but you get to enjoy them just the same.

If I must reincarnate again and again until all my karma is exhausted, it will never happen if I'm responsible for national karma as well.

You are responsible for a portion of that karma *only* while you are a part of that group. Some individuals reincarnate again and again in the same nation or in the same religious group because they have developed strong emotional ties with that country or religion. It is a powerful example of attachment. This is a serious impediment to spiritual growth and often prevents our experiencing the variety of circumstances we need in order to grow.

Once you leave a particular group, you no longer share in the karma of that group. Incoming members will take up a share of the karma and you will no longer be a part of it.

Every month there are ethnic groups that cease to exist in the world. This happens when all the group karma is exhausted and the energy of that particular group is no longer necessary to the progress of current humanity. Every two weeks, another language disappears forever from the world when the last remaining speaker of that language dies.

It makes me sad when I hear you say that.

Did you feel sad before you heard it?

No, but now that I think about languages and ethnic groups becoming extinct, I feel a sense of loss, like we've lost an important part of our heritage.

Notice first of all that you only have an emotional response when you think about a situation. As long as you were not thinking about it, everything was fine, but once you thought about the fact that languages and ethnic groups are dying out, you conclude that we have lost something important, although you did not think it was important before. Your emotional reaction is a sense that *you* somehow have been diminished and *you* feel sad. Do you see how this is related to your ego?

Yes, I do.

You are still addicted to the emotional drama of life and to the part the personal ego plays in it. It is important to realize that the world is ephemeral. Nothing lasts forever, not a flower, or a tree, or a human being, or a pet rabbit, not even a stone, or a star, or a planet. Everything lasts for a certain period of time, and then it is gone forever.

But am I not eternal?

You, the personality, are not. At the end of your life, your personality will cease to exist. Not even your soul or your monad is eternal. The only thing that endures forever is the divine spirit that dwells within the form. When you identify with that instead of with the form, whatever it may be, suffering and the sense of loss will cease.

When we accept everything that occurs with equanimity because we know that the universe is just and that everything has its reason, there is no sadness, because we know everything is exactly as it should be.

Chapter 8

THE CYCLES OF LIFE

When I was a child, I spoke as a
child, I felt as a child, I thought as a
child. Now that I have become a
man, I have put away childish things.

1 Corinthians 13:11

AS ABOVE, SO BELOW

Nature does not reinvent itself. Instead, it uses patterns
that have existed forever, adapting them to the level of
building under construction. The analogy of a Great Architect is valid but must include the recognition of a group
of workers. The Spiritual Hierarchy consists of beings
who know how to build using natural elements. Each one

155

has passed, or will pass, through the experience of human existence, and some are still using a human form. Once we have gained a certain amount of experience, and apply it intelligently in alignment with the plan of nature, we too will be members of the Spiritual Hierarchy, but there is much work to be done first.

An architect never re-designs every item in a structure. Instead, based on previous experiences, some successful and some resulting in failure, he adjusts, expands, re-orients, or otherwise modifies the current blueprint based on experience gained from previous projects. Some things have proven to work well while others are still experimental.

The Hermetic axiom, "As above, so below," demonstrates that everything in nature is based on the same principles of building. The same patterns are used, but are adjusted to the current conditions and scope of the project. As eloquently expressed by one of the Adepts, "Nothing in nature springs into existence suddenly, all being subject to the same great law of evolution. Nature follows the same groove from the 'creation' of a universe down to that of a mosquito."

One of the great patterns used on all levels of creation is that of cycles. There are major cycles and minor cycles. There are cycles that last trillions of years and cycles of less than a billionth of a second.

At the beginning of this book, we discussed the cycle we are all currently experiencing, that of the Prodigal Son. We, not as humans, but as sparks of Divinity, came forth from the Spiritual Source. These divine sparks "fell to earth." That is to say, the various realms of existence were created within our solar system, from the most sublime downward until the physical, or most dense, was built. After millions of years of preparation, forms were created for these divine sparks to inhabit, beginning with the simplest and continuing in complexity over eons of time until "coats of skin" were made for them to wear. This is a symbolic way of saying that physical bodies were created for the spiritual beings to use in gaining experience.

When these divine sparks had advanced in consciousness and experience, reaching the threshold of the human kingdom, a remarkable event took place. Human souls were created, and an additional outpouring of spiritual force made them distinctly different from all other life forms on our planet. We had now gained the potential of becoming gods in our own right. We can learn the fundamentals of becoming builders and later architects of our own solar systems. Obviously, we are a long way from that stage, but every human is making progress toward the goal, whether he is aware of it or not. The spark of Divinity returns to its source, much enlightened and much wiser, just as the Prodigal Son returns to his ancestral home.

All cycles proceed through the same stages:

- Reawakening from a period of sleep.
- Growth and development, reaching a peak.
- Decline and slowing down.
- Unconscious sleep and preparation for the next cycle.

The cycle of the Prodigal Son follows these steps and is one which lasts billions of years. We experience another cycle which lasts 365 days called the seasons.

In winter everything is asleep, dormant, appearing as if dead. When springtime arrives, there is a reawakening and stirring, and in summer, rapid expansion until maximum growth is reached for the current cycle. Autumn follows, with the decline and slowing down of all systems. It is the harvest time. Winter arrives, and everything is dormant again. It is a time for rest after a strenuous year of growth and new experience. The essence of that experience has been extracted in the form of seeds which will continue the growth experience the following year.

Each acorn contains within it the essence of every oak tree that has ever lived. It also contains the essence of experience gleaned from life forms through which the indwelling spirit has passed in other kingdoms of nature. Nothing of value is ever lost. The forms we inhabit are only of temporary value, and they are destroyed once they have served their purpose. The real value is the experience gained and the increase in consciousness, carefully preserved in order to manifest again in the next cycle. When we focus on the life within the form, its spiritual energy, we are less attached to the forms we inhabit and suffering will cease. It is because of our attachment to forms that we suffer.

Just as the acorn contains the essential experience of all previous oak trees, so our soul maintains "seeds" of all essential experience gained from previous lifetimes. The details of the daily drama experienced, the emotional desires and wishes, are not preserved; they are not important to the soul. The soul recognizes and responds to essential matters, to the quality of vibrations, not our personal reactions to everyday life events.

The essence of the rose is contained within its petals, but once that essence is extracted, the dead form is no longer necessary. It has served its purpose, and the materials are recycled for the use of other life forces in new physical forms.

Are there other cycles in nature?

There are many similar cycles. Every day you experience one of them. We experience the same stages nature goes through—reawakening after a period of rest, getting "up to speed" again, resuming our work where we left off before, followed by a period of winding down, a decline in energy, and finally sleep and much needed rest. The first period of sleep is generally unconscious. As our energy is recharged and we get closer to beginning the new day, consciousness increases until we are awake again and ready for a new period of experience. Just how "awake" we are depends on our level of enlightenment.

THE HUMAN LIFE CYCLE

The cycle of prime importance for most humans is that of an individual lifetime. Again, it follows the natural pattern. We come into the world still in a relative state of unconsciousness and spend several years adapting to our environment, which may have changed considerably since our last incarnation. There is a period of "getting up to speed," regaining knowledge from previous lifetimes and downloading it into a new brain.

Why don't we remember our previous lives?

You, the personality, have never lived before. You have no connection to previous lives except through the connection to your soul, and the soul pays no attention to the everyday details of any lifetime. It is aware of and retains only the essence of the life experience, not those emotional events you find so important. In addition, it would not be helpful to remember past lives.

Why do you say that?

If we remembered all the emotional reactions we had in another lifetime, such as anger, revenge, and resentment, we would never make progress. We would spend each lifetime obsessing about the past, especially if we encounter the same people with whom we experienced these negative reactions. Nature is kind in preventing us from remembering the details. Each lifetime is a chance for a fresh start. Don't waste time trying to find out who you were in a previous lifetime. You, the personality, have never existed before and will never exist again. Let go of all the personal drama and focus instead on contact with your soul.

You would do well to imitate nature and forget the past even in this lifetime. It is only the eternal now that is meaningful. This concept is so important that it will be discussed in detail in the next chapter.

Once the physical body has achieved maximum growth and we have reached the point where most of our previous experience has been recaptured, we begin the real work for this lifetime, that of learning new lessons and increasing our understanding of how life works. Later, our energy gradually decreases, the body we have been using wears out, and death ensues. The physical body is discarded, as well as the astral-emotional vehicle and the lower mental vehicle, kāma-manas. Then follows a period of rest and regeneration.

We can gain much insight by observing and analyzing the phases of life through which we pass in a given lifetime. In India, people have long recognized three primary phases of a person's life, each approximately twenty-five years in length.

THE FIRST TWENTY-FIVE YEARS

The first twenty-five years is a period of physical growth and development, a recapitulation of things learned in previous lifetimes, and preparation for additional growth and further development. The recapitulation begins immediately and is predominant during the first twenty-five years of life, although it continues even longer. Much of this period involves becoming accustomed to a new physical body. The soul has guided its development, not just from birth, but from a time prior to birth, sometimes even before conception.

Newborn infants are still very much in touch with the soul, although the little brain is not able to express much that would indicate it. Still, we subconsciously recognize something special about babies and young children. They have access to realms of consciousness that adults do not. Children of three or four years old are delightful in their interactions with life. Because of their soul connection, they see the divine nature in all creatures, not just humans, but also animals and plants. They also may see things we adults do not see, including nature spirits. They may have invisible playmates we can't see but are very real to them. This is not fantasy on their part. They are interacting with beings that have no component on the physical plane. Although these beings may not be humans, the child often ascribes human characteristics to them. Children live in a world few adults can access.

One proof of this soul connection is children's uncanny ability to learn new languages. Place a young child in any language environment and, within a short time, he will be speaking it fluently and with the same accent as those around him. A young child can easily learn five or six languages, provided there is someone around to reinforce the language skills on a regular basis. Take the child out of that environment before he has reached the age of about eight years, and he will completely lose the ability to speak the language within a few months. Later, if he decides to re-learn it, he must start all over, learning through study and effort, just like adults learn a language.

The soul has access to methods of understanding and learning that the personality does not. Because the young child still has a strong connection to the soul, he can learn certain things with incredible speed. Is there something we can learn from this? We can. If we can re-establish the connection with our soul that we had as a child, we can learn new things as easily as he learns a new language. A new area of consciousness opens up. The person who has developed soul contact lives in a very different world from that of the average individual.

Throughout the early years of this cycle, we are gradually increasing in consciousness in the physical world and losing consciousness to the higher realms of existence. A veil is drawn between us and our soul, enticing us to focus on the world around us and participate in the drama unfolding in our environment.

During this first twenty-five year period, the individual is recalling things learned before. School teachers are familiar with this phenomenon. For example, some students have no difficulty learning math. With a little guidance from the teacher, they have grasped the concepts and are able to put them into practice immediately. Other students struggle with it. They may eventually learn the fundamental concepts, but further learning comes at the cost of hard work and effort. The same is true for music, art, or any number of subjects. Some students have an innate talent for the subject and others have little or none. Obviously, the ones who learn quickly are recapitulating what was already learned in a previous incarnation.

By the end of this first twenty-five year period, the individual has grown to full stature physically, has come up to speed on previous learning to a large extent, and has already made inroads in new learning, especially in areas of new development in the world since his most recent lifetime. The period of time that was spent out of incarnation can vary from a few months, or less, to well over a thousand years. For the average person, it is probably between fifty and a hundred years, although in the case of an enlightened individual, it can be much longer.

THE SECOND TWENTY-FIVE YEARS

At the beginning of the second twenty-five year period, the individual is ready to begin making a contribution to the community through working, raising a family, learning from others, and teaching others.

Every individual, from the least advanced to the most advanced, is both a student and a teacher. This never changes, even after we have passed the human phase of evolution. We learn from those who have gone before us, and we serve as teachers and sources of inspiration to those who come behind us in the evolutionary process. In a given lifetime, you may be "teaching" someone younger than you are, when, in fact, he or she is more advanced than you are in that subject. Even though the student has more experience than the teacher, he must be brought up to speed in this lifetime and will quickly pass the teacher as he takes his proper place with regard to the subject matter.

Often, an individual has married and is raising a family during this second period, with varying results of success or failure. Obviously, this will depend on experience from previous lifetimes as well as the ability to observe others and learn from their mistakes or their successful results. Family groups often serve as our primary means of learning, teaching, and understanding human psychology. We learn from our parents and we teach our children, but sometimes the reverse is true—we learn from our children and teach our parents.

For most people, this is the period of greatest physical strength and stamina. It is not by accident that raising a family generally occurs during the first part of this cycle. The need for physical strength while raising a family is tremendous and is an investment in the future of humanity.

If you have children of your own, it behooves you to examine honestly and carefully your motives for bringing them into this world. Often it is simply animal instinct, the biological impulse to perpetuate the human race and, from a personal perspective, to be sure that your own genes are passed on to future generations. Others have a strong emotional need to feel needed. They sometimes have children because they feel unloved and think that by having a child, they will always have someone who loves them. They often unconsciously create co-dependency, raising their children without teaching them to be independent. The thought of having independent children is abhorrent to them, because the ego of the parent requires someone who is dependent as long as the parent is alive. This is the basis of some very dysfunctional family relationships. Look at your own family, extended family, friends, and acquaintances. You will recognize some very unhealthy relationships among them.

Are there ever people who have children for unselfish reasons?

It is a rare individual who has children strictly for altruistic purposes. It would have to be someone who is relatively enlightened. Sometimes it is based on karmic relationships, and sometimes on the willingness of the enlightened parent to serve as a teacher for an advanced soul entering a new incarnation. By being raised by another advanced individual, this younger person will have the best chance of making tremendous progress in the current lifetime.

Work is generally a major factor during this second twenty-five year period. In previous generations, the mother was in charge of the household work and raising the children, either doing it herself or supervising servants. The father's role was to provide for the financial needs.

Today things are very different. It is now rare to have a stay-at-home mother. This came about because of World War II. Many women were hired to fill work positions vacated by men leaving to serve in the war, and it was discovered that, not only could they do the work, but often better than men could. As the consumer age gained momentum during the '50s and '60s, families decided they needed two or more cars, electronic devices, exotic vacations, designer clothing, and other items that would enhance the ego. The advertising industry blossomed during this time and has continued to thrive ever since. Economic downturns do not dampen consumers' desire for things but serve as a wakeup call to those who are ready to become enlightened with regard to consumerism.

THE THIRD TWENTY-FIVE YEARS

The third twenty-five year period, from fifty to seventy-five, is a major shift from the previous one. In some ways it resembles the first twenty-five year period, but in reverse order. This is the time when the person can, if he chooses, retire from active work in the outside world and spend more time in study, contemplation, and meditation. He is beginning the return to a more spiritual state of being. In India, a person at this phase might even decide to leave his or her family and go into a retreat. It is felt that he has served the community by raising his family and working hard for many years. He has earned the right to devote the remainder of his life to spiritual practice. This is not seen as being selfishly motivated. It is recognized that each person who attains a new level of awareness paves the way for all around him. "And I, if I be lifted up, shall draw all men unto me."

Compare this concept to the current one in so many countries of working until retirement age, which might be anywhere from 60 to 70, and then spending the remainder of life watching television, traveling, socializing with friends, and waiting until death comes. In some cases death is welcomed, but in many it is feared because of uncertainty. The person avoided analyzing life and refused to acknowledge his immortality as a personality, fearful of what might be encountered. Those who fearlessly accept life as it is and who recognize the transient quality of all forms, have nothing to fear. Their focus is on the life within, not the form. They have laid up their treasures in heaven. These treasures are the life lessons learned, and they can never be lost.

The person who spends the final part of his life in spiritual practice almost always is prepared for death and accepts it as a necessary part of the life process, confident that he has earned the right to a period of rest before resuming his labors.

In this third twenty-five year period, what are the final years like?

During the last few years of life, this person hopefully has made peace with the world, has let go of all resentments, no longer experiences anger, and accepts whatever comes with equanimity and grace. No longer does he react with strong emotions to outer events. The drama that consumes so many others in the world has lost its attraction. He finds joy in the peace of quiet moments, for that is when the voice of the soul can be heard.

Regardless of the beliefs of the person—and many spiritual people belong to no organized religion—one who has spent a number of years in contemplation and meditation is able to return to the state in which he first entered the physical world, more in touch with the soul and at home in higher realms of consciousness.

The final few years then would show a retreat from the outer world and a growing awareness of the more spiritual part of our being. When the last few days or weeks arrive, he or she often manifests a beautiful inner light and exudes a peacefulness that is a joy to experience. He spends long hours apparently asleep or unconscious, but in fact is in communion with the soul, and at the same time is subconsciously aware of all that others are doing or saying nearby.

By the time death occurs, he is completely accepting of the process, and is more aware than ever of the great strain of physical life. Few people at the moment of death are aware they have left the physical body behind. The process of natural death, even if it is sudden, is no different than falling asleep at night as we drift into a period of unconsciousness. We die to the world every night, so when the final falling asleep arrives, it is an old friend with whom we are comfortable.

We can learn something profound by observing and understanding the different phases of life. There is no reason to wait until the end of life to experience the enhanced soul connection. We can enter that state at any time, provided we are willing to accept the conditions.

What are the conditions for experiencing soul contact?

The same ones the elderly person goes through in the natural process—withdrawing from the drama of the everyday world, long periods of contemplation and meditation, and a willingness to let go of all emotions, whether "good" or "bad." We must get our relationships in order, leaving nothing unresolved. Only then can you create the peace in your physical existence which will allow your soul to contact you. The soul is always ready for contact and communication. It is we who are distracted by the physical world and not ready for soul contact. We must ascend to its level of existence. It cannot descend to ours, because the vibrations in our world are incompatible with those of the soul.

To die before you die is the secret of eternal life. This is reflected in the last line of the prayer of St. Francis, "It is in dying that we are born to eternal life." It is not the physical death process referred to in either of these phrases, but rather dying *to* the physical life, giving up our attachment to ego, desires, passions, and emotions, letting go of all the things most people think are important in life. Few people are ready to do that, but if they are, they will experience more power than ever before.

The willingness to give up attachment to the physical world must be a conscious and well thought out decision, not resulting from disappointment, disgust, or a feeling that life has failed us.

SEVEN-YEAR CYCLES

Students of the Ancient Wisdom often notice that their development follows cycles of seven years. The milestones of 35, 42 and 56 years are often significant, not necessarily at the anniversary, but close enough to be noticed.

One astrological event that often affects students is known as the "Saturn Return." When Saturn returns to the same degree of the zodiac it occupied when you were born, and this occurs somewhere between 28 and 30 years later, you may have an event in your life that opens up a new direction of travel. It may also occur again 28 to 30 years later. Saturn is not the grim hand of authority described by many astrologers. It represents the power of Shiva, who destroys in order to rebuild.

The period between the ages of 56 and 63 is especially significant for most students. By this point they have often reached the "high water mark" of this lifetime for spiritual growth. The remainder of the lifetime is often devoted almost entirely to study, contemplation, and teaching.

Travelers on the spiritual path often experience distinct and sometimes drastic changes at various points in their lifetime. Many describe it as if they had lived several lifetimes in one. To make rapid progress, we must accomplish far more than the average person and accept whatever life lessons are presented to us. We must learn to "go with the flow."

Chapter 9

THE ETERNAL NOW

Time is the sequence of the stages of consciousness, as registered in the human brain. It is therefore a physical event.

— *Discipleship in the New Age, Vol.2*

THE PAST NEVER HAPPENED

I have heard of the power of now, but I'm not sure I agree with it or understand it. I have distinct memories of the past. I'm here now because of the past.

You are not here now because of the past, but because of the eternal now. As you go through life, you are experiencing a series of *now*. Think about this very moment in time. There are trillions of energy patterns in the universe, and not one remains static for even a split second. Out of all those countless energy patterns, how many of them are you aware of?

A minuscule portion, I guess.

And of that tiny portion you *do* perceive, how accurate is your perception?

I would like to think it's fairly accurate.

And yet it's not. Close your eyes and try to describe in minute detail everything you just saw.

I just tried it, but I can only describe in general terms what I saw before. After I opened my eyes and looked again, I saw much more detail and realized how much I had missed. Even so, I couldn't shut my eyes again and describe everything in great detail, the way I can with my eyes open.

Your mind has the ability to focus on things, but that area of focus is necessarily much smaller than the area we are observing. The human mind, wonderful as it is, is very imperfect. Have you ever compared your memories of childhood with those of other family members?

I have, and was shocked to find their memories are very different from mine, sometimes diametrically opposed.

Whose memories are more accurate?

I would like to think mine are, but to be honest, I'm not certain anyone's memories are completely accurate.

How much stock should you place in those memories?

I'm not sure. Before I thought my memories were quite accurate, but now you have me doubting myself.

A CASE OF FAULTY MEMORY

The judicial system deals with this problem constantly. In 1984, a college student was raped. The man who committed the crime was in her home for more than an hour. She had several opportunities to observe him, and made careful mental notes so she could identify him later. From photos at the police station, she easily picked the one of her attacker and picked the same person in a lineup. Based on her eyewitness testimony in the courtroom, the man was convicted of the crime, despite his protests of innocence, and was sent to prison.

In prison, a fellow convict greeted him by a different name. When questioned about it, it became obvious that someone else looked similar to him. When confronted with this evidence, the man who resembled him admitted the rape, and a new trial was requested. Unfortunately, on the witness stand, this man recanted his earlier confession and denied being the rapist. The victim, incensed that her reliability was in question, adamantly insisted that the first man was the perpetrator, and he was sent back to prison, convicted for a second time.

While watching television one day, the prisoner heard about DNA testing and asked that it be done in his case. Fortunately, a small DNA sample had been saved and, when tested, proved that the perpetrator was not the man who had spent eleven years in prison, but the other man, who had since died.

The victim was devastated, and was forced to admit that her inaccurate powers of observation and faulty memory had caused an innocent man to lose eleven years of his life and to be branded a rapist.

Now I'm really not sure about my own memory. I wouldn't want to be the cause of a loss like that.

And yet we do it on a smaller basis all the time. We make judgments and form opinions about people based on appearances and speculation, and then talk about it to others as if it were fact. If we are persuasive enough, others will believe what we say. Millions of lives have been ruined by malicious gossip by people who were convinced they had the facts right.

Would you want to be responsible for the loss of someone's reputation because you talked about him or her to others and convinced them to believe something you thought was true, but in fact wasn't?

I would feel terrible about it, and I'm sure I've been guilty of that in the past.

Today would be a good day to stop judging, wouldn't it?

It would, and I intend to stop making judgments, not just in conversations, but even to myself. I can see why judging others is a dangerous game to play. What happened in the case of mistaken identity?

The real rapist died in prison from cancer before he could be brought to trial on the rape charge. The victim was so upset that her compelling testimony had taken eleven years from a man's life that she asked to meet him so she could apologize in person. He told her he had never hated her or felt angry toward her, but couldn't understand why she was so adamant in her testimony. After a two-hour conversation, they hugged for a long time.

After that, they became friends and visited each other from time to time. They also have presented seminars for law enforcement personnel to teach them how to avoid the pitfalls of eyewitness testimony.

You've convinced me now that no one's memory is infallible, including my own. But what about photographs and videos? They capture everything.

Do they? When you are present in a situation, assuming you're awake, your eyes perceive certain energy patterns, your ears perceive other energy patterns, you physically feel certain sensations, smell different things, and even telepathically sense many things. Do you know of any camera or sound recording device that can record everything you perceive?

No, of course not.

What you are able to perceive by being physically present, even though it is only a minuscule part of the billions of energy patterns present, is still far greater than what can be recorded by machines. That's why being present at a concert is an entirely different experience from watching it on television, and why being present in a class on spiritual development is very different from listening to a recording of it.

Presence, and especially when one is truly *present*, is completely different from a secondhand experience. Regardless of how good the machines are, they cannot capture all that you can experience by being physically present and that, in turn, is only a tiny fraction of what a more advanced being can experience. An Adept, a Buddha, or a Planetary Logos can experience far more than we can, and even they cannot experience everything.

THE AKASHIC RECORDS

There is one recording device far superior to any device invented. It is called the akashic records.

What is that?

The akashic records are nature's way of recording events. They exist on the etheric, astral, and lower mental realms. They don't record events, but rather perceptions.

I don't understand.

A camera is an artificial eye, and a recorder is an artificial ear. They record certain sound or light patterns, whether or not someone is present at the time. Then, when a human or an animal watches or listens to the recorded vibrations, he or it reacts mentally and emotionally to the recording. The akashic records are more like a recording of those mental and emotional responses, although they include more than that.

It is similar to looking at a painting and not seeing our own interpretation of it, but rather the ideas and emotions the artist experienced before and during the creation of the painting. Our own judgments and perceptions are suspended; instead, we perceive the ideas, concepts, desires and knowledge the painter had, even if the painting was created thousands of years ago.

I've never heard of that before. So every thought and emotion I've ever experienced is in the akashic records?

Every person experiences a life review as he or she is dying. In a matter of seconds, every perception—whether physical, emotional, or mental—that you have ever had since the moment your consciousness "quickened" the tiny body prepared for you, is re-lived again. It is a literal life review, the final event of your lifetime, as the physical brain scans one last time everything it has ever experienced. All these perceptions are part of the akashic records, but you do not necessarily have access to yours from previous lifetimes any more than anyone else does.

Do the akashic records only contain perceptions of human beings?

No, they contain records of all conscious beings—minerals, plants, animals, humans, and even non-physical beings. They also contain the perceptions of more advanced beings, at least as they pertain to these lower levels of consciousness.

Psychics have partial access to the akashic records, but they generally require some kind of connection, either your physical presence, an item you have worn, a photograph, or a telephone connection with you. In this way, they can tap into the part of the akashic records that contains your personal history. The problem is, their connection is feeble, and they inject their own opinions and prejudices into the situation instead of viewing it clearly, with no personal interference. This is the reason they can see the past, but with varying degrees of accuracy. Their ability to predict the future is even less accurate as we will see presently.

Why is it so difficult for them to see accurately?

For the same reason your recollections are faulty. Yours are inaccurate even though you were present at the time. However, your opinions, prejudices, emotions, and expectations color everything you experience. Then, the tiny bit you remember of the event is further transformed each time you review it in your mind. It does not become more accurate with each review, but less accurate.

The psychic is seeing your memory of things, but through an additional set of filters composed of his or her own opinions, prejudices, and emotions. So the accuracy at that point is very suspect.

Now I'm beginning to think nothing in the past is accurate.

Even in the present moment you do not see accurately. You have a perception based on the sum total of your eons of experiences, interacting with the overwhelming array of vibrations in which you are currently immersed, but you can only perceive a tiny part of it with any degree of clarity.

If I wanted to learn how to be clairvoyant but with greater accuracy, how would I proceed?

First, you must gain mastery over your emotions. Eliminate all prejudices, stop judging others, and then you can begin to start developing some degree of accuracy. Clairvoyance is nothing more than a heightened degree of perception of the vibrations around us. All of us are clairvoyant to some degree, but of the billions of souls connected with our planet, only a handful have a degree of clairvoyance that is highly accurate.

If you want to develop your ability to perceive higher vibrations, get in touch with your Higher Self through contemplation and meditation, and your ability to perceive will unfold automatically.

What about practicing mediumship or channeling? Wouldn't that help?

Absolutely not. It will delay rather than hasten your spiritual development. We cannot emphasize strongly enough the need to avoid these activities.

REMOTE VIEWING

There is one practice we might recommend, and that is remote viewing. Although it is still quite undeveloped, it is by far the safest method of exploring the ability to become more perceptive. There is no contacting of spirits or channeling of entities involved. The emotional element is almost completely absent, so it is not as popular as channeling, but it has much more to offer in the long run and will be far less likely to interfere with your spiritual development.

You said the past never happened. Do you mean it didn't happen because my memory of it is faulty?

It didn't happen because it never happened. Even if you could perceive and remember accurately, it never happened. The past simply does not exist.

But I thought you said it was recorded in the akashic records.

It is the present that is recorded, and not even the present, but our perceptions of the present that are recorded in the akashic records.

Time is not a continuum consisting of past, present and future; it is a single point, which is now. This point is eternal, it is all there is, and that is why it is so powerful. As one teacher expressed it, "Time is the sequence of the states of consciousness, as registered in the human brain. It is therefore a physical event."

But without the past, I'm nobody. I'm somebody because of my past. If I lost my memory of it, I would feel unimportant.

You have never been "nobody," and at no point will you ever cease to exist. You have always been important and will always be important, but not in the egotistical way you think of it.

At the end of your life, you will lose all memory of what occurred during this lifetime, at least in the way we think of memory. You will not remember any names, any parties you attended, or any movies you watched, and yet you will have lost nothing.

I can't imagine living without memories of people and events.

You don't have a choice. At the end of your life, you will lose all the memories you think are so important. They are only important to the personality and to your ego. To the soul, they have no importance whatsoever.

I don't believe that. I think my soul is very interested in my personal life.

You can believe what you like, but believing something that is untrue can only delay your progress. Our spiritual progress cannot take a giant leap forward until we grasp the concept that our personal desires and the drama we create in life are only temporary. They are important only because they propel us forward. They are not the goal; they are a means to an interim goal. When that goal is reached, a new goal will be set, and so on ad infinitum.

It is extremely liberating to let go of the past. Make a practice of it yourself. Get rid of mementos and old memories and begin to live in the present.

I could never let go of the past. I love to look at old photos and reminisce about things that happened when I was younger.

You mean about things that never happened?

What do you mean?

You admitted that when you compare your memories with others, the memories seldom are the same. You are the only person in the world who has the "memories" you have, and those memories are constantly changing. You live in a universe that has only one inhabitant—you. The other people who seem to exist with you are simply perceptions of yours. They are bit players in your personal universe, and you are a bit player in theirs.

I can kind of see your point, but it's frightening to think about it. It makes me feel that nothing is real and life is meaningless.

Nothing in existence is real. It is temporary, and anything temporary is an illusion, or māyā. Only the Absolute is real. Even though existence is not real, it is also not meaningless. Moving forward and expansion of consciousness can hardly be considered meaningless.

Once you let go of your attachment to this illusion, you do not feel a sense of loss, but a sense of expanding consciousness. You experience more, not less. Your ability to love others is no longer based on personal needs, yours or theirs, but on your connection with the One Life. You become more aware of energy fields and are less focused on the forms used by the indwelling life.

Time, as we know it, exists only on the physical plane. In other realms of consciousness, there is only now. The past and the future do not exist separately. They are an integral part of now.

I can understand intellectually what you are saying, but I don't think I'm ready to let go of my past.

You have a lot of company, and no one can force you to let go of your attachments. At the very least, be aware of the attachments to what you perceive as the past. When you look at old photos or indulge in swapping stories with friends, ask yourself how much of it is real and how much is imagined.

I can do that.

If you do that over a period of time and are honest in your observations, you will one day realize that your entire life happened in your mind; you will discover that life does not consist of the events of your life, but in recognizing the life force which *is* you.

Even if you lose your memories, you will have lost nothing. You are who you are because you embody the sum total of all experiences you have ever had, in this lifetime and all others, which you cannot remember. That experience is yours and can never be taken from you.

THE FUTURE WILL NEVER OCCUR

So if there is no past, there is also no future?

It is even easier to disprove the existence of the future. Your past is a collection of imperfect memories about something that may or may not have occurred, but the future is nothing more than your fears or hopes about something that might occur. It never does, at least not exactly in the way you thought it would.

I have personal experience with that. Many times I've worried about something I was sure would happen, but it didn't.

You probably didn't realize you were creating negative energy affecting not only you, but also those around you.

I didn't at the time, but I'm more aware of it now. I still worry sometimes, but not as much as before.

Analyze what changed in your attitude. Once you can clearly see what caused the anxiety, then you are in a position to eliminate it before it ever happens. You make progress by using your mind as a tool. The mind, combined with wisdom, creates will, and will is very powerful. The mind combined with emotions creates desire, resulting in suffering and confusion.

If the future is nothing more than my fear or expectation of what will happen, how do psychics predict the future?

With very little accuracy. Most psychics predict your future the same way they tell you what happened in the past—they read your mind. For example, a woman consults a psychic regarding her marriage. She and her husband are not happy together, and she has been thinking for some time about getting divorced. The psychic tells her, "I see that you will be getting divorced in the near future." The woman leaves, having received confirmation that she is going to get divorced.

Time goes on, and not only does the couple not get divorced, they somehow come to terms with their life together. It may never be the fairytale marriage that most people expect, but they can co-exist together in a tolerable but less-than-perfect relationship. The psychic's prediction was not based on "seeing" the future, but on reading the clues in the client's mind.

Even a trained seer cannot predict the future with any degree of accuracy, and certainly not at the microcosmic level. What they are able to predict are general trends. For example, if you know a young man who is dishonest, selfish, and completely irresponsible, who consistently makes poor choices and hangs out with the wrong people, you can, with some degree of accuracy, predict that he will one day end up in prison or convicted of a crime.

If you are in a helicopter and can see two cars speeding toward a common point, each driver unable to see the other, you can predict that they will collide. Economists predict an economic collapse based on existing financial conditions if nothing intervenes to change the equation.

Seers predict the future based on current conditions, and we know that the present is the sum total of past events. Too many things can occur which will change the current dynamics, mostly caused by millions of human beings and their personal desires and goals, which change constantly.

Not even the spiritual head of a solar system can predict with great accuracy what will occur in his solar system.

We should therefore not be surprised if even the best psychic is only partially accurate.

Whether or not you agree that the past never happened and the future will never occur, contemplation on this subject will open your eyes. Living in the past or in the future is a sign of avoidance and is not healthy. It indicates you are not willing to live in the present and accept the reality you have created, but prefer to live in a fantasy world in your mind. It is a dangerous place to be.

Be at peace with yourself and with the world you have created. Accept responsibility for your state of being. After all, you are its creator. Once you admit that, everything falls into place. Life is easy. We make it hard.

Where are we?

Right here!

What time is it?

Now.

What is missing in your life at this moment?

Nothing.

You see, life is perfect.

Chapter 10

THOUGHT CONTROL

> The goal of meditation is the ability
> to contact the divine inner self, and
> through the contact, to come to a
> realization of the unity of that self
> with all selves and the All-Self, and
> this, not just theoretically, but as a
> fact in nature.
>
> — *The Light of the Soul*

THOUGHTS

Energy follows thought. Thought is the creative force in the universe, and nothing can be created without it. Every action, emotion, piece of music, painting, sculpture, building, planet, or solar system was first a thought. And once a project is started, thought continues to change the evolution of it, by observing, analyzing, and comparing, then making adjustments to guide the future direction of the work in process. Periodically, the current state of affairs is compared with the original plan, and adjustments are made to re-orient the project, bringing it more in line with what was proposed, or the original plans are modified to account for current conditions.

Until the consciousness within us reaches the human stage, real thought is not possible. Animals are motivated by instinct, and thought is barely beginning to show in their nature. Plants are capable of feeling, but not of thought, and although minerals are conscious, they are not able to think.

Thus, at some point in the human stage of evolution, we acquired the potential of becoming gods because we have a mind—still in an early stage of development—which is learning to direct energy in order to create. Mind exists at all levels above that of the human being. The Logos uses thought to create forms for planets, elementals, minerals, plants, animals, angels, and humans to inhabit in order to grow in life experience.

Thought does not originate in the human brain as some scientists believe. The mind exists apart from the brain and continues to exist after the death of the physical body. Remember that there are two levels of thought for humans, at least in the mental realm. The lower mind embodies concrete thought—images, symbols, and language—and the higher mind embodies abstract thought, those ideas which cannot be expressed in any language or image, symbols being the only method of conveying some hint of the thought. Nothing can convey accurately at a lower level that which exists at a higher level. We must raise our consciousness to that level in order to experience it directly. As the Buddhists say, "The finger pointing to the moon is not the moon." Language can hint at, but never express, the great truths and concepts that exist at higher levels.

Thought does not exist only in the mental realm of consciousness. It exists at the mental level and all those above it. What changes with each level of consciousness is the manner in which thought functions. For example, at the buddhic level, it functions as intuition, a type of thought, but different from thought at the mental level. At higher levels, the wonders of the thought process are unimaginable to us. Only in a state of pralaya, the resting period between active phases of existence, does thought temporarily cease, but it awakens again when the rest period is over.

When we sleep, our consciousness generally leaves the physical body and remains with the astral and mental vehicles, usually staying in the general vicinity. We seldom remember what is experienced by our astral and mental vehicles at night, and in most cases it is nothing profound. Most dreams are created by energy patterns coursing through the physical brain. They are often influenced by what happened during the day, emotions we felt, images we saw, and what we last saw on television before falling asleep. Their quality is also influenced by what we ate, how heavy it was, how spicy, and how recently. They are often vivid, but seldom very meaningful.

On the other hand, we sometimes have a dream that is very meaningful and is not the result of brain activity. This is what might be called a vision rather than a dream.

It generally communicates something of importance for our spiritual development and is a result of recalling something experienced on the mental plane. Most often it is a communication from our Higher Self and can occur because we are in a receptive state of mind when we sleep.

Think about these concepts and put them into practice by watching your own thoughts and seeing the results of those thoughts. Our thoughts create everything—what we experience in life, our karma, our relationships with others, and our relationship with the outside world. Everything is created by thought. No action or emotion originates on its own. There is always a thought behind it.

Once we realize the power of thought and begin to take control of it through contemplation, visualization, meditation, and analysis, we start learning how to use thoughts to direct energy. If you own a business and want it to grow in a certain direction, not only must you have a plan, but you must put a certain amount of thought energy behind it, guiding it along the way. It is not enough just to supply the physical effort. There must be thoughtful direction as well. It is the energy this thought process carries with it that creates the final result.

We are all gods in the making, and it is in learning to direct energy through thought that we learn to become creators in the universe.

What is the first step in learning how to control thoughts?

Awareness. We are convinced that we know how to think. We do not, or at least few people know how. Most of our thoughts are emotions put into words or actions.

We react to everything around us, and any reflex action is based on emotion or instinct. One of the first words a child learns is "mine." His tiny developing ego is already expressing desire. We saw this in the story of the magic toy.

Thought is a force, just like electricity or magnetism. Each thought we think creates a pattern along which energy can and does flow. So the first thing we must do is become aware of our thoughts. You probably remember your first attempts at meditation. You sit quietly in a calm environment and wait. Generally, the first thing that happens is your mind goes wild, jumping from one idea to another with little rhyme or reason. We call it the "monkey mind." In fact, this does not occur only when you sit quietly. It is the natural state for most people.

Most of us are only able to turn off the mind when our physical brain is too tired to process the signals. Then it goes into dream mode, with more random, meaningless images and disconnected thoughts coursing through the brain.

Even when we are convinced we are thinking, there is only a small amount of focus and a large amount of background activity in the mind. Those who insist they can focus on several things at once are mistaken. Having multiple thoughts means your focus is divided and none of them has your full attention. You cannot be functioning in the now in three different places.

Each thought has two qualities—a frequency and a strength—just like a radio wave. The frequency is the quality of the vibration. Just as with emotions, we have negative thoughts, neutral thoughts, and positive thoughts, and some thoughts we believe are positive are not exactly that. Only thoughts that are completely un-selfish in nature can be characterized as being of the highest quality. Anything prompted by ego or personal need falls somewhat lower on the scale.

The strength of the thought is determined by the individual who creates it. A highly advanced being can create a thought far more powerful than the average human, whose thought power has great potential but is not yet well developed.

How can I increase the power of my thoughts?

The goal is not to become the creator of more powerful thoughts. If that is your aim, it is personally motivated and any success in that direction will be used to satisfy your ego. Focus instead on character development, and the rest will follow naturally.

There is one way we can increase the power of our thoughts now, and that is by repetition. It occurs all the time in people who are obsessive by nature. They anguish and worry for hours every day over some trifling matter that has no real importance and does not help humanity in any way. Or they obsess about someone they feel has "done them wrong," an ex-spouse or other individual upon whom they heap fierce anger and scorn. What they probably are not aware of is the amount of accumulated negative energy that is created. This energy causes even more damage to the creator than to the object of scorn. It results in mental imbalance, emotional disturbance, and physical illness. It is estimated that at least 75% of our illnesses are caused by thoughts and emotions.

We can also use repetition of thoughts in a positive manner. It is called affirmation. In the 19th century, Emile Coué, a French psychologist, coined the phrase, "Every day, in every way, I am getting better and better." He taught his patients to use it and they saw results in the form of improved health. We can't change anyone's karma by sending positive thoughts, but every thought has its result, whether positive or negative, and the thinker reaps the positive or negative karma from the thought, based on his motives.

What about prayer? Isn't that a way of helping others?

Many prayers are well-intentioned but not well thought through. We generally feel that a divine being has somehow neglected us or someone we know and we need to call his attention to the matter. The supplication for help is often done in a matter of seconds or is repeated parrot-like with little thought behind it. Prayers of this nature have almost no effect whatsoever.

It is far better to engage in active visualization and affirmation. This requires more effort on your part than prayer does, but it is more certain to have a positive effect, even if the result doesn't look exactly like what you want it to.

How does visualization work?

Visualization and affirmations are covered in chapter 11. What is important to realize is that you take responsibility for the results. It is far more than a request for someone else to step in and help.

Once you become aware of your thoughts, you realize just how little control you have over them. Your thoughts and emotions control your life; you seldom control them. Own your thoughts. Take responsibility for them. Throughout your life you have given control to parents, authority figures, public opinion, and your peer group. You gave away your ability to think. Now is a good time to take it back and own every thought you think. As long as we go along with the crowd, we can claim we're not responsible for our thoughts, but we still suffer the consequences of them, so you may as well strike out on your own. Stop letting others create thoughts for you, and become a generator of thoughts that are well-conceived.

How do I do that?

By creating lots of quiet time in your life. Turn off the television, forever if possible. If you're not ready for that, limit your viewing to three hours a week and choose those hours wisely. Turn off the radio in your car and at work if you can. Spend a day in silence once a month, not uttering a word, just being alone with your thoughts the entire time.

Many people are terrified of being alone with their thoughts. They do not trust themselves. It is one of the reasons people feel the need to talk non-stop and have noise constantly in the background, usually the television or radio. Anyone who is addicted to this constant noise will not be able to control his thoughts.

By creating some open space around us, we can begin to examine our thoughts and observe their effects. Start the day with a period of meditation, even if only for five or ten minutes. At noontime, arrange again for a few minutes of quiet contemplation.

What should I be thinking about during this time?

Nothing. Learn first to quiet the mind. Until you can create a blank screen, you cannot choose what you want to think about.

Be very cognizant of the two-hour period before you go to sleep. If you attend a cocktail party, a football game, or watch something dramatic on television, it will affect the quality of your sleep and your ability to meditate for hours afterward. Make your surroundings as monk-like as possible.

My parents always wanted me to live in a cloistered environment, but I'm not sure I'm ready for that.

Then your development will be for another lifetime or a later phase of this one. You will never make progress without sacrifices.

Part of the difficulty in controlling your mind is that you are trying to counteract years of built-up energy patterns. You cannot simply re-configure them in one afternoon. It generally requires a concerted effort over a period of years. Another effect of working on thought control is that we gain more clarity in our thinking. Our thoughts are no longer fuzzy and incomplete. They become more powerful and well-formed, with substance to them. As you be-

Thought
Control

197

come a reliable force for good in the world, you will automatically receive help in learning to direct your thoughts and make them more effective.

When I read, my thoughts wander, and I often must re-read a section because I wasn't focused.

This will improve as you work on meditation and mind control. You will be able to read with greater comprehension, understand the matter more fully, and retain it much longer. You will also find that your intuition comes into play more. You may read something that triggers a memory of something else you read or heard, and from the combination of these, you understand something which before was a mystery. This is a real result that comes from efforts at thought control.

THREE SPIRITUAL PRACTICES

For the person desiring to follow the spiritual path, there are three things that must be included in his spiritual practice—study, meditation, and service to humanity. Of these three, service is the most important, but without the first two, our service will be limited to what any kind-hearted person could provide. It is through study and meditation that we gain a greater understanding of how life works, and the wisdom which comes through contemplation and meditation makes us valuable instruments in lifting up our fellow men.

Study, which includes reading books, attending classes and lectures, and watching educational programs, builds our base of knowledge. But knowledge alone is not sufficient. You must do something practical with the knowledge you have gained. You must put it to work in order to make the world a better place. The student of life is a perpetual student, always striving to learn more. It is not enough just to learn "stuff." There is a tremendous amount of useless knowledge in the world that will only help if you are participating in a trivia contest. Practice discernment instead, and spend your available time on carefully chosen topics that will help your fellow human beings.

MEDITATION

Meditation and contemplation are crucial to spiritual progress. Without them you cannot hope to go far. Unfortunately, few people really know how to meditate, even among those who go through the motions of "meditating" every day. For some people, meditation is simply a form of prayer, a kind of mental recitation of affirmations. This can be, and often is, an important step in the meditation process, but it is not, in itself, meditation. Nor is sitting quietly and thinking, even though this is also a helpful practice and can lead to true meditation.

Meditation has a very definite goal, and the one who meditates sees specific results which can be identified.

What is the goal of meditation?

The development of a reliable contact with one's Higher Self, the soul. As long as there is emotional drama in your life, you will not achieve a meaningful level of meditation. You may learn to sit quietly, but the emotional vibrations you have been surrounded with during the day do not simply disappear when you sit down to meditate. If you have not achieved a degree of thought control in your everyday life, you are not able to control your emotions, and if you have not learned to control your emotions, the results of any attempt to meditate will be minimal at best.

Meditation is not an activity—it is a state of being. You must enter into that state in order for meditation to occur, and once you enter it, meditation happens automatically. Preparation for meditation does not take place five minutes before you meditate, but five days before.

What do you mean by that?

You must live every day in such a way that your outer life is a reflection of the character of your soul. If you get angry with people, spend your time idly chatting inanely with others and voicing opinions about people and events, there is nothing in that activity which is attractive to your soul. If you spend your free time watching movies or television shows built on emotional drama, those vibrations do not dissipate in a matter of minutes. One incident involving a violent emotional reaction—excitement, hatred, anger, or fright—often requires three to five days to calm down completely, assuming nothing happens in the meantime to re-vivify it.

Any strong emotion is like a violent storm on a placid body of water. Imagine a crystal clear lake whose surface is completely calm. Not only can you look deep into the water and see clearly at any depth, but the surface perfectly reflects what is in the sky above. As if in a mirror, mountains, clouds, birds, sunsets, and stars are reflected accurately on its surface.

When a violent storm arises, the surface no longer reflects accurately, if at all. Anything reflected is horribly distorted, and if enough disturbance takes place, nothing at all can be seen reflected in the water. The disturbance of the water causes even more disturbance beneath the surface. Sediment is stirred up, and all becomes cloudy and murky. Nothing can be seen clearly any more, either on the surface or below it.

Our emotions work exactly the same way. The number of people who proceed placidly through life with little or no emotional disturbance is extremely small. Most try to keep disturbances to a minimum, or at least try to hide them and pretend they are not there, usually with little success. There are some people, however, who love the disturbance and will purposely stir things up if they become too calm. The only ones who can avoid emotional disturbance are those who consistently practice non-reaction. Those who make no effort have no choice but to endure the results of these emotional upheavals.

If you have made no effort to learn non-reaction by controlling your thoughts and emotions, you cannot hope to be successful in meditation, and without meditation, you will not learn how to control your thoughts.

If learning to meditate involves controlling my thoughts and learning to control my thoughts depends on meditation, it seems I will never learn either one.

You must work at both simultaneously. You have some degree of control over your environment even now. Turn off the television, decline the invitation to attend a noisy cocktail party, avoid the "friend" who always wants to argue or loves to criticize. Stay away from those who are addicted to drama. Make a firm resolve to do everything you can to create the conditions in your life that are conducive to meditation. Keep everything as calm and tranquil as you can.

Make it a point to meditate every day, even if only for five or ten minutes. This is not usually enough time to achieve a deep meditation, but consistency is of vital importance. It is much better to meditate ten minutes daily than an hour once a week. If you are sporadic in your efforts, your results will not be great.

Every time I try to meditate, my mind jumps from one thought to another, and I can't seem to focus on any one thing.

The "monkey mind" is experienced by most beginning meditators. It may take months or even years to control, but it must be done. If you have made little or no effort to control your mind in the past, you will not learn how to do it overnight. Remember that you are trying to speed up your own evolution if you are on the spiritual path. It's not easy, but it must be done. The average human will drift along at the current rate of evolution, which is fairly slow. Those who want to move forward more rapidly must become strong swimmers. Even though you are going in the same direction as the natural current of evolution, accelerated progress means you must be moving faster than the current carrying our fellow men at a more leisurely pace.

CONTROLLING THE MONKEY MIND

A good practice for controlling wandering thoughts during meditation is this—whenever you find your mind wandering, trace the thoughts backward. What thought currently is in your mind? What was the thought before that? And the one before that? If you practice this consistently, you become proficient in tracking your thoughts. You begin to realize the truth of the statement that "thinking" happens to us and we seldom control our thoughts.

Training your mind is like training a wild horse. It doesn't want to do what you want it to; it wants to run free. To the wild horse or the untrained mind, freedom means doing whatever it feels like, with no restrictions. If you have never tried to control your mind before, you may be surprised that it resists your efforts. Be patient and be persistent. Eventually, just like the wild horse, your mind will give in, but only if it recognizes that you are in charge and have proved it by your persistent intention. Once the mind settles down, it is willing to be trained, but you must continue your efforts, and you must be clear about your intentions. A trained horse is eager to do what its master wants, and a trained mind does likewise.

The astral-emotional plane is the potential reflector of the buddhic plane, the source of true inspiration. The real man consists of ātma, buddhi and manas, or spirit, intuition and the higher mind. As long as the emotions and the physical body run wild and are in charge of the thinking process, there is no chance of reaching a state of perfection. The emotions must be tranquil and a perfect reflector of your buddhic nature to grow spiritually. The word buddha means enlightened. An enlightened person is one who has developed intuition by controlling his thoughts and emotions; he is able to contact his soul through meditation. To become a Buddha is to have achieved an even higher level of enlightenment.

RĀJA YOGA

Meditation is the key to controlling thoughts and emotions. In the East, the science of meditation and mind control is contained in the teachings of rāja yoga.

I've heard of rāja yoga but I'm not certain I know what it is.

The words yoga and religion are similar in derivation. Religion comes from Latin and means to re-connect, re-tie, or re-unite. What is it that is re-connected? The lower self, the personality, must be re-united with the Higher Self, the soul. In the descent of spiritual consciousness into the "underworld," or matter, there comes a time when there is a disconnect between the higher nature and the lower, or "animal," nature.

In allegorical terms, a "veil" is drawn between earthly realms and spiritual realms. Whether you call it a veil or a disconnect, it is very real, but it is also necessary at a certain stage of development. We are enticed by the allurements of this underworld. These allurements or magic toys, in the form of emotional desires, are the basis for growth during this period. If we remained fully conscious of our more spiritual nature, we could not be enticed, and we would not have the experience required for continued growth in consciousness. Without this veil, we would not be able to move forward.

Religion, therefore, should be the means of reconnecting with our spiritual self, but it only works for the most discerning of human beings. For the remainder, organized religion becomes just one more means of satisfying personal emotional needs. Many religions have been augmented and distorted from their original purity in order to serve the personal ambitions of the "authorities" of those religions, and they operate these organizations as effectively and purposefully as any large corporation. That type of organized religion has little to do with reconnecting to the soul. If you don't believe it, observe carefully the most ardent and fervent members of a congregation; you will find no lack of ego, pride, and personal ambition. Those members who do make spiritual progress generally do so in spite of the organization, not because of it.

THE SCHOOLS OF YOGA

Yoga is a Sanskrit word which means union or connection, and it also purports to give humanity the ability to reconnect with the Higher Self. Of the millions who practice various forms of yoga, few have found the means of connecting to the soul. It makes no difference whether you try to achieve this connection through religion or some other practice. The few who succeed will do so because of their ability to discern what is true and what is not, as well as from an intelligent and concerted effort to make it happen.

The key to enlightenment can be found in every major religion, but you will have to dig deep and know how to distinguish between gold and iron pyrite. All of the Abrahamic religions have pure truth at the core. The teachings in the Kabbalah, Gnosticism, and Sufism have all the essentials required for enlightenment, but only the earnest student will find them because it depends not simply on learning certain information, but on learning how to apply that knowledge in a way that will help us understand the laws of the universe. "Give me understanding and I will keep thy laws." Learning is not enough. Until we develop wisdom, we are simply collecting data.

In the East, the same profound truths are included in yoga, esoteric Brahmanism, and esoteric Buddhist teachings. No matter where you look for the truth though, it is not easy to find. You must search through tons of ore in order to find a single nugget of truth. Without having developed discernment, and without practical knowledge of the world we live in, it is an impossible task. Meditation is necessary in order to reach the goal.

There are several schools of yoga, just as there are numerous interpretations of any particular religious philosophy. Nearly everyone in the western world is familiar with hatha yoga, a form of yoga for the physical body. While it is a great form of exercise and a beginning toward reconnection with the soul, it is limited in its scope and requires the practice of other forms of yoga to gain enlightenment.

Karma yoga is another form of physical yoga, and in fact, karma means action. Those who work in shelters and volunteer to help the poor and the needy are practicing karma yoga. Mother Teresa is a perfect example of one who practiced karma yoga. But it also implies something more. It means we should be present in everything we do. Whether you are washing dishes or reading this book, be present. Be in the now. This is a form of yoga anyone can practice.

Laya yoga encompasses practices concerning the chakras, the whirling vortexes of energy found at specific points in the etheric body. The major chakras include the root chakra at the base of the spine, one at the sacrum, and one at the solar plexus. These three centers are all associated with our lower or animal nature and are well developed in most people. The higher centers are associated with our higher nature and include the heart center, throat center, and two in the head, one associated with the pineal gland and one with the pituitary body. The ājñā center is at the level of the forehead about midway when measured from front to back, and the crown center is farther back, at the crown of the head. The ājñā center especially is involved in the meditation process. The four higher centers are far less developed than the three lower centers in most people.

Many books depict the chakras as facing forward and being more or less near the anterior surface of the body. Others say they face backward except for the two head centers, and are approximately three inches in back of the spinal column.

KUNDALINĪ YOGA

A specific variety of laya yoga is kundalinī yoga. The purpose of kundalinī yoga is to awaken the latent power which lies asleep at the base of the spine and thereby develop psychic abilities. Even though it is dormant, kundalinī is the basis of energy in the physical body. It is the "fire" or "electricity" which is a vital part of our physical existence. It is foolish to try to awaken this energy prematurely through the practice of kundalinī yoga.

Why is that?

If you succeed in awakening the sleeping kundalinī, it is no less dangerous than playing with an angry cobra. You essentially have torn the veil between the physical and astral realms before you are prepared for the consequences. You would find yourself face to face with entities you never knew existed and over which you have little or no control. The same thing happens to people who destroy that veil through uncontrolled use of alcohol or drugs.

Once the veil is torn, it can seldom be repaired, and the poor victim is often driven insane by voices and astral beings, some visible and some unseen. Anyone who practices kundalinī yoga is literally playing with fire. Some people have also experienced the arousal of kundalinī when they were struck by lightning, but they are almost always ill-prepared for the results.

Why does kundalinī yoga even exist if it is so dangerous?

There are powerful forces in nature, and through gradual and persistent effort, we learn to work with them. We have great respect for electricity because we know it can kill, so any sane person is extremely careful with it and only interacts with it in ways he knows are safe. Kundalini is just as powerful and can kill the careless person just as easily. There will come a time for each individual when he or she will be taught how to awaken it safely for the benefit of humanity, but not for any selfish reason. For most people, that is in the far distant future, lifetimes from now.

Fortunately, there are few instructors who know much about kundalini. If they knew more, they would have developed amazing psychic powers. As it is, a little knowledge is dangerous. The best advice is not to practice certain breathing exercises unless you have a teacher in whom you have complete trust. If you would not trust your life in the hands of this person under any and all circumstances, walk away. There are plenty of other things you can be working on in the meantime. Tantra practices fall into the same category as kundalini, and in the West they are sometimes the basis for sex magic and black magic. These practices should be scrupulously avoided.

Much of what is called kundalini yoga in hatha yoga classes is not dangerous and is not the same as that taught by advanced yogis. As long as the techniques do not have the intention of developing psychic ability, you are probably safe. However, always be on guard. You alone are responsible for your success or failure as a student.

Bhakti yoga is the yoga of devotion, but in reality it operates almost entirely in the astral-emotional realm. The vast majority of religious devotees, regardless of whether they are devoted to Buddhism, Hinduism, Christianity,

Islam, or Judaism, are operating from an emotional basis. It matters not whether the object of devotion is an ideal or a personage. Emotion is emotion, and it is not very helpful in attaining enlightenment.

Do you mean to say that the millions of religious devotees in the world are deluded?

In a word—yes. If that devotion is based on emotional fervor, which is the case for the majority, it comes from personal desire and ego. In a very small minority, the devotion is based not on personal desire and emotions, but on a real desire to be of service in the world. If it is truly unselfish and altruistic in nature, there is a much better way than devotion.

And what is that?

Rāja yoga. Rāja means royal. This is the king of yogas. The oldest known treatise on rāja yoga is found in the yoga sūtras, or aphorisms, of Patañjali. No one knows when they were written, but it doesn't matter. What matters is that they constitute a succinct scientific method of learning mind control through meditation.

Why aren't more people aware of these yoga sūtras of Patañjali?

Many people have heard of them, but it is easy to dismiss something written in archaic language which is hard to understand today. But also, learning to control our thoughts is hard work, and few people want to be bothered. There are always a hundred things more important and more pressing than an effort that would lead to enlightenment.

What exactly is covered in these yoga sūtras?

Much of it is covered in various discussions in this book. Rāja yoga involves using great intellect, combined with spotless purity and dauntless courage, to do whatever it takes in order to reconnect with the Higher Self. You must be willing to sacrifice and let go of much that has been important to you for many lifetimes if you are to move forward. You cannot move forward *and* hold on to the past. "No man can serve two masters." You cannot be immersed in the spiritual life and at the same time be immersed in the material world.

Can you give me some practical advice on how to meditate?

As we said before, create the proper conditions within yourself first. Practice non-reaction and non-judgment. Let the world pass you by with all its glamor, drama, and illusions. You are too intelligent to remain caught in its net. You have discovered something much more valuable than the outer world has to offer.

YOUR SACRED SPACE

Find a location that is conducive to meditation. If you are fortunate enough to have a room in your home that can be dedicated exclusively to meditation, that's great. Select a room, or even a portion of a room, where there are no discordant vibrations. It should not be a room where anyone watches television, listens to loud music, or where many people pass through, leaving behind a trail of thought forms and emotional vibrations. Make it a sacred space reserved for study, contemplation, and meditation.

Should I use incense or candles to set the mood?

You should use whatever helps you meditate. Some think incense helps, but others are distracted by the smell. Music is seldom helpful, although some people find that "white noise" helps by masking ambient sounds, allowing the mind to withdraw more easily from the outer world. Candles also are optional, although a flame inherently has a quality of spirit about it, and almost all religions use candles in their services. This is not by accident.

You can also use a gong or chime as part of your meditation practice, and this is particularly useful in coordinating a group meditation. What you use as an aid to meditation is not important. Just be sure it does not detract from the experience. Some people get very wrapped up in the ceremony. It has to be done just so, with certain accoutrements, and in a certain order. If you get caught up in the ritual, then it becomes a superstition and you have lost sight of the true objective. The person who has achieved a degree of ability in meditation needs nothing special, just a quiet spot and, within seconds, he or she is deep in meditation, completely oblivious to the surroundings.

Sometimes when I meditate I see colored lights or images. Does that mean I'm making contact with my soul?

Not usually. For the most part, you should ignore things you see of this nature. They are astral phenomena and will do nothing to help you make contact with your soul. Focusing on them will lead you down the path of lower psychism, which is a trap. If you create the forms yourself as an exercise in visualization, that is different. When you experience visions, which are very different, it is a much more complex scene, more intense than any movie you have watched. You are most likely to experience it first during sleep and perhaps later during meditation.

THE STATES OF CONSCIOUSNESS

Is meditation a form of self-hypnosis?

Not at all. There are various types of consciousness that we humans experience. During waking hours, we are in what might be called our normal state of consciousness. In the aphorisms it is called jāgrat. Our mind is functioning through the physical brain, and we are able to think and reason with a degree of clarity.

When we sleep, there are generally two main phases, unconsciousness, called sushupti, and semi-consciousness, svapna. During unconsciousness, the brain does not transmit anything that registers as thought. It does not cease to function, but it does so in a subsistence mode. This phase is crucial to the well-being of the physical body. Without it, the body and the brain do not gain the rest they need to function properly.

When the physical body is asleep, there is an aspect of our existence that watches over it. It is sometimes referred to as the physical elemental. If anything occurs that it perceives as a danger to the body, it will attempt to awaken you. It does not have the intellect that you do, and its level of consciousness is quite low. Its function is to do everything possible to preserve and protect the body. It is not necessary to go into detail about it, but it is helpful to be aware of its existence.

Semi-consciousness, or svapna, occurs during the dream state. You are aware of your dreams but are generally not able to control them. You are more like a spectator watching a very strange and disjointed movie.

Alcohol and drugs also induce a state of semi-consciousness, even hallucinogenic drugs. With alcohol and most mood-altering drugs, the more you ingest, the less conscious you become until you drop below the level of consciousness completely. A high enough dosage results in death. If you are unable to control your thoughts and cannot end the experience immediately at any time, you are in a state of semi-consciousness; you are not in control.

Hypnosis, or mesmerism, results in a state of semi-consciousness. The hypnotized person has purposely become passive and has given control of his body over to another person. Now that person is in charge and the one hypnotized is only partially conscious, in a state of consciousness similar to that of the dream state. The same thing happens in the case of a medium. The medium purposely puts himself into a passive state, and then any entities passing by can operate through him by impressing thoughts and images on his brain. In the case of a trance medium, he becomes completely unconscious and is entirely at the mercy of the possessing entity, which uses the medium's body as if it were his own.

Self-hypnosis or auto-suggestion is more like the use of affirmations. You cannot be both the hypnotizer and the hypnotized. You cannot be in control and in a state of sleep. What you can do, however, is practice using affirmations during normal consciousness or during meditation. Then, during states of partial consciousness, your brain will repeat the affirmations because they were firmly impressed on it by the strength of the thought or through repetition. This is why affirmations are so effective.

Most people only experience normal consciousness, semi-consciousness and unconsciousness. What many describe as heightened consciousness is often a rush of emotional energy combined with a feeling of great devotion, a sort of emotional ecstasy. It is still normal consciousness infused with emotional energy.

Heightened consciousness, or super-consciousness, is something altogether different. Some people have never experienced it. Some have only experienced it once or twice in a lifetime, and then only to a slight degree. Some people experience it on a regular basis. Once you experience it, there is no doubt in your mind as to whether or not it was an episode of super-consciousness. It is extremely rare to experience it every time you meditate. This super-conscious state is called turya in the aphorisms.

It is only during these moments of super-consciousness that you achieve soul connection. The connection between the soul and the personality is the antahkarana. In most people it is practically non-existent, rather like a tiny filament. After years of meditation, you may achieve some degree of enlargement of the antahkarana, but it requires several lifetimes of concerted effort before it is fully functional. Then the personality is a fully-developed instrument the soul can use in service to the world. Transfer of control is passed to the Higher Self, and the personality is dedicated entirely to the welfare of our fellow men.

While the primary goal of meditation is the development of the antahkarana and complete communication with the soul, the secondary effect, which occurs at the same time, is a heightening of vibrations on every level.

What does that mean?

It's not easy to describe. Perhaps it is best to give an example. We have already seen that emotions exist within a certain range of frequencies. At the lower levels are what we call negative emotions—hatred, resentment, greed, jealousy, and anger. In the intermediate range are such emotions as anxiety, worry, and irritation. At the higher end of the scale are emotions like compassion, affection, and kindness, provided they are unselfishly motivated. Although we think of them as emotions, some of them are aspects of our spiritual nature, and only the highest level of the emotional realm can reflect them. As you practice meditation on a regular basis and at the same time practice the concepts presented in this book, you discover that the lower emotions appear less frequently until, for you, they cease to exist. There is no longer any material in your emotional being which can vibrate in sympathy with these lower emotions. You are on your way to human perfection.

This phenomenon affects more than the emotions. The physical body itself is changed. Every atom in your body is replaced by new ones over time. Not one atom in your current physical body was there seven years ago. Each time one is replaced, the frequency of the new one matches the current frequency of vibration that you have achieved through meditation and thought control. In the average person, this happens normally over eons of time, but we don't have eons to wait. We must do the same thing ourselves through a determined effort. Fortunately, we don't have to be a molecular biologist to make it happen. It occurs as a natural effect of our concentrated effort at enlightenment. It occurs during deep meditation and because of our spiritual practice in everyday living.

Does the heightening of vibrations also affect the mind?

It does. Every aspect of our lower nature must be brought into alignment with the Higher Self. The personality must become a perfect instrument for the use of the soul. The mental, emotional, and physical vibrations must all be tuned to those of the Higher Self. This is the purification process of the refiner's fire. All that is coarse, all that is dross, must be burned away, leaving behind only pure gold. It is not a process without pain or sacrifice.

Why is that?

Think about it. You must eliminate from your being everything that is most dear to many people—emotions, drama, and attachments. For long ages there has been nothing in the personality that was of any interest to the soul. Then, over a period of time, the personalities of various lifetimes made an effort at alignment with the soul and finally, after several lifetimes of concentrated effort, the goal has been reached. One more human being has reached the other shore. This is the true meaning of salvation. It has been a long, arduous effort at tremendous cost, but the rewards outweigh by far the effort required. This particular individual has become a valuable instrument and is a member of the Spiritual Hierarchy.

Only those who have achieved this exalted level of enlightenment can be said to have achieved eternal life.

Don't we all have eternal life?

We do. We are life itself, and life is eternal, but there is a great distinction between the life of an ordinary human being and that of a member of the Spiritual Hierarchy. As long as you have periods of unconsciousness like the ones you experience during sleep and after the death of the physical body, there is a discontinuity of consciousness which causes anxiety for many people. People have many fears and especially fear death because they are afraid they will cease to exist. This fear is well founded as long as that individual identifies with the personality. The personality *will* cease to exist when the body dies, so the person who identifies with his personal being has every right to fear death. Only when a person is constantly in contact with the Higher Self and has learned to retain complete consciousness, not only during sleep, but also after the physical body dies, can it be said that he has achieved eternal life. Only then is there no longer any break in consciousness.

To die before you die is the key to eternal life.

I've heard that phrase before, but I didn't understand what it meant.

It means that the personality is no longer in charge. Through long and sustained effort, it has become a perfect instrument for the use of the soul. It gives new meaning to the final phrase of the Prayer of St. Francis— "It is in dying that we are born to eternal life."

Chapter 11

YOUR SPIRITUAL PRACTICE

> When you move in the world of the
> senses, free from both attachment
> and aversion, there comes a peace
> which ends all sorrows, and you live
> in the wisdom of the Self.
>
> — *Bhagavad Gītā 2:64-65*

YOUR MEDITATION PRACTICE

What are some things that will help in meditation?

There are a number of practices that will help. Each student should try several of them and then continue to
practice those he or she finds useful. A spiritual practice
may include some of the following—reading, writing, mu-

sic, painting, or other forms of art, hatha yoga, nature walks, contemplation, periods of silence, meditation, and teaching. You may think of others as well. The key is to do your practice consistently, every day if possible.

THE CENTER OF MY UNIVERSE

Take a large sheet of paper and put a dot in the center of it. This is you, and the page is your universe. Think of different people who have played a part in your life, now or in the past, living or dead. Don't dwell on each one, but as that person flashes into your mind, put a dot on the paper. The proximity of their dot to yours should indicate your relationship with that person. Those close to you will have a dot close to yours. Casual acquaintances or enemies will have a dot farther out. As soon as you think of someone, make a dot and move to the next one that comes to mind.

Go way back in your life. You have interacted with thousands of people. You may be amazed at some who come to mind that you have not thought of in years. You can include pets also. Do this for ten or fifteen minutes, or until it becomes more difficult to think of new ones.

Now spend a few minutes looking at your paper, visualizing your connection to these people and the fact that they are also connected with each other. Close your eyes and spend some time in contemplation, especially on your connectedness not just with people, but with everything in the world. You may gain some interesting insights, especially with regard to the most difficult relationships in your life.

CONNECT WITH A PLANT OR TREE

This practice is designed to help develop your sensitivity. There are two types of sensitivity in people. The first is a sort of victim mentality in those whose feelings are easily hurt and who habitually react to the slightest hint of criticism as if it were intended to wound. We all know people like this. It is difficult to interact with them because you always have to be careful. The most innocent observation can cause a flare-up of anger. "How dare you say that!" They are quick to let you know you have offended them, whether you intended to or not.

This type of sensitivity is based entirely on ego. The stronger the ego, the more fragile it is and the more "sensitive" the person is to anything that can be construed as criticism. This person is not a candidate for spiritual growth.

The type of sensitivity we want to develop includes no sense of ego. It can only manifest when you are in control of your thoughts and emotions and are at peace with yourself. It is receptive instead of reactive, altruistic instead of selfish, directed outward instead of inward.

Select a tree if you can, in your back yard or a nearby park, one you can visit almost daily. If this is not possible, choose a plant, even one on your balcony or kitchen table. Take your time and select a tree or plant with which you feel an affinity. Now spend some time with this living being. Don't project your thoughts or ideas onto it. Instead, practice being receptive. Make your mind a blank slate and simply observe any ideas or impressions you receive.

You can touch the tree if you want, but this is not about a physical experience of texture or any other physical attribute. Your goal is to tune in to the essential nature of the tree, to feel its energy. The tendency at first may be to project human traits onto it. We tend to anthropomorphize anything we feel connected to. Many of your initial impressions may be caused by your imagination. It takes time to learn to perceive accurately without the interference of our own energy. The goal is to perceive objectively, to "see" clearly without our expectations and prejudices getting in the way.

There is no need to analyze anything or make judgments. Continue this practice daily, or as often as you can. See if you feel a difference in the tree as the seasons pass, as summer turns to autumn, then enters the dormancy of winter, only to re-awaken and begin a new cycle of growth in the springtime. You may want to keep notes in a spiritual journal.

YOUR SPIRITUAL JOURNAL

Many people find a spiritual journal to be helpful. It should not be a diary, but should reflect the results of your spiritual practice. Some people like to keep a dream journal, but your spiritual journal should only include dreams that are especially significant, ones that could be called visions rather than dreams.

The spiritual journal should be more about contact with your soul. It may have only a few entries each year, or it may have many. You don't have to write in it every day, but if you do, keep it succinct and concise. You may make notes on a concept that has acquired new meaning, a note on what you are reading, or the results of your meditation practice.

If your journal becomes too introspective and focused on you, you have missed the point, and it is just one more way of massaging your ego. If you feel it is important because it is a part of you, you have failed to practice non-attachment. If it is ever lost, it should cause no reaction. We can't be too careful about falling back into the realm of the ego. It is very clever, though not particularly intelligent, and it intends to survive at any cost. The ego has no integrity and will try to make you compromise yours in order for it to survive.

Glance through your journal from time to time; you may find you are making more progress than you thought. Some of our greatest advancements come from the most difficult trials we encounter. It is only after we have climbed a little higher up the mountain and turn to look back that we see the true perspective of the past, and everything becomes more clear. A spiritual journal helps us remember previous experiences and incorporate them in a meaningful way when we can see with greater clarity.

THE NATURE WALK

It doesn't actually have to be a walk, and it doesn't have to be outside, although being outside with nature is helpful. Be where you can connect with natural objects—trees, flowers, birds, squirrels, clouds, fish, mountains, rocks, anything in nature. Then, just as in your practice with the tree or plant, experience the energy you feel. Marvel at the movement of the clouds or the shifting colors of the sunset. Resist the desire to share this experience with others. This is your experience. Everyone else has his own experience in life.

Have you ever seen something so wonderful you felt you had to share it with others? Perhaps you saw a magnificent sunset or an incredibly beautiful flower, so you took a photo in order to share it with them. On sharing the photo, their reaction is either minimal or obviously feigned in order not to offend you. You look again at the photo to see why they don't see the marvelous things you saw, and are shocked to realize that the beauty and majesty you experienced are not there. You try desperately to explain in words what it was you experienced. All efforts are futile.

Even if that person is with you physically during your experience, he or she will have a completely different experience. Each of us lives in a universe of our own. No one else can experience what you perceive, and you cannot perceive what others are experiencing. Give up. Stop trying to make others see and experience what you do. It is only another form of attachment and an indicator of ego.

One goal of the nature walk is to connect with the powerful energy around us. We enjoy it thoroughly only when we do not feel compelled to share it. If you are walking with someone else, walk in silence. If you see something interesting, point it out, but no words are necessary. After you return, you can bask in the memory of the experience. Trying to put it into words or share it with others will only diminish it. Learn to keep silent. This is also true of meditation experiences. Keep it to yourself unless there is some lesson that can be helpful to others. Sharing spiritual experiences often has more to do with ego than with helping someone learn something new.

During your walk, practice observing without words. Any words, mental or spoken, will detract from this meditative experience. The most profound concepts of the universe will never be conveyed in words. External forms always reflect interior energy fields and patterns, but there are always energies in the inner expression that the outer form cannot convey.

The purpose of this exercise is to stop the incessant chatter of the mind. When we observe something in nature, our mind wants to make notes and create phrases so we can share it with others as well as remember it ourselves.

There is no reason to recall that experience and, in fact, it can never be recalled. It happened in the moment and belongs to that moment. Once that moment has passed, the physical experience ceases to exist. It is gone forever, and all you have is a poor memory recorded in your mind. The true recording of the event is engraved in your soul's experience. It can never be erased, but it also can't be shared with others. Learn to be okay with that.

ULTRA-SLOW MOTION

This is a practice anyone can do. It can be done indoors or outside, individually or in a group, sitting or standing. It is extremely simple and extremely powerful.

The practice is this—move very, very slowly and with intention. Be fully present the entire time. Be completely focused on the physical movement, even though it is barely perceptible. If you do it correctly, you will not be able to think of anything else. The only thought in your mind is your current position at this precise moment.

The motion of setting down your pen and taking a sip of water from the glass in front of you, an action that normally requires five seconds, now may take five minutes. But don't worry. There is nothing more important during those five minutes than what you are experiencing.

You can do this simply while walking. Each step may require a full minute. If you are really brave, try it in a public park. If there are birds feeding nearby, an interesting experiment is to see how close you get before they fly away. If you move extremely slowly, they become mesmerized, and you may be surprised just how close you get before their natural instinct overcomes their curiosity.

If you have trouble quieting your mind for meditation, this is a perfect practice for you. Try it with children. If they are old enough to understand the concept, they are often eager to try it.

VISUALIZATION

Part of learning to control the mind is being able to stop the thought process and make the mind perfectly still. People are often surprised to find how difficult this is. Once you have achieved a degree of thought control, the next step is to start directing the mind and using it as the powerful tool it can be. A perfect practice for this is visualization.

The ultimate goal of visualization is to help others, but to learn it, various practices, in the form of guided meditations, are useful. Deep meditation, samādhi, will not occur through visualization, but it is a fundamental part of the process and is a practical application of meditation. Use any guided meditation that appeals to you, or create your own. Here is one you can practice and modify to suit your needs. Read it over several times until you have it impressed on your mind. You don't want to interrupt the process to refer to notes.

Sit quietly in a comfortable position with the spine erect and close your eyes. Starting at the top of the head, focus your attention on each part of the body in turn. As you focus on it, feel all the muscles and nerves in that area relax. Continue on to the muscles and nerves of the face, back of the head, ears, chin and neck, relaxing each area as you go.

Continue downward to the upper back, shoulders, arms and hands, then the chest, abdomen, and lower back. The hips and buttocks are next, then the pelvis, thighs, knees, ankles, feet, and toes.

When all muscles and nerves are relaxed, do the same with the organs—the heart, lungs, spleen, and pancreas, liver, gallbladder, stomach, and digestive system. Now feel your connection with the earth and with all beings. By now you should be in a state of relaxation and ready for a walk.

Imagine you are walking through a wooded area on a beautiful day. In sunlit areas, you feel the warmth of the sun on your back and shoulders. In shaded areas, you feel the cool breeze on your face. Breathe deeply and slowly. With each inhalation, breathe in life and revitalizing energy. Notice the sweet scents of the flowers, the earthy smell of damp forest, and the pungent odors of the evergreen trees.

Travel slowly. There is nowhere you need to be except here. Become aware of the sounds of the forest. The birds are chattering, each species in its own language. Bees and other flying insects are buzzing, each one experiencing life in its own way. From time to time, you hear a creature scurrying in the underbrush. Far in the distance you hear the sound of a stream, and in your mind you see the stream you will encounter before long.

Walk slowly, enjoying every moment of your adventure. Relish the sights, sounds and sensations. Marvel at the exquisite colors surrounding you. After a while, you stop in a clearing and lie down on a bed of soft grass. Feel the living energy that surrounds you in every blade of grass, every flower, plant, and animal. A lizard is doing pushups on a rock nearby, his head tilted toward the sun, eyes half closed. This brings a sense of drowsiness to you, and as you watch the mottled white clouds scuttle across the blue sky, your eyelids close as you drift into a peaceful, dreamless sleep.

When you awake, you have no idea how long you slept, but the quality of the light has changed, and the world around you is even more magical than before. Everything seems to be enchanted.

As you walk on, you are led by the sound of the stream, beckoning and enticing, growing louder as you approach. When you see the brook, you continue to follow it, smiling at its persistent effort to reach its final destination. Coming around a bend, you catch sight of a magnificent lake of clear blue water extending in front of you. Without hesitation, you dive into it and enter a completely new world. Beneath the surface, and perfectly visible, are many varieties of fish and aquatic animals. Some are curious, never having seen a creature like you, and they do not hesitate in swimming over to investigate. Others are more timid and peer out from rock caves and thick plant growth.

After interacting with these underwater beings, you swim to the opposite shore where a waterfall drops directly into the lake, the force of the water creating bubbles, foam and whirling eddies in the lake's surface. Once close to the waterfall, you notice a ledge behind it and swim through the falling water to investigate. Pulling yourself up, you stand for a long time behind the water in the humid space, feeling the mist of the droplets on your face and the power in the ionized air.

Continue climbing up the rock face beside the waterfall until you reach the top, high above. Standing tall, you look down at the scene below. You can see everywhere you have been, from the beginning of your walk, to the meadow where you rested, the stream you followed, and the lake below, with the waterfall at your feet. Everything has meaning. Each step of the way was necessary for you to reach the point you have attained.

Looking up at the sky, you see a bird of prey searching below with all-seeing eyes. His wings are fully extended, and he instinctively takes advantage of the subtle air currents, gliding and soaring effortlessly in the invisible energy fields. Closing your eyes, you become one with this being. You see everything he sees. You share the results of every experience he has ever had. His knowledge and expertise are yours as well.

In a flash, you know that you are one with all life and can experience everything that any being has ever experienced, by expanding your consciousness to include what previously seemed separate from yourself. You are Life itself.

While this is a powerful exercise, it must be used with caution. There is always the possibility of using it as a tool to emphasize the self, *my* experience. Remove any thought of you as a personality, and focus instead on you as a point of light, one among billions, in the One Life. Your experience is no more important and no less important than that of any other point of light.

There is also another potential problem with this practice. The more powerful it is for you, the more real it becomes.

I don't see what problem there could be.

The question is this—is it real or not?

If it's just something I imagined, then it's not real. Or is it?

The dreams you have are real because they exist. You wouldn't dream of denying that, and as long as you are in that dream state, they definitely exist. Every thought you create or experience is real, and the more powerful the thought, the more real it becomes. Other people can feel the effects of your thought, and some can even "see" or "read" those thoughts.

If you repeat this practice a number of times and imbue it with enough energy, a psychic may be able to see it more or less clearly. One psychic might see it as a walk you had taken, convinced he was seeing a series of events that took place in the physical world. A highly trained clairvoyant would distinguish that it was a mental practice with no corresponding physical component. When you are operating in the astral-emotional and the lower mental realms, it is easy to be deceived.

Every physical object also has an astral counterpart, but not everything that exists on the astral plane has a physical counterpart. Likewise, everything that exists on the astral plane has a mental counterpart, but there are mental "objects" that have no astral or physical components. Thus, there is more that exists in astral form than in physical, and even more that exists in mental form.

Being able to sort out these different realms of existence is no easy task. The ordinary psychic is at a severe disadvantage. None of them have the training necessary to make much sense of it, and very few have the level of intelligence or purity required for this training.

Many psychics are completely delusional. They create a universe within their mind, and the thought forms can be so powerful that they are surrounded with them at all times. If they believe this self-created universe is anything but that, they will continue believing in it for the remainder of this lifetime, and it is a severe impediment to further progress. The potential problem is the same for us. We may create a universe in our mind and choose to live there instead of in the outside world. It is tempting, but it's not helpful. Learn to be okay with things just as they are.

EVERYONE CAN READ MY THOUGHTS

An interesting and useful practice is to act as if everyone were psychic and could read your thoughts. Do you want to know the truth? They can. Every individual, not just humans, can perceive the energy patterns created by your thoughts and emotions. Sometimes it is a subconscious perception, but never underestimate other people's ability to "read" you. The reason they can seldom read you with accuracy is because their perceptions are filtered by their own prejudices and expectations. A person who is dishonest will assume everyone else is as well, and will not be good at discerning who is telling the truth and who is lying.

People are probably more perceptive than you give them credit for. Even the worst criminal has a divine spark within and subconsciously respects the more advanced individual, the one whose light shines more brightly than the rest. The most unenlightened sometimes have more insight as to another person's level of advancement than a semi-enlightened person. Why? Because the ego of the semi-enlightened person often gets in the way. He refuses to believe that someone nearby could possibly be more enlightened than he is. A prophet is not without honor except in his hometown and among his own family.

The point of this practice is that people can perceive our emotions and thoughts, some more accurately than others. Our job is to control our thoughts and emotions so they always reflect the kindness and compassion which are natural characteristics of our higher nature.

Chapter 12

EMOTIONS: FRIENDS OR FOES?

That which you seek desperately,
you will lose.
That which you release,
you will have in abundance.

THE ELUSIVE BUTTERFLY

A man had collected butterflies since he was young and
had an enormous collection of different species. It was the
largest collection of its kind and he was very proud of it.
Each day he strolled through the rows of displays and
admired his specimens, some smaller than a fingernail,
and some as large as a plate. He smiled with pride as he

gazed upon them and thought about the adventures they represented; he had caught many of them himself.

But there was a bit of sadness in him. One particular species was missing. It was a rare one found only in a particular area of a remote rainforest. Other collectors reported having seen it, but none had been able to capture it. He made up his mind that he would obtain this specimen, regardless of the cost in time, effort, or money.

He began preparations for an expedition to the rainforest where the butterfly had been spotted before. After weeks of planning, he arrived in the area after having made a long and arduous trip, the last of it in a canoe paddled by indigenous people.

For weeks they travelled about, setting up camp each day, and he spent hours searching for the object of his desire. Day after day he met with disappointment, frustration, and despair. He began to falter in his determination, but he thought about how much this specimen would enhance his reputation among his peers. He would be famous. Having the only one in the world would bring him esteem and the envy of others, so he pushed on, having received new motivation.

Finally one day, it happened. There in front of him was the object of this long ordeal. He knew it immediately from the markings described by other collectors. He raised his net and then, just as it swooshed through the air, the butterfly soared away to a different resting spot. Again and again, when he was on the verge of attaining his goal, it escaped at the last second, almost as if it were playing a game with him.

After several hours of fruitless effort, he was exhausted. He sat on a fallen tree to rest and set his net down beside him. Cradling his head in his hands, he thought about the dreadful possibility of returning without having attained his goal. He would have to face everyone he had told about this adventure and admit he was a failure.

After a few minutes of musing about his fate, something caught his attention. His eyes were still closed, so it wasn't anything he saw. Or did he? He perceived a certain energy field, something that had not been there a moment ago. Slowly, he opened his eyes and looked carefully to the left. There, resting gently on his shoulder, was his elusive butterfly. He was careful not to get excited and frighten it. What to do? He slowly reached with his right hand for the net, but it had fallen down, just beyond his reach. He didn't dare swat it with his hand as this would destroy it as a specimen.

Pondering over his predicament, he was more and more fascinated by this creature, the object of his fondest dreams for years. Here it was finally, resting on his shoulder, but with no way to capture it. He gazed at the exquisite, iridescent colors shimmering in the sunlight, pulsing with the ebb and flow of life. Suddenly, a sense of despair came over him. He was shocked to realize that, just a moment before, he had been plotting to kill this poor defenseless creature. Then he thought about all the other defenseless beings he had killed in order to have a collection to be proud of. How many thousands of lives had he destroyed because of his selfish needs? The horror of it shook him to the depths of his being. His heart contracted in pain as tears of regret filled his eyes.

The butterfly shifted its stance slightly and turned as if looking directly at him. It was his farewell glance, and he flew away, high into the sky and out of sight.

He didn't know how long he sat there. He had fallen into a deep reverie and had seen visions he couldn't fully remember. He wouldn't be able to explain anyway the transformation that had just taken place. He knew he would never add another specimen to his collection, but the transformation that had occurred within him was worth far more than any collection ever could be.

In chapter 2 we read the story of the magic toy. In that story and the one above, we see the effects of desire in our lives. It is desire that impels us to action. If there were no desire to provide the impetus, we would have no purpose in life and would simply exist. Whether we are referring to the actions of a solar system, planet, man, ant, or atom, desire is the motivating factor that causes us to move forward.

At our current stage of human evolution, it is emotional desire, that which the ego craves, that motivates us. We want a relationship, money, power, and material objects that will provoke envy and jealousy in others. Within a few hundred years, personal emotional needs will have begun to wane as our motivation in life and will be replaced with a different type of desire.

But wouldn't we cease to be human if we no longer had emotions?

It's not emotions that make us human. It's true that animals have fewer emotions than we do, but their emotions are driven by instinct, not by the mind. As humans, we have powerful and well-developed emotions, but in general, our minds still have much development ahead. We are human because of the level of consciousness we have attained, not because we have emotions.

As we have seen, the majority of humans are propelled forward in gaining experience by kāma-manas, the lower part of mind linked to emotional desire. More enlightened individuals are propelled by buddhi-manas, the higher part of mind linked to intuition. The buddhic realm of existence vibrates with a much higher frequency than emotions do.

How would we recognize some of these more enlightened individuals who no longer need emotions for their impetus?

Surprisingly, few of them are found among the so-called "spiritual" people of the world. They are often found among scientists and philosophical people, those who ponder deeply over the mysteries of life. Einstein, who wanted to "know the mind of God," is an example of this more enlightened individual. They are not concerned about their own personal needs but rather dwell on matters of planetary and even cosmic importance. It might be said that their feet barely touch the ground, they are so often deep in contemplation of higher matters. You would probably not find them often attending sports events, movies, or other venues filled with emotional excitement.

Why do you say that few are found among the spiritual people of the world? I should think they would make up a large percentage of this group.

Unfortunately, the majority of "spiritual" people have simply exchanged one type of emotional drama in life for another, a type of "spiritual" drama. In organized religions, we often see it in the form of services that have the flavor of a rock concert, with loud music, fervent singing and praying, and high emotional drama. There is nothing especially spiritual in this type of religious theater. It is designed to appeal to the personal ego and its need for emotional drama.

Other individuals, though more quiet and studious, are often not much more advanced. They may no longer thrill to the vibrations of loud music and emotional group events, but they still are driven by the need for drama in their lives; their egos are not only intact, but powerful. They have substituted "spiritual" emotions for lower, more primitive emotions.

For example, students of esoteric studies often grasp a tiny fragment of a concept, and then, rather than guard it carefully in their hearts where it can develop and grow to a greater understanding, they become greatly excited and can't wait to "share" it with others, which means their ego will receive a boost by being the one to announce it to the world.

Over the centuries, there has been no lack of individuals who formed groups around themselves in order to announce to the world the imminent return of Christ to earth. Even in the Bible this occurred within a short time after Jesus died, and it has continued unabated up to the present day.

Look at some of the groups who loudly proclaim the return of Christ, have any number of miraculous signs as evidence, and strange stories to corroborate their message. You will find at the center of such groups one or more individuals with enormous egos who make a great show of being a spiritual guru, specially selected to announce the great event to the world. Take a look at their prophecies, and you will find that time after time they fail to materialize. You will also find that many of the things they write have no more substance to them than the writings of the average high school student.

Does that mean there is no such thing as the second coming of Christ?

There is only one coming of Christ which is of any importance to an individual, and that is the birth of Christ consciousness within his heart. Obviously, this is a very personal and precious event, something to be kept private and pondered over carefully. It is not something to announce to the world. Hence the parable of casting pearls before swine.

There are Avatars—divine beings—who, from time to time, come from a much higher level of existence to help in the spiritual development of humanity. They even sometimes are born to human parents and occupy a physical body, although this is rare. More often, they overshadow human beings who have purified their own physical bodies and thoughts, and have greatly reduced or eliminated negative emotions in their own nature.

The individual who fills the position of the Christ—the World Teacher—will come into the world at some point. He may decide to use a physical body, but it may be that the lowest vehicle he occupies will be on the astral level. No matter how he chooses to appear, it will not be the public event so many proclaim will happen. Only those who are enlightened will be aware of his existence in the world, and they alone will be able to benefit to any great extent by his being here. The average person would not be able to tolerate or appreciate the higher levels of vibration and would not recognize his exalted status.

Be wary of those who dress themselves in spiritual garb—and here we speak both literally and symbolically—in order to impress others with their spiritual development. Anyone who does this is simply enhancing his personal ego. There may be some kernel of altruistic motivation at the center, but it has been obscured by the still potent ego of the "guru."

Keep in mind that all energy vibrates at a particular frequency. That which vibrates within a certain frequency range is called astral, or emotional. When we talk of vibrations, they include not only physical vibrations, but the vibratory frequencies that animate matter on all planes of existence. Each type of vibration can only be perceived at its own level.

There are many teachings that "seem true" and make sense, but you can't necessarily "prove" them to someone else. Every concept must be grasped at its own level. Unfortunately, words become almost useless at some point in explaining higher concepts. They then serve only as symbols, hints and suggestions for the perceptive individual who contemplates and meditates on them in order to gain more enlightenment.

In the higher vibrational range are positive emotions such as compassion, benevolence, kindness, concern for others.

I wouldn't consider those emotions but rather good character traits.

As long as there is the slightest personal desire involved in the action, it is emotional in nature. Examine the motive carefully. If you give someone a gift because you want him to recognize your generosity, then it wasn't really a gift. You gave it because you wanted something in return, even if it wasn't something material. You wanted to enhance your ego. Few people in the world are completely honest. It is most difficult to be honest when your ego is involved and it feels threatened. It will try everything possible to convince you that your motives are pure and unselfish when they are not. Why? Because it knows if there is no selfishness in you, it will no longer exist.

Many acts that appear kind and compassionate on the surface contain mixed motives, both selfish and unselfish. Many charitable foundations in the world would never exist if it were not for the fact that the founder receives accolades and recognition for being so generous. But how many would donate the money anonymously, without any need of personal gratification? There are some who do that, but their numbers are small compared to the former type.

Unconditional love, joy, loving kindness, true compassion—things that have no selfish motive or emotion involved—are characteristics of the soul and are only re-flected in the highest levels of the astral-emotional realm. Those who exhibit these traits are a joy to work with. There is never a question of motive or the need to appeal to their egos, because there is no ego and their motives are always pure.

THE POWER OF THOUGHT

No emotion ever existed without a thought behind it. Im-agine a hungry lion behind you. As long as you are una-ware of it, do you have any emotion? No. You continue blissfully unaware, doing whatever you were doing. Now imagine that you turn around and see it crouched, ready to spring upon you, having marked you as lunch. Are there any emotions involved? For the majority of people, the answer is yes. There is a rush of adrenalin, and the body immediately is in fight-or-flight mode.

Think about this carefully. What changed between the state of no emotion and that of high emotion? Only one thing—a thought. As soon as your mind told your brain you were in mortal danger, your body immediately re-sponded with an emotional and a physical reaction. Would it make any difference whether the danger were real or imagined? None whatsoever.

Have you ever dreamed you were falling from a high place? What happened? The same thing that would hap-pen if you saw a lion behind you. Your mind tells your brain you are in mortal danger. There is an emotional and a physical reaction. You would probably awake in a panic and find your heart beating wildly. Although there is no way to prove it, it is probable that many people have died of a heart attack in their sleep because of a dream.

Is a dream real or unreal? While you are experiencing it, we can certainly say it is real. We could just as easily say it was not real because it is nothing but an idea, an image.

IS LIFE REAL OR UNREAL?

It certainly seems real. We experience birth and death, dramatic events, and have a long series of experiences. We feel happiness and heartbreak, joy and sorrow, hope and despair. Is it real or not? It doesn't matter. Just as the dream was real while you were dreaming it, life is real while you are living it. But there will come a time when the life comes to an end, and the consciousness within you will reflect on it as if it had been a dream. It will no longer seem real because you are now in a different state of consciousness. Simply stated, we will awaken one day and find that life was just a dream.

That sounds terribly pessimistic. Why would we have to endure the pain and suffering we do only to find it was nothing but an illusion?

Because that's how life works. That's how we gain experience. Someone learning to fly may use a flight simulator with mock controls to learn how to pilot a plane. This gives the illusion of flying, but it's not real. Then he gets in a Boeing 777, takes off, flies several hundred miles, and lands safely. Is this real? It's not any more real than the flight simulator. All that we experience as reality is an illusion. But it doesn't matter. We gain the same experience, whether it is real or imagined. Remember, the gain in experience and growth of consciousness are the only things that are important. What we perceived as reality to get there is an illusion and of no importance.

So does that mean we should never make any effort in life, since it is only an illusion? Why wouldn't we choose to do nothing instead?

Try doing nothing and see what happens. You may sit there for a while, but eventually you get bored and feel the need to do something. What is it that impels you to stop doing nothing and do something? Desire, the life impulse deep within all creatures. Remember, an ant, a planet, a solar system, and a hydrogen atom all have desire. The consciousness within you is in ceaseless motion. Its nature is to evolve, and nothing will change that innate nature.

THE POWER OF EMOTIONS

Whom the gods would destroy, they first make angry.

A young boy was playing one day with his friends. He often suffered from asthma attacks and always made sure to keep his inhaler handy. While playing, one of his friends made a comment that upset him. He became so angry that he experienced shortness of breath and realized he was having an asthma attack.

He turned from his friend and ran to his backpack for his inhaler. After rummaging through it, he realized he had left it at home. The realization that his source of relief was missing brought on a panic attack, and the resulting panic increased the intensity of the asthma attack until he was no longer able to breathe. He lost consciousness, fell to the ground, and died, with his friends anxiously gathered around him.

Unfortunately, this is a true story. What did the emotion of anger cost this young boy? His life. A sudden surge of emotion can kill immediately, as in this case, but we suffer every day from the effects of emotion. Each emotion adds its impact to the accumulation of stress in our lives. Look at those around you who have frequent and strong emotions and you will see the effects in their physical demeanor.

Each time you have a surge of emotions, your immune system suffers. A fit of anger reduces your immunity to the point that you are susceptible to almost any disease-causing agent nearby. Although immunity is affected by many different things, emotional stress will affect it immediately and in a negative fashion.

But what about good emotions? Wouldn't those be helpful instead of harmful?

Emotions are emotions, and whether "good" or "bad," each comes with a cost. Imagine an elderly lady with a weak heart who answers her door one day to find a van outside and a group of people filled with anticipation to announce that she has won twenty million dollars in the lottery. The emotional reaction may be too much for a weak heart, and could easily cause her to die, just as the boy died from an angry emotion. Every emotion has its cost.

Remember that no emotion ever occurs without a thought behind it. It is the thought that causes the emotion. And every emotion has a physical component. You can't have an emotion of any type without also experiencing a physical reaction. Think about this carefully, observe it in life, and you will find it is true.

CONTROLLING EMOTIONS

You can't control emotions by focusing on them and saying, "I'm going to gain control over this emotion." They come in numerous guises. Not only do we have the ones mentioned earlier, but also the need for drama, the addiction to the highs and lows of emotion. Relationships are often built on the common need for an emotional experience. Things go smoothly for a while and then boredom sets in, so one of the partners will do something to create drama, the other reacts, and both are happy again. Many couples stir up fights on a regular basis because they are addicted to the cycle of fighting and making up. They love the emotional roller coaster ride. Without it, life would be meaningless, or so they think.

The majority of mankind is addicted to this emotional roller coaster ride. We seek it in movies, concerts, religious events, boxing matches, car racing, personal relationships, television commercials, and thousands of other situations. If we don't have enough drama in our own lives, we look for it in the lives of celebrities or acquaintances.

The suffering that humans experience is caused by our addiction to emotion. And although many people claim to dislike emotional drama because of the suffering, even the suffering is part of the addiction. Without suffering, how would they experience joy? Without unhappiness, how would they know happiness? You can't have the highs without the lows. This is the nature of emotion and is also why it's such a powerful addiction. We have strong physical reactions to it and it makes us feel alive.

So you're saying if I'm not ready to control my emotions I'm doomed to suffer? That doesn't seem fair.

It has nothing to do with fair or unfair. It is simply how life works. If there were no consequences to your actions and you could engage in emotions without experiencing the results, what would happen? First of all, you would feel lifeless, like there was nothing of value in life. But also, there would be no reason for you to want to change your habits. It is the negative result of emotions that impels us to find a higher type of desire which will replace emotions as our impetus in life.

Few people are ready to let go of emotions, first of all because they have nothing with which to replace them, and secondly because there are still many life lessons to be learned in the current phase. Trying to pass too soon to the next phase is not helpful. The best thing to do is to recognize you are motivated by your emotions if that is true, and realize that at some point, whether in this lifetime or another, that will cease to be the case.

Watch your emotions carefully. Examine them and their results in yourself and in those around you. You will see how emotions are used by some individuals to control or manipulate others. You probably know someone who uses anger like a blowtorch, brandishing it menacingly toward anyone who dares cross them or question their motives. Emotions are effective weapons. People walk on eggshells around those who are emotionally volatile.

COMPOUND EMOTIONS

Emotions are seldom pure emotions. That is, there is generally a combination of several feelings that arise at the same time. If someone says something to you and you take offense at it, not only do you erupt in anger, but there is a degree of hatred aimed at the person who made the remark. This may be fairly mild, or moderate, but it may be strong enough that you would be tempted to harm that person if you thought you could get away with it.

Outrage often accompanies anger. Every emotion is either directed at the object, usually a person, or at yourself. *You* feel outraged. *You* feel you are under attack. *You* feel you have been wounded or diminished by someone else. We generally assume their actions were meant to harm, seldom stopping to consider that we all say and do things which might be perceived as motivated by evil intentions, but often it is simply lack of awareness.

CLAIRVOYANCE

A good clairvoyant can see these emotions in a vivid and graphic way, but good clairvoyants are rare.

I don't agree. I know several people who are psychic and receive communications from their spirit guides.

A good clairvoyant does not rely on spirit guides. A spirit guide, or astral entity, is not very advanced and often is less advanced than the average person. They have no more insight into the mysteries of nature than any other unenlightened individual. A good clairvoyant, a seer, is one who has been trained over a number of years by those who are highly advanced. He or she learns to distinguish the subtle variations of vibrations and interpret them with accuracy. Their talent is never wasted in fortune telling or to boost someone's ego. This ability comes at a high cost in terms of work and effort. It is used judiciously and only for the good of humanity. All efforts by an enlightened person are for the good of all, never for the benefit of one's personal ego.

Still, I would love to develop clairvoyance. Can you tell me how to do it?

Trying to develop clairvoyance should be scrupulously avoided.

Why would you say that?

If you have a desire to become clairvoyant, there is a personal aspect to it. Your real desire is to impress others and have them revere you as someone with an unusual ability. For those who are born with a degree of clairvoyance, it is often a curse. Yes, they are able to "see" things on the astral-emotional plane, but their vision is extremely limited, nothing at all like what we see with our physical eyes.

Imagine you are walking through a dense, heavy fog. From time to time, and only through intense mental effort, there is a brief opening in the fog and you perceive something, then your vision clouds over again. You are left to interpret and describe what you saw as best you can. This is not unlike the experience of a clairvoyant. Using your imagination, you fill in the missing parts in order to make some sense of it. If you are being paid for a psychic consultation, you are under pressure to produce something. It would hardly do to be vague. The client came to you because of his or her personal ego. You are being paid to appeal to that ego.

Psychics are under great pressure to perform, and they almost always produce information, some part of which is somewhat accurate. Some psychics claim to be 80% accurate in their readings. In truth, it is far less than that.

I know some psychics who have been surprisingly accurate in what they say.

Some are good at telling you about the past, remarkably so in many instances. But they are not receiving this information from dead relatives of yours or from spirit guides. They have an uncanny ability to tap into and read your mind. Some of the things they tell you are astounding because you have not thought about them in years, yet here they are telling you about the pet dog you had as a child, and they even know his name was Butch.

Still, that's pretty impressive.

It *is* impressive, but usually the information is quite useless. You already know you had a dog as a child, and you know his name was Butch, but this does nothing to help you become more enlightened, does it?

I guess not, but it's interesting and fun to get a psychic reading.

Unfortunately, it's not so great for the psychic. She often pays a heavy price for the session. The money you paid her doesn't begin to compensate for the damage done to her spiritual advancement.

I don't understand.

When a psychic goes into that passive state of mind where she can tune in to the astral world, she opens herself up to every passing entity, and many of them are abominable in nature. Have you ever seen a person on the street ranting and raving at an invisible person?

I have. It's frightening to see the vacant look in their eyes. I'm always careful to avoid them.

The psychic encounters the same types of entities the deranged person does. Some are able to avoid the worst of them, just as you cross the street to avoid the deranged person coming toward you, but what if that entity is the one that is attracted because of the client in front of her? She has no choice in who appears to bring a message. Some of these entities are not horrible but still are not very advanced either.

Psychics are stuck in a world of unhealthy vibrations. The lower levels of the astral-emotional realm are full of harmful vibrations, and psychics are completely at the mercy of them. The emotional and physical toll on them is huge. It is not unusual for them to become ill or die much younger than normal because of the stress. It is better to leave psychic activity alone.

What about spiritualistic séances and trance mediums?

"Spiritist" is a more accurate term for these activities. There is nothing very spiritual about them. Trance mediums are playing a dangerous game. When they allow an entity to occupy their physical body, it is an activity far more intimate than sexual intercourse. Would you be willing to vacate your body and allow some entity to use it while you are unconscious, only learning later what occurred while you were away?

I probably would have been tempted to try it before, but maybe not after what you just said.

The astral world is extremely tricky. It is entirely illusory and emotional in its vibratory rate. If you have even the slightest bit of ego still in your nature, you will become hopelessly lost in the labyrinths of this astral-emotional realm. You only see accurately when you have completely overcome all ego and emotional desire. Obviously, it is a highly enlightened individual who has achieved that, not one who makes a living giving psychic readings to emotionally needy people. Don't get caught up in the desire to develop psychic abilities. It can only harm your spiritual development. Do you see now why viveka and vairāgya are so important?

Remind me again what they are.

Viveka is discernment, the ability to see things clearly without the emotional filters that cloud our vision. It is completely dispassionate. There is no sense of self that enters into the equation. Without great intellect, this is not even possible, and relatively few people have great intellect, even when they are convinced they do.

Vairāgya is often translated as desirelessness, but it is much more than that. It is also non-attachment and non-reaction. There can be no attachment and no reaction when we have gained complete mastery over our emotions. Perhaps the best way to describe vairāgya is "indifference to pleasure or pain," in other words, equanimity. Our composure is unruffled by the events of life that send less enlightened individuals into an emotional tailspin. We are unflappable.

Spend your time and efforts developing your character, not in psychic development. Learn to be scrupulously honest in all things. This is harder than you realize, and being honest with yourself is the hardest.

Develop your own spiritual practice. Spend time in quiet contemplation, observing life, making notes, analyzing, figuring out how things work. Every minute you spend in idle conversation, involvement in drama, or indulging in emotional pursuits, is a minute that could have been more effectively employed in contemplation.

Learn to do good in the world. It is not enough just to *be* good; you must *do* something as well. Radiate peacefulness and kindness wherever you go. Some people radiate frustration, distrust, and anxiety. Do the opposite and radiate that peaceful glow that indicates a more enlightened being, assuming you are that being.

Once you have made significant progress in character development, you will be able to develop clairvoyance with less chance of it being detrimental to your well-being. Until that time, be content with what seems to be slow progress. As long as you maintain steady pressure in the right direction, everything will work out. Slow and steady wins the race. Impatience and desire for rapid progress are a sure sign you are not yet ready, and the harder you push for achievement, the more certain it is you will fail. Your spiritual goal should cover several lifetimes. If you only care about what you can accomplish in this one, it indicates that ego is involved. The Higher Self is not concerned only about this lifetime. It has a much greater range of vision.

Keep in mind the story of the elusive butterfly. The more ardently you desire something, the more certain it is you will fail in obtaining it. If your motive is entirely altruistic, progress will be slow and steady, but far safer. There are many wrecks along the road to spiritual development, each one caused by impatience and personal ego.

As we said, emotions are compound in nature, but each person at any time carries an aura that reflects the sum total of his or her emotional and mental energy and, most importantly, it is cumulative.

How is it cumulative?

If you never resolved an emotional issue that occurred when you were five years old, you are still carrying that energy with you. It still affects you and everyone around you. If others also have unresolved issues of a similar nature, your energy patterns reinforce theirs and their energy patterns reinforce yours. Until one of you makes the effort to eliminate that energy from your life, nothing will change.

Once you have eliminated that frequency from your aura through an intense effort on your part, you will no longer be inflicting it on others and, in addition, you can no longer be affected by others who still carry it with them.

Too many New Age students simply pull the drawstring tighter on their bag of unresolved emotions. They think if they ignore them long enough, they will go away. Not only does this not occur, but the opposite is true. As long as you ignore them, they continue to gain energy.

Then what can I do to eliminate them so I can start making progress?

Your question is well stated. Until you do something about emotions, you can't make real progress. Once you make significant progress in resolving old issues, you will have the ability to prevent new ones from taking hold and, little by little, they will stop being the dominant force in your life. At that point, the rate of your spiritual growth will increase significantly.

Only through learning to control your mind will you learn to control your emotions.

Chapter 13

HOW EMOTIONS AFFECT US

Most folks are about as happy as they
make up their minds to be.

— Abraham Lincoln

LOVE AND HAPPINESS

If you ask most people what they want most in life, they
will probably say, "To be happy," often followed by, "and
to be loved." Let's examine these concepts of love and
happiness to see why so many fail to achieve these seemingly simple goals.

261

It is said that indigenous people who live in arctic regions have more than twenty words for "snow." When you are surrounded by snow and ice, and especially when your livelihood and ability to survive are based on your knowledge of them, not only must you know the various conditions, but also how to communicate that information to others. While snow is falling, it can be soft and gentle, driving sleet, pounding hailstones, or a blinding whiteout. On the ground, it can be fine and powdery, icy crystals, dry and crumbly, or wet and easily made into snowballs.

We talk about love a lot, yet that one simple word can mean anything from primitive, animal lust to the most sublime unconditional and spiritual love. There is no other word that covers such a wide range of emotions and vibrational frequencies.

When we "fall in love," it is completely beyond our control. Satisfying this emotion becomes more important than anything else, even food. "All the world loves a lover." It's easy to smile at the star-struck lovers and feel an emotional response, either relating because of our own experience, or perhaps jealousy because it's happening to them and not us.

The theme of every love song in the world is—I will die without your love. Without you, life has no meaning. I'm nobody without you. When we "fall in love," we enter into a contract, generally without the help of a good attorney. This contract states, "I will love you as long as …" Then follows a list of conditions, covenants and restrictions. Whether the contract is express or implied, it is there.

Almost never is it a unilateral contract that states, "I will love you forever, no matter what."

Unfortunately, in many cases, what we were certain was a pure and exalted feeling turns into just the opposite—hatred. Those who were so in love with each other become bitter enemies and fight viciously. Was it really love in the beginning if that "love" can devolve into bitter hatred? It is not possible. If you truly love someone, that love is forever and can't be annulled like a marriage can. Regardless of what happens or who is at fault for the breakup, true love will always exist if it was ever there in the beginning. Otherwise, it was not really love at all, but emotional neediness.

We should look at our love contracts carefully and honestly. It's easy to insist our love is unselfish, especially when it involves the love between a parent and child. Seldom is it true unconditional love, even in the latter case. More often it's based on emotional needs. I'm emotionally needy and am in search of another emotionally needy person so we can fill each other's needs. This is the very definition of co-dependency, and it's hardly indicative of enlightenment.

Does that mean we should never enter into a love relationship?

If it's based on emotional needs, you will enter into the relationship no matter what. Emotions are all-powerful in most people, and we're unable to change the situation. Until you have developed control of your mind to a degree, avoiding emotional situations isn't even an option.

There's something else that must be considered—karma. Few of our strongest love relationships can be avoided because they are karmic. We reincarnate again and again with the same group of individuals.

ABUSIVE RELATIONSHIPS

Some relationships are distinctly negative in nature, and sometimes abusive, whether physically, emotionally, or mentally. Often those who are abused are just as addicted to it as the abusers. It is an unhealthy relationship no matter how you look at it. While physical abuse is harder to deny, emotional and mental abuse often occur without anyone acknowledging it.

Abuse is characterized by a need to control others or an emotional desire to be dominated by someone else. If you are in an abusive relationship, regardless of which role you play, you should take a long, hard look at it. The price of abuse is enormous.

I know someone who is in an abusive relationship. I've tried to help her get out of it, but she keeps going back. I finally had to stay away from her.

It's heart-breaking to see people so addicted to the emotional pattern that they are unable to break the cycle. To us it seems simple—to them, it's impossible to make the change. And there is often a real threat of physical danger.

You can't save everyone who is suffering. In fact, there's only one person you can ever save—yourself. We can offer suggestions, but it turns into nagging if repeated too often. In most cases, we can only stand by and give loving support. However, we must never be an enabler. Those involved are the only ones who can change the situation, and it may be their most important lesson of this lifetime. If they don't learn it this time, the cycle will continue lifetime after lifetime until they wake up and realize what they are doing. Only then will anything change.

Our responsibility lies not in recognizing the abusive relationships of others, but in examining closely our own life to see if there remains the slightest need to control others. This can manifest as a boss no one can ever please, a parent whose children can never quite achieve enough to make them happy, or a lover who uses sex or affection as a tool to control the partner. Abuse can manifest in very subtle ways, and it is our responsibility to recognize and eliminate it wherever it occurs in our own life.

Lust, whose vibrations exist at the lower end of the astral-emotional realm, is relatively easy to recognize. The majority of love relationships occur somewhere in the mid-range of emotions. They are neither very coarse nor very evolved. There's still a lot of selfish, personal need involved on both sides and, for the most part, it is emotionally fulfilling without causing the negative energy found in abusive relationships.

UNCONDITIONAL LOVE

The highest form of love, unconditional love, is not an emotion at all, but a soul trait. The lower forms of love have a strong emotional-physical aspect, characterized by the need to be together or in frequent communication.

There's always an element of fear associated with lower forms of love, the fear of loss. Only the ego can feel loss, grief, or the sense of being diminished. There's nothing about the soul that can respond to these feelings.

True unconditional love is far more powerful than any of the other types. Not only is it a soul trait, it is a quality of the One Life. When our consciousness is focused at, or above, the higher mental level, we experience oneness with all life. There's no sense of separation, anxiety, or fear of loss. Once you have felt this abiding universal love, you can never confuse it with the lower vibrations we also call love.

If we feel only unconditional love, does that mean we love everyone equally?

We will always have those for whom we have a special love. It is so because we have shared much of our journey together lifetime after lifetime, but there's no sense of clinging. Our love for each other exists at the soul level, and it spills over into the realm of the personality, without making it less spiritual in any way. There is always space in a true love relationship. There is no neediness, only a transcendent and abiding joy, knowing that person is a part of our life experience. When he or she dies, there may be a sense of sadness, but not the grief that is often felt by people.

How do you distinguish between grief and sadness?

In both instances there is a temporary feeling of loss. With grief, it is a profound emotion; there's an element of anger and resentment attached. "How could you do this to me?" "How could you leave me, knowing how much I need you?" There's a sense of outrage, and a distinct feeling of being injured by the loss of the person, whether through death, divorce or other form of forced separation. It is the ego that is incensed at being injured, and the emotion exists at the low end of the astral-emotional realm.

THE POWER OF SADNESS

There is a distinct difference in the case of sadness. There is none of the anger and nothing in the lower range of vibrations. Instead, an opening appears, a vacant space that once was filled, but now is a void that seemingly cannot be filled, and therein lies the key—wherever there is a space, Spirit can dwell there.

You can't make a flute out of a length of bamboo until you remove the pith. There must be an opening through which the breath, or ātma, can move. This is true also in other aspects of our life. We feel our life must be chock-full of things—physical objects, emotions, people, and relationships. Even in our concepts of the ideal situation, whether the Garden of Eden or Heaven, we're certain it must include everything that "makes us happy."

Sadness brings us back to reality. It reminds us there is more to life than the things we think are so important. When an empty space opens up, all the things we thought were so important assume their proper perspective and, at least for a time, we exist at a slightly elevated level of awareness.

I hadn't thought of it like that before, but when I reflect on the times I experienced loss and sadness, there was also a kind of spiritual energy at the same time.

We can't live fully on two different levels. We can either be fully present in the physical-emotional-mental world and partially aware in the higher realms, or we can be more fully conscious at the soul level and interact only as necessary in the outer world. When we operate in that manner, we are still far more present in our actions than the average person.

The goal is to function in the world without being worldly, to be in the world but not of the world. To be worldly means we are unable to separate ourselves from the constant drama around us.

Thus we see that sadness is a special emotion, unlike any other. Some people have experienced a quantum leap in consciousness after a loss when sadness was experienced rather than grief.

Someday there will be a better way of expressing the range of emotions referred to as "love." In the meantime, we must be observant, recognize the level of vibration involved, and decide if it is one that is helpful to our spiritual growth. At the very least, we can be somewhat cognizant of what true unconditional love is and recognize it when we experience it. Just as you can't control whether or not you fall in love, you also can't control whether or not you experience unconditional love. It's an integral part of the higher life and cannot be separated from it.

JOY VS. HAPPINESS

If we define happiness as the opposite of unhappiness, we will never be entirely happy, but will continually experience variations of the happy-unhappy cycle of drama. Some cycles last for minutes, some for days, and some for weeks, but none of them last forever. It's far wiser to let go of our attachment to the elusive goal of happiness, but that can only happen when we substitute joy for emotional happiness.

How is joy any different from happiness? Aren't they two words used to describe the same thing?

Just as unconditional love is characteristic of the soul, so is joy. Hatred is the opposite of selfish love, unhappiness is the opposite of happiness, but there is no opposite of unconditional love, and there is no opposite of joy.

Joy is the profound sense of peace you feel when you contact your soul and have relinquished attachment to the things of the outer world. You are not diminished in this process. You have far more than ever before. There is, however, some sense of loss in the process, and this occurs because relatively few people are able to share that level of awareness with you. Though the outer world is full of people, the higher realms of the inner world are still sparsely populated.

I think I might prefer to stay with my friends and family. I'm not sure I want to leave them behind.

This is a common problem with people who are on the verge of a great leap in consciousness. We are torn between two worlds. The personality, the ego, wants to stay behind and move at the pace of the rest of humanity. The soul urges you to run ahead and experience a higher level of consciousness so you, in turn, can show others how to attain it.

SOUL MATES

Does everyone have a soul mate? If so, I haven't found mine yet.

The concept of soul mates, like many others, has been greatly misunderstood. Commonly, the idea is that there exists somewhere a perfect mate who will fulfill my every need, a reliable companion in a warm, caring relationship, someone who will never abandon me. Often, it implies a great sexual relationship as well. In most cases, when one is convinced he has found his soul mate, it is simply a matter of good chemistry, a seemingly perfect match, at least for the time being, and our common needs are met.

While some people are able to maintain a relationship like this for a number of years, and perhaps even the remainder of this lifetime, it is not entirely unselfish. Often there is great inter-dependence, otherwise known as co-dependency.

There *are* soul mate relationships, but they exist at the soul level, the part of our being that continues from lifetime to lifetime. Over the course of numerous lifetimes, we create recurring patterns of relations with people, some harmonious and some inharmonious; the majority are comprised of a combination of these two extremes. At some point, when an individual has become somewhat enlightened, another individual may be a more or less constant companion in spiritual growth. The two may not incarnate together in every lifetime, but very often. These two souls form a pair bond, each one encouraging and supporting the other in spiritual growth.

Over time, through various lifetimes, all traces of selfish needs and personal desires are eliminated, and the result is an exquisite and beautiful relationship, not for the benefit of the personalities, but for the good of the world. There's no sense of clinging or neediness. If the two are apart, even for long periods of time, there's no sense of loss or loneliness, because their bond is at the soul level where there is no separation. The physical plane connection is only secondary.

A significant aspect of this relationship is that both are at approximately the same level of advancement, although outwardly this may not always be obvious. Although the relationship in any given lifetime may be that of married partners, it can just as often be a parent-child, best friends, pupil-teacher, or any other close relationship. The two may be of the same sex or opposite. It doesn't matter, because the relationship is at a spiritual level where sex doesn't exist.

Don't go searching for a soul mate. If you do, it is inspired by your own needs, and any mate you find will fall short of your expectations. You may not have established a soul mate just yet, and it's not likely everyone will have one, even in a future lifetime. Not everyone is inspired to work in this manner; some work best by themselves.

If you do have a soul mate and that person is in incarnation at the same time, you will find him or her without any problem. You will automatically be brought together. In any soul mate relationship, there are a number of other individuals who are connected with this unit; they drift in and out of various relationships over many lifetimes. The combined energy of the soul mates—which is greater than the sum of the two individuals—not only has the power of attracting others, but it provides a strong energy field for teaching and inspiring those who are around them.

Like two mountain climbers, sometimes one ascends until there's a safe stopping point and then helps pull the other up to that level. Then the roles are reversed and the second one goes first. In this manner, they are able to progress much faster than each working alone.

Don't worry about whether or not you have a soul mate. If you do, fine. If not, that's okay. Do the work in front of you right now, and everything will fall into place.

THE HOUSE BY THE SIDE OF THE ROAD

A married couple had lived nearly fifty years in a little house in a remote area near a busy interstate highway. One New Year's Eve, while they were watching television late in the evening, they heard a knock on the door.

They thought it might be a relative or friend, or perhaps a stranger in need of help. Over the years they had helped hundreds of travelers with car problems or who otherwise were in need of a helping hand. Their tales of woe always found a sympathetic ear, a meal if they were hungry, and a little money if they were broke. The husband got up to answer the door.

Stepping outside, he conversed with someone on the front porch and re-entered presently, followed by two men brandishing semi-automatic weapons. "Do whatever they say—these men are desperate," he advised his wife.

Unknown to them, the two men had been traveling with a cache of weapons. When stopped on the highway by a suspicious police officer, they shot and killed him, then sped off again. They knew that every law enforcement agent in the area was looking for them; they had to switch cars quickly.

They demanded the car keys from the couple, ripped the phone off the kitchen wall, and tied them up with the phone cord and a rope. All this time, neither of the victims had screamed, panicked, or caused a commotion.

It became obvious that one was in charge and the other was following his orders. As the latter nervously tied up the wife, he leaned his head against her shoulder and let out a quiet sob. At that moment, she felt he was experiencing great remorse for what he had become involved in, and she felt a wave of sympathetic compassion for him.

With the couple secured and no means of calling for help, the two men jumped in the couple's car and left. They didn't dare get back on the highway, so they drove in the opposite direction, toward the railroad tracks, hoping to find a small country road.

The couple eventually was able to work free from their bonds and contact family members who lived nearby. Soon police officers arrived to make sure everyone was okay and to fill out their report.

The following day, the men were discovered holed up in another house twenty miles away. They had not gotten far in the stolen car. It was stuck in the mud near the railroad tracks, and they had hopped a freight train to make their escape.

After a standoff with police officers, the leader turned his gun on himself and committed suicide. The other man surrendered.

What happened to the couple? Weren't they traumatized by their experience?

They never showed the least bit of anxiety, anger, or outrage, just a genuine feeling of regret that these two men had made such a mess of their own lives. Whenever someone asked about the incident, they related the details as if it were a movie they had watched, not a real-life drama in which they had been personally involved. The wife often said they both felt protected at the time, and that whatever happened, it would be for the best. They had always treated strangers with respect and kindness, and there was no reason to think the universe would not repay them in kind.

Even the coarsest and least evolved of human beings have a spark of divinity within. When they encounter people who are kind and whose inner light shines brightly, they recognize that and respect it in some way. If these desperate men had encountered someone else, the outcome might have been very different.

This couple did not even own a gun, even though they lived in a remote area. If they had come to the door with a gun in hand, both would have been shot on the spot. Their faith in the innate goodness of humanity and expectation that they would be protected by their past good deeds is really what saved them.

There is one other thing that saved them.

What is that?

Non-reaction. Not reacting emotionally when their lives were in danger was paramount to their survival. These men had just killed a police officer and had nothing to lose. If either of the victims had screamed or reacted emotionally, the adrenalin-charged desperados would not have hesitated to pull the trigger.

If you don't practice non-reaction in your everyday life, you will not be able to learn it on the spot when your life depends on it.

What happened to the criminal who surrendered?

The couple had to appear and testify against him in court, and he was sentenced to a long prison term. He became a model prisoner, taking full advantage of all opportunities for education, and has done everything possible to atone for his actions. Eventually he was paroled and became an honor student in a community college.

What about the elderly couple?

They lived to celebrate not only their fiftieth wedding anniversary, but their sixtieth as well. Both died of natural causes, three years apart. Both died at home with loving family members by their side, in the house by the side of the road.

THE STARFISH STORY

There is a story that often makes the rounds of New Age groups. A wise old man goes down to the seashore each morning to contemplate and write. One morning, after a violent storm, he sees a human figure in the distance who appears to be dancing. As the old man gets closer, he realizes it's a boy, and he's not dancing, but reaching down again and again to pick something from the beach and throw it into the water.

"What are you doing, son?" the old man inquires.

"The sun has come out, and these starfish are stranded on the beach. If I don't get them back in the water they will die!"

The old man smiles. "Son, there are miles and miles of beach and thousands of starfish. Your efforts may be well-intentioned, but you can't possibly make a difference."

The boy picks up another starfish and flings it into the water. With a flourish he turns to the old man and says, "I made a difference to that one!"

What do you gain from this story?

I think it's great! Obviously, this is someone who cares about all life and wants to make the world a better place. Even if he saves only one starfish, he has made a difference in the world. I wish more people were like him. How do you interpret the story?

This is an example of what may be called a "feel good story." Each is designed to tug at the heart strings and maybe bring a tear to the eye as one recognizes the basic goodness in people.

Is that a bad thing?

Not a bad thing, but it serves no useful purpose. We know already that there is basic goodness in people, even in the least advanced of our fellow human beings. A story that produces a little surge of emotion has the motive of producing a bit of drama. Some dramatic stories are long and complicated. This particular genre is known for being succinct, easily told or forwarded by email, and resulting in a momentary emotional reaction.

That seems a little mean-spirited. It kind of takes away the good feeling most people get from these stories. How would you react to a story of this nature?

First of all, we hopefully wouldn't react. Reaction implies a reflex emotion. Instead of looking at the story through emotional filters, what if we looked at it from a different point of view? The first premise is that living is good and dying is bad.

Isn't that true?

What is life? It's not the physical form. It's what, for a given period of time, animates the physical form and uses it as a vehicle for gaining experience. The life-force does not cease to exist when the physical body dies.

What happens to the starfish that died, the ones the boy couldn't save?

The life-force from the dying starfish enters a period of unconsciousness, just as it does when sleeping. Then, when a newly-formed body is available, the same life-force returns to occupy the new vehicle. It recapitulates the same process of growing up that it has done many times before, and then continues in its acquisition of knowledge of how life works. There's no sense of loss or having missed anything. Life continues through countless episodes of experience, each unique in its own way. Death is not worse than life—it is part of life.

The second thing we want to look at is how our actions may be interfering with the natural process. It's easy to adopt the attitude that nature has made a mistake and we must try to fix it. More often than not, regardless of our intentions, we create more imbalance, not less. Part of the lesson the starfish is learning is how to survive. Often it is the most intelligent of the species, not the strongest, that survives, and that knowledge is transmitted to future generations. By helping the unintelligent creatures survive, we are unwittingly postponing their starfish education.

Biologists, and those who create nature documentaries, are careful not to interfere with nature. They, of all people, understand animal behavior, but they also recognize they don't have all the answers. Often they become emotionally attached to the animals they work with. Being objective is not easy, whether dealing with animals or humans.

I see the point you're making, but does that mean we should never try to help animals, or human beings, for that matter?

We should always try to help if we think we can. Responding emotionally, however, is never helpful. When there is an accident and someone is injured, the emotional person is not only *not* helpful, but makes the situation worse. The dramatic situation is a perfect excuse to redirect everyone's attention to one's own emotional needs. It's the ego that reacts emotionally to an event. The helpful individual is the one who observes quietly in the background to assess the situation and then, if he can be of assistance, quickly and efficiently proceeds to do so. When he is no longer needed, he slips away as quietly and undramatically as he appeared. No stories, no drama, no seeking of attention or praise, just simple service to humanity.

When we try to help other human beings, whether it is a homeless person, a friend, or a family member who has financial or emotional problems, more often than not, we make the matter worse. If we're honest with ourselves, our desire to help is an emotional need on our part, not a well-thought-through attempt to help someone who has earned a second chance. We unwittingly get sucked into other people's drama, and often they don't want to be saved. They simply want some company in their misery. Look carefully at the times you have tried to help someone who was suffering, and in many cases you will see this is true. We are enablers and co-dependent unless we look at the situation from an unemotional point of view.

That seems very cold-hearted.

It's not cold-hearted at all. The most advanced individuals in our solar system are not cold-hearted, but they also don't react emotionally to the dramas created by humans. If they did, they would be unable to help. They know how nature works. They know that every human is exactly where he needs to be for his continued education and development. Everything is exactly as it should be.

Does that mean they just look on and do nothing to help?

Not at all. They work twenty-four hours a day to guide and educate humanity. But they are aware that it is a work in progress and takes time. It's not a matter of waving a magic wand to make everything "perfect." Everything is perfect just as it is because each individual is at the level in the School of Life where he should be. Their attention is not directed to individuals unless they believe that individual can be a useful instrument in educating and training humanity. They cannot be enticed into catering to anyone's personal emotional needs.

Notice that the old man in the starfish story was a wise man. He was wise enough to know that nature was fulfilling its role perfectly and had not made a mistake. He was also wise enough not to waste time trying to convince the boy to change. The boy was caught up in the emotion of the moment, convinced he was doing something important. The old man was wise enough to leave him alone in his conviction.

We often associate emotions with the heart. We call people who do not react emotionally "heartless" or "cold-hearted." The heart chakra is not associated with emotions, the solar plexus is. If you think about it, you will realize it is true. When you're emotionally upset, what part of the body reflects the emotion? The digestive system. When you're nervous, you get "butterflies in your stomach," a graphic way of describing the peculiar sensation felt in the solar plexus.

WORRY

The Dalai Lama was being interviewed by a television news reporter who referred to a terrible earthquake that had happened in Tibet. She asked him how he handled the sadness in him, realizing that he was not able to go help his own people.

The Dalai Lama replied along these lines, "When I see some problem, some tragedy, I remember the advice from an ancient Buddhist master. A tragedy happened. He thought and analyzed the situation. If there is a way to overcome that, then there is no need to worry. If there is *no* way to overcome that suffering, that tragedy, then there is no need to worry."

There is great wisdom in this simple advice. If you can help, help. If not, then accept the situation with equanimity. What do most people do instead?

They worry about it and feel bad they're not able to help.

And how does this help the situation?

It doesn't.

Not only does it not help, it makes things worse.

How does it make things worse?

Because you are adding more negative energy to an already difficult situation. The best thing you could do is to send thoughts of goodwill and wellbeing. Instead, you're adding worry and anxiety to the same thoughts and emotions that millions of others are creating. If you look carefully at the situation, it is your personal need for drama fueling the fire of emotional reaction. *I feel bad because I can't rush in and save the situation.* Have you noticed that the energy field of a worried person is not very different from that of an angry person?

I have. It's not very pleasant. Usually I want to get away from them.

Every emotion has a frequency of vibration as well as a distinctive quality. The emotions of anger and worry are slightly different in frequency, but both are negative in their effect. The energy in each case is focused on the thinker, and he uses the disaster as a means of creating personal drama. We perceive these energy fields and are affected by them, whether or not we're conscious of it.

I understand, for example, that if someone in my family is ill, it doesn't help to worry about it, but I can't seem to stop. How can I change the way I react to a situation so close to me?

Think through the situation carefully. Maybe there *is* something you can do. The physical presence of an enlightened person in a group of worried and anxious individuals can be extremely comforting. The aura of peaceful acceptance you exude, if you choose to, can do more to help than you might imagine. You can only do this though if it is a natural state of being for you. You can't develop in on the spot, and you certainly can't fake it. Many people pretend to be a certain way, but no one is fooled. Everyone is perceptive enough to feel the energy field you carry with you.

There's another important aspect to the idea of worry. Worry and anxiety are emotional reactions, either to something that affects us personally or someone else. In either case, it is our thinking about something that stirs up the emotions, isn't it?

Yes, I guess so. As long as I don't think about something it doesn't bother me, but when I have nothing else on my mind it comes back.

Worry is a habit, and a very bad habit. With many people, when they have nothing else to think about, they find something to worry about. It's an addiction, just like smoking, overeating, or shopping. We derive a certain pleasure out of worrying and re-affirming our belief that life is unfair.

How Emotions
Affect Us

283

Why is that? It seems almost like an illness.

It is an illness, a psychological one. At least seventy-five percent of human illnesses are caused by thoughts and emotions. If you think about it, you will realize that everything you worry about involves your ego. Your ego thrives on emotions, and it needs a variety of them to be satisfied. Worry, anxiety, anger, frustration, and resentment all feed the ego's sense of importance. If it doesn't have emotions to keep it occupied, it will create a situation to inject emotion into its environment.

I know someone like that. If things are going too well, she purposely starts an argument or finds some kind of drama. She doesn't seem to be happy unless there is drama in her life, and it always affects everyone around her.

This is another example of addiction to emotions. Emotions create drama in our life. If we can't find drama in our own life, someone else's drama will do. Look at the postings on social internet sites. You will notice that some people are content with a low amount of drama; others constantly have high drama going on, usually in the form of an argument or strong opinions about something. Regardless of the level of the drama, it is still an addiction. As long as we are addicted to the drama, our spiritual progress is limited. How can we discover what lies beyond when we are involved every day with emotional drama?

Do you have any suggestions for overcoming addiction to worry and anxiety?

Yes. Start by sitting quietly and analyzing the situation. How did it happen? Was it an act of nature, such as an earthquake or tsunami? Was it due to lack of foresight or even greed, as may be the case in economic collapse, whether international or on a personal level? Is it due to bad habits, emphysema caused by smoking, or heart problems caused by excess weight?

Spend some time on this. You've probably spent hours worrying about the situation. You will accomplish far more good by spending two or three hours using your mind to understand it instead of indulging in emotional reactions. Emotions never solved any problem. Only your mind can solve a problem, and only if you use it as a tool.

Ask yourself, "What's the worst that could happen?" For example, if you're struggling financially, worry can only make the situation worse, and your worst fear may become reality because you created the scenario over and over, and had an emotional reaction every time you thought about it. Get emotions out of the picture. Until you do, you will not be able to think clearly, and there is no possibility of a solution.

How does it help to ask myself what's the worst that could happen?

Once you have determined the worst that could happen, the next question is, "Could I deal with that?" The answer is always yes. Perhaps you have friends or family members who would help you.

I wouldn't want to depend on someone else to help me. I want to do it myself.

That's your ego speaking. Pride is the number one attribute of the ego. It is immensely proud. Did it ever occur to you that you're depriving others of a desirable opportunity when you refuse to let them help?

I have friends who have asked their parents for help so many times they don't want anything to do with them anymore. They've asked me also, but I finally realized they are simply irresponsible.

Some people abuse the offer of help from others. This is a case of ongoing drama and a need to be rescued. Some people are addicted to rescuing people, and some to pretending to want to be rescued. It's called co-dependency. In both cases, it's the ego that is addicted, and in the case of the ones needing rescuing, they don't want to be rescued because that would be the end of their drama. Their goal is to get others involved in their drama, not put an end to it. Are you one of those people?

I think I was at one time, but when I realized what I was doing, I was shocked. Ever since then I've been careful not to do it.

Awareness and mindfulness are always necessary to overcome any addiction.

Once you have thought through the situation, using the two questions, "What is the worst that could happen?" and "Could I cope with that?" you come to the realization that you can cope with anything. After all, only the personality can suffer. You, the soul, have nothing within you that could suffer in the way the personality can. As you focus more on the qualities of the soul and get in contact with it, everything is easy. Life is easy. We complicate it with our emotional drama. Once we end the addiction to drama, we have achieved true freedom.

ADDICTION TO DRAMA

A friend sent me a text message early this morning. She said she had been awake since 2:00 a.m. and was afraid she was having a nervous breakdown. I don't know how to help her.

What is it that's worrying her?

She's been watching the news coverage for weeks about a murder trial. She even has a television set next to her while she works. When the verdict reached by the jury was "not guilty," she was so distraught that she can't sleep and worries because she's convinced the defendant got away with murder.

There's little you can do to help someone like that. You can make some suggestions, but ultimately she's the only one who can help herself. This is a prime example of addiction to drama. It's not her personal drama, so there's no reason it should affect her, but her addiction to drama is so out of control that she will seek it. Her ego requires drama in order to thrive, and if there's no drama immediately at hand, it impels her to go find some.

Do you recommend counseling for someone like this?

Counseling can help, but only if you find the right counselor. Too many are willing to listen week after week to their patients' stories, collect their money, and send them home again. A good counselor will hold her responsible for what she has created and give her a chance to see clearly the mess she has gotten herself into. Then she must decide whether or not she wants to get rid of the addiction. If she chooses to keep it, then perhaps there's no real reason for counseling except to fool herself and others into believing she's doing something about the problem. A good counselor would probably refuse to be a participant in such a farce and suggest that she try a different solution.

Do you think medication can help in this kind of situation?

Each person must decide for himself, taking into account the advice the medical professional is giving. Many people want a pill, a procedure, or a magical elixir that will cure their problems. There's no such thing. The suffering is caused by something created by the patient, either in this or a previous lifetime. The solution must come from the same source as the one that created the problem, the human mind.

So if I suffer from high blood pressure or diabetes, I'm responsible for it?

Something in your thought patterns, and often in your emotional reactions, has created the situation that resulted in an unhealthy, out-of-balance situation. Why do you think we stress so much the need to control our thoughts?

I'm beginning to see that thoughts are far more important than I realized.

Stop worrying so much about life being unfair, and start taking responsibility for your life. No one can make serious progress until the thoughts, emotions, and ego are at least somewhat under control. The goal is complete control. Everything in your life that causes pain and suffering to yourself and those around you is a reminder that you have not yet attained that goal. There are still some life lessons to be learned.

So there's not much I can do to help my friend.

No. You can give some suggestions, and you can be supportive if she really wants to overcome her addiction, but whatever you do, don't become an enabler. People with addictions will find others who support them in their addiction. Don't be surprised if she alienates herself from you because you don't empathize with the drama in her life, drama caused by her addiction to emotions.

It's not easy to see someone you care about suffer like that.

You can't change the addiction. Only she can do that. But you can practice non-reaction.

How can I do that?

If everyone were miserable because someone else is unhappy, no one would ever get out of the cycle of emotional drama. Someone has to rise above and set the example, but this can only happen when you have overcome any addiction to emotional drama in your own life. Once you do, others naturally look to you as a leader for clues on how to proceed. You do this by being caring and compassionate, not by reacting to their drama, and definitely not by being sucked into the whirlwind of their emotions. Misery loves company, but the enlightened person always declines the invitation to attend the pity party.

Chapter 14

THE SPIRITUAL PATH

Be humble, if thou would'st attain to
Wisdom. Be humbler still when
Wisdom thou hast mastered.

— *The Voice of the Silence*

THERE IS ONLY ONE PERSON YOU CAN SAVE

Just as you can't save anyone but yourself, the soul can't
save the personality. The personality is in charge all along
until it's ready to pass control to the soul. It never happens instantaneously. The war for control between the
personality and the soul is one that includes numerous
battles, but there is one decisive battle which marks the

291

turning point. From that time forward, the outcome is certain and only the timeline can change. There's still a long process of letting go of old attachments and a period of growing pains from the spiritual growth occurring.

The early stages of this period can be lonely and sometimes daunting. We can't always see clearly and often wonder if we made the right choice. Sometimes we feel we're losing our mind, and that is always a possibility. Until we gain some spiritual ground and are more secure in our new experience, there are some distinct dangers. That's why we must be well-grounded and have gained a degree of control over our thoughts. Trying to develop astral clairvoyance at this point would almost certainly spell failure.

Once started on this track of advanced learning, there is no turning back. In the words of Eliphas Lévi, "You must either reach the goal or perish. To doubt is to risk insanity; to come to a stop is to fall; to step back is to tumble headlong into an abyss."

Turning over the reins to our Higher Self brings great rewards, not for us personally, but for all mankind. But it is not without risks, and many shrink back when face to face with the choice. "Many are called, but few are chosen." You decide whether or not you are among the ones chosen, and it is based on your preparedness. Everyone who offers himself for the task is given a chance and undergoes basic training, otherwise known as "trial by fire."

I'm not sure I understand what you mean.

The Spiritual Hierarchy is aware of every individual who is even remotely approaching the spiritual path. If a person forms a definite thought in his mind that he wants to be considered for rapid advancement, the Hierarchy is aware of that proposal. There are no flowery messages from exalted beings or encouragements from a cheering section. Instead, there are great trials, one after another. Read the story of Job if you want an indication of the scope of these trials. There's nothing fun or exciting or glamorous about it.

The path to higher learning is protected by adamantine gates. You must take heaven by storm, not by prayers and pleading. Once you have made enough progress to pass through those gates, they slam shut behind you forever and there is no turning back. From then on, you must wend your way silently and with determination, overcoming one obstacle after another. In the beginning, there is much solitude and loneliness, but eventually you encounter a few individuals with whom you can travel from time to time.

A tiny fraction of those who apply make the cut, yet every applicant is convinced he is the exception and will not fail. The failure rate is staggering, and it is almost always caused by the ego. A failure is temporary, but it could mean the end of advancement for this lifetime.

Before offering yourself as a candidate for advanced spiritual education, spend several years in preparation. Study and ponder over carefully what is contained in this and other books. Work on developing moral character. Are you scrupulously honest? Have you made progress in controlling your thoughts and eliminating your ego? Have you overcome the love of power and attention? Are your emotions completely under control? Until the answer to each of these questions is yes, you are advised to wait, because the chance of failure is close to 100%.

Make haste slowly. Be clear about what you want to accomplish, and then proceed methodically toward that goal. You still have much to attend to in the outer world. You can't simply walk away from karmic obligations.

Do what you feel you must do, keeping always in mind the final goal.

Many use spiritual development as an excuse to ignore responsibilities. This is not true spiritual work, but pseudo-spiritual. "I'm tired of life. It's too difficult, too painful, and too frustrating." Some people escape through alcohol and drugs, some through physical or emotional isolation, and some through other activities—television, reading, or hobbies.

The pursuit of spiritual growth for many is just one more way of escaping the doldrums of everyday life. The person who uses spiritual practices as a means of escape will not go far. It must be done for the right reasons, and if not, they are selfish in nature. Don't think you can fool anyone. Nature is not stupid. It is far more intelligent than you are. You may know what you desire, but nature knows what you need. Fortunately, there is no easy solution to the unhappiness in the world.

I think you meant to say "unfortunately."

No, it is fortunate because unhappiness and suffering are great motivating factors. Just as desire and ego were earlier motivating factors in our lives, at some point we realize that by achieving our goals, along with it there is pain and suffering. Life is smart. It knows how to move us through the learning process. We can kick and scream all we want, just like the child who doesn't get his way, but eventually we settle down and figure out that it is not what we want from life that is important, but what life wants from us.

At some point we have to grow up.

SEX AND THE SPIRITUAL PATH

You mentioned several times that one of the requirements for spiritual advancement is spotless purity; I assume that includes sexually.

It does, but perhaps not exactly in the way you are thinking. In order to gain some understanding of the subject, we need to know something about the history of human sexuality. Then perhaps we will be in a better position to understand what the future holds. Any time we want to see what is ahead for us in our spiritual quest, it's a good idea to look both to the past and to those who are in advance of us to find out what they have learned.

There are a number of things to keep in mind regarding human sexuality. First, the soul does not have a sex. It is neither male nor female. Angels also are neither male nor female because they have no physical body. Humans have given male and female names to certain angels because of characteristics they embody, but they truly have no sex. Only when one occupies a physical body is there a need for sexuality.

Once you establish a reliable connection with your own soul, sex will assume its proper place in your life and will not be the all-consuming obsession it is with so many people. You have only to watch television for thirty minutes to see how obsessed people are with sex. Since it is on their minds most of the day, the amount of energy built up by these thought-forms and the emotions associated with them is tremendous.

The true human, the Higher Self, is not a sexual being. Our true nature has nothing to do with whether we currently are using a male or female body. Once we gain complete control of our thoughts and are in tune with our soul, we will use sex only as a means for producing physical bodies to be inhabited by other souls, and will no longer be obsessed with sex as a means of emotional excitement and drama.

The physical bodies we occupy were developed from animal bodies, adapted for use by human souls. These bodies retain many of the animal instincts, remnants of a far distant past. Much of our struggle as human beings revolves around this battleground on earth, with our inherent animal nature arrayed on one side and our true spiritual nature on the other. The spiritual side always wins eventually, but the battles are fierce and sometimes appear desperate. This is often the case with disciples and their sexual nature. There is a tendency to anguish over it.

Whenever we anguish over something, we're sending out negative energy which affects everyone in a detrimental way. It is also important to realize a little-known fact—whenever we begin to make real spiritual progress, there is a heightened energy that comes into our life. The effect of this is to emphasize all aspects of our nature, both the most sublime and the coarsest. Things we were able to ignore or control before, suddenly are brought to the forefront, and we're forced to deal with them. The first reaction is often dismay at realizing this part of our nature even exists, and often embarrassment at having to acknowledge that it does. We have no problem acknowledging the higher characteristics brought to the forefront at the same time.

If you're struggling with thoughts of sex and sexual habits, then be okay with that. Don't stop trying to control them, but stop making an emotional drama out of it. Accept it for what it is and keep moving forward. Eventually everything assumes its proper place in the disciple's life, but there are periods of time when everything appears to be out of control.

One of the most revered spiritual teachers of the 20th century had a twenty-five year clandestine love affair with the wife of his best friend and manager. It did not become known publicly until several years after his death.

Does that mean we should not pay attention to his teachings, since he was obviously not the highly spiritual being everyone thought he was?

Not at all. What took place in his private life does not affect his teachings. His teachings should, at all times, be evaluated on their own merits and not based on the assumption that they are important because thousands of followers revered him as a great teacher. Never believe something just because a well-known person said it. You alone are responsible for analyzing each idea and deciding if you can apply it in your life. Otherwise, it has no importance to you, regardless of the source.

Overcoming sexual inclinations is far less important for an aspirant than other things. Character development should be of utmost concern. Honesty, non-reaction, control of thoughts, non-judgment, elimination of drama, and respect for life should all be on your list of character traits to work on.

We humans must deal with some biological instincts that are still prevalent among animals. Foremost among these is preservation of the species and the instinct to pass on our own genes. We have an inborn instinct to propagate, to pass our genes on to future generations. In some cases this becomes obsessive. A couple unable to have children, instead of adopting, will spend thousands of dollars to conceive a child that carries their own genes. There's no rational reason for this. It is instinctual.

A male lion who finds a female with cubs will often kill them so the female will be responsive to bearing a new litter, this time carrying his own genes. Although we have progressed somewhat beyond such animalistic behavior, we still feel the deep desire to keep our genes going. It is part of our animal instinct and part of our ego.

The males of many species are programmed to have sex with as many females as possible. Fierce battles are fought with other males for the right to mate, and the females pay close attention to the outcome. They want the strongest genes possible for their offspring, and instinct guides them to accept the stronger male, not the weaker one.

Females, and we still find this behavior among humans, are looking for two things—good genes and a good environment for raising their young. In humans, this sometimes results in a curious situation; the two requirements may not be found in the same individual. The male who has money and the capacity to provide a good home, education, and all that is required for "success" in life for his offspring may not be strong physically and may not be very attractive. He doesn't have the right genes.

A woman may marry a man of means but secretly engage in sex with a more physically attractive man in hopes that her children's genes will be stronger and more desirable. It is estimated that as many as ten percent of the children in the world are not the biological offspring of the supposed father.

What do women look for in a potential mate? They look at facial symmetry, strength, height, weight, and overall attractiveness. They watch to see if there are any indications of illness, either physical or mental.

Men look for the same features in women, but they also pay particular attention to the breasts and hips. They may not realize that this is an age-old instinct to see if she has the right physique for bearing his children and the proper equipment for nourishment. Women may not recognize that artificially reddening their lips and cheeks is an imitation of nature's signal that they are young, healthy, and sexually receptive.

The amount of money spent each year to dramatize and indulge in carnal lust is incredible. Think of the good that could be done if these billions of dollars were spent on world education instead. But we are where we are as humans in our journey. We can be more aware of our animal instincts and look forward to what the future will be. This helps us know what the next step is for our own personal growth.

We all spend many lifetimes as males and as females. Each lifetime has a certain set of circumstances that fit the needs of the individual for the advancement possible in that lifetime, and that includes our sexuality.

I've heard that homosexuals still have a strong identity with the opposite sex, the one they experienced in a past lifetime. Is that true?

This is one of those New Age myths that spring up from time to time. It seems plausible on the surface, but life tends to be somewhat more complicated than people would like. Many people want things to be black or white, true or false, right or wrong. Life is almost never accommodating for them. There are many shades between pitch black and snow white. Few things are one hundred percent true or one hundred percent false. None of our observations are completely right or completely wrong.

It's not important to delve into the reasons for the existence of homosexuality. What is important is to recognize that every individual is born into the circumstances that provide for growth in this lifetime, and that includes his or her sexual nature.

What about people who say homosexuality is a sin and must be punished?

Are you the one who would determine the punishment?

No. I don't feel any need to.

Some people do, and they personally take on the responsibility of ostracizing those who don't fit their ideas of propriety. They spend millions of dollars to pass laws that make sure they are branded as second class citizens. Or they invent ill-conceived programs guaranteed to change the unlucky individual. If there is anything out of balance, karma will take care of that. The universe does not need us to act as policemen, judges, and juries. There are far more pressing issues in our society than worrying about other people's social habits. As long as we're talking about private actions among consenting adults, it's not our place to worry about what they do. It's our own ego that insists on meddling with other people's lives.

Seen from the highest spiritual perspective where sex should only be engaged in for reproduction and no other reason, any sex act that is for personal pleasure would be perceived in the same manner. The truth is, some people have an emotional reaction based on fear.

What fear is that?

The fear they may have the same nature within themselves. In fact, they do. No person is a hundred percent heterosexual or a hundred percent homosexual. Everyone's sexuality lies somewhere along the continuous scale between the two extremes.

What about those who say it is unnatural?

How can it be unnatural if people are born that way?

That's just it. They claim they were not born that way and that someone has enticed them to engage in deviant behavior.

This viewpoint gives those who choose it license to judge people and make their judgments known to others. It's their ego that demands it. Hopefully our understanding of human psychology has reached a point where this sort of argument will soon be just another once strongly-held, but now embarrassing, popular opinion to be relegated to the dust bin of the past. Homosexuality occurs among animals in more or less the same percentage as in humans. Are animals acting in an unnatural manner?

Some would argue that we're more advanced than animals and shouldn't engage in animal behavior.

Then give up sex altogether, unless you intend to have a child.

I don't think I'm ready to do that just yet.

There's your answer, and until the people who hold such strong opinions about others' sexual behavior are willing to forego all sex for pleasurable reasons, then perhaps we shouldn't listen to their ranting.

That's exactly what I plan to do.

It's helpful to keep in mind the qualities of the soul that have to do with sex. There are none. The soul is sexless and has no interest in sex. "They neither marry nor are given in marriage, but are like angels in heaven." As far as the Higher Self is concerned, the only reason sex exists is to produce a physical body it can use as an instrument. We humans turned sex into the emotional drama it has become. It occurred during Atlantean times when our minds were turned to purely selfish goals, and we're still dealing with the consequences. It's not easy to eradicate the enormous quantity of emotional energy built up over millions of years. It is part of our group karma as a human race. When we reach the point in spiritual evolution where the personality becomes a perfect instrument of the soul, we will have complete control over our thoughts, including thoughts about sex.

EARLY STAGES OF HUMAN DEVELOPMENT

We have not yet touched on a very important aspect of human sexuality. In the early stages of human development, there were not yet physical bodies available that were adequate for us to use. Humans existed for millions of years in a stage in between that of the soul in the higher mental realm and the physical world we would eventually inhabit. At first this was at the astral-emotional level and eventually the etheric level, which is part of the physical, but more rarified than what we can visually detect.

The physical bodies we would eventually inhabit were being prepared eons before we could occupy them. Even when ready, some souls refused to accept the primitive and unattractive vehicles prepared for their use. This is one origin of the story of the War in Heaven, where one-third of the heavenly hosts rebelled and two-thirds were willing to go along with the plan.

When we began to inhabit more dense physical bodies, they were not yet divided into male and female. This resulted in unusual forms of reproduction, some of which are perhaps more closely related to amphibians than to mammals. The legend of Zeus related by Homer says that he visited Leda, the daughter of Thestius, who was the king of Aetolia. After the "visit," Leda gave birth to eggs, and in due time humans hatched from these eggs. Our myths and legends are not nearly as fantastical as we think. The separation into male and female bodies did not occur instantaneously, but over millions of years. It is difficult for us to even conceive of what these early physical bodies were like. They were not like anything we have on earth today.

When the Bible says Adam and Eve wore coats of skin that were made for them, this is the period referred to. There was no need to wear clothing before, because "Adam" and "Eve," who represent us in the far distant past, were not in dense physical form at first. The "coats of skin" were the physical bodies created for them, and it was not until much later that anyone thought of wearing clothing. There was no need, as we were still in a stage of innocence, not unlike that of small children today who run around naked until some adult has an emotional reaction and creates a drama.

The separation of the sexes occurred over a long period of time, and was only complete approximately eighteen million years ago, according to some ancient texts.

That's far more remote than scientists say humans have existed.

Nevertheless, we have reason to believe it is accurate. Spiritual science has information not known to physical scientists.

Up until about this same period, sin, as such, did not exist. Our mental development had not yet reached the stage where we could be held accountable for our actions, but that would change over time.

How do you define sin? I've heard many definitions, but none that really make much sense.

The typical definition of religious people is that sin is anything contrary to the laws laid down by their deity, and these laws are generally spelled out in the religious writings of their prophets, often in great detail. The idea is not far removed from the truth, but there are hundreds, and sometimes thousands, of "laws" and "rules" in these texts, and most people disagree as to what is required, apart from the most basic, such as—do not commit murder, honor your parents, do not steal, and do not lie. Few people in the world can honestly claim they've never broken any of these, as basic as they are.

A more helpful concept of sin is to define it as any action, willful or otherwise, which is contrary to the natural flow of spiritual evolution, but it also takes into account your present level of consciousness. As an example, pride, ego, and emotional desire play an important role in the development of relatively unenlightened individuals; we would be out of place to force them to eliminate habits that are still useful for them. On the other hand, if you are a somewhat enlightened individual, you may be at a stage where you should begin eliminating them from your nature.

As you see, what is not a sin for someone else may be a sin for you because it no longer serves a purpose in your spiritual growth. "From him to whom much is given, much is required." Thus, apart from the basic requirements for human behavior, what is a sin will depend on your own personal stage of advancement.

No one is *at* a particular stage of development of consciousness. We operate within a range of consciousness. In our most elevated states of mind, we operate at one level of consciousness which seems very exalted to us. At other times, we operate at a distinctly lower level of consciousness. There are beings whose range of consciousness is remarkably higher than ours, and those whose range is definitely lower. There are also many whose range of consciousness is partly contiguous with our own.

We push against the lower limit of our consciousness and strive toward the upper limit, constantly aiming to raise it. It's this polarity that propels our spiritual growth. Each time we eliminate some of the lower qualities in our nature, we have finished forever with that area, and the lower boundary of our consciousness range moves higher. There is no such thing as final enlightenment. We are all enlightened to some degree and are constantly working, hopefully, at becoming more enlightened.

You might want to spend less time concerned about what sin is, or is not, and spend more energy focused on what your next step is for spiritual growth.

I can do that.

We discussed how humans existed at other realms before achieving the densest point in our outbound journey. Language did not exist in the early periods when we were at the astral-emotional level and the etheric level. We were still much more spiritual in nature than we are now. We lived in close proximity with those who were far more advanced than we were and whom we revered as gods. We could communicate telepathically because all were aware of each other's thoughts.

In the distant future, a similar state of affairs will occur, albeit on a higher turn of the evolutionary spiral. Little by little our bodies will become less dense and more rarified, we will again be able to communicate telepathically with each other, and we will once again live in closer communication with the Spiritual Hierarchy, those who are far in advance of us in consciousness.

A good practice to develop is one mentioned earlier, to act as if everyone can read our thoughts, whether we are alone or in public. Since this will one day be true, it is useful for us to act as if it were already the case. You can imagine, can't you, how your thoughts and actions would change if everyone could read your mind?

I don't even want to think about it. I'm sure I would be terribly embarrassed at times.

There's no need for embarrassment; many people have far worse thoughts than you. Even if people can't read our thoughts word for word, they still perceive the energy of them and are affected by them.

As you work to control your thoughts, remember that you want people around you to be affected in a positive manner.

Have we adequately answered your questions regarding sex?

[Laughing] It wasn't exactly what I thought it would be, but then I've come to expect the unexpected when I ask you questions. It has definitely given me some things to contemplate.

Complete sexual purity will be important at a certain point in your spiritual growth, but few people are there just yet, and those who worry about it are creating negativity from their worry and anxiety. This affects themselves and others and is more detrimental to spiritual growth than whatever activity they engage in. Work on other character traits first. Get your thoughts, emotions, and ego under control, and the rest will fall into place.

HONESTY

One of the most important qualifications for spiritual advancement is honesty. In a letter to A.P. Sinnett, one of the Adepts said that never during his entire life had an untruth polluted his lips. How many of us can say that truthfully? Without scrupulous honesty, we will not advance far spiritually. Those students who spend their time learning more information would do well to spend less time learning and more time applying what they have already read or heard in order to improve their character. You have not really "learned" anything until it has been applied to your own life and the results are proven.

We learn early in life that lying sometimes saves us from being punished. If it works once, we're willing to try it again, even if it doesn't work every time. Later, we lie in order to get what we want. We claim to have abilities or experience we don't really have, or we pretend to be wealthy in order to attract attention or entice someone to enter into a relationship with us. Internet profiles are proof of this. The truth always comes out eventually, and we reap the benefits of the karma we have created.

There is a curious thing about lying. No one ever lies all the time. If they did, we would simply ignore everything they said. Instead, those who lie also sometimes tell the truth. The problem is, we can never be sure if they are lying or telling the truth. We always have to be wary. The rare individual who invariably tells the truth is always reliable, and if this is a person of great intellect and depth of experience, he is someone we want to be with.

What if someone asks me a personal question I don't want to answer?

Nothing requires you to comply with anyone's curiosity. If that person needs to know that information for a valid reason, then you must tell the truth.

How do I tell someone, "That's none of your business," without being rude?

Non-reaction is the key. If your body language and the tone of your voice indicate that you are offended, it may react on your inquirer and cause another reaction. You can always ask a question in return: "Why would you ask that?" If the person is at all sensitive, he will realize it shows indiscretion on his part and will drop the matter. You can always change the subject yourself, simply by ignoring the question.

What about "white lies"? If I say something that isn't quite true in order not to upset someone, especially a child, surely that wouldn't be a problem.

It wouldn't? Do you think the child will not at some point realize that you lied? And when he does, he will no longer trust you completely. Besides, who are you trying to protect? Are you trying to protect the child's ego or yours?

The child's, I guess.

If you think about it, it's really your own ego you're trying to enhance. You want to look good in his eyes, so you're willing to tell a lie in order to keep things calm and not upset anyone. It may seem to work in the short term, but it is simply a bad idea. If you are always completely honest, you will be highly regarded by all, even your enemies. The number of people who are scrupulously honest is small, but you could be one of them if you choose to be.

THE END DOES NOT JUSTIFY THE MEANS

All too often, individuals and members of organizations are convinced that the end justifies the means. According to them, since they are working on behalf of a religion or organization which is "right," it is okay to use any means necessary to achieve their goals, even if they are injurious to others. This was the attitude of those who took part in the Inquisition, which resulted in the deaths of hundreds of thousands of individuals. All through history, abusive individuals have hidden behind the shield of "right" in order to inflict their abuse on others, hoping the law of karma would not apply to them because they were on the side of "right."

We may become complacent by saying, "Well, we don't kill them anymore. We use other ways of manipulating them in order to 'save' them." It doesn't matter. Any time you use unethical methods to influence others, you are simply in the wrong. Ignore the warning at your own risk. The end never justifies the means. Everything must be ethical and honest from start to finish.

ETHICS AND THE SPIRITUAL ASPIRANT

There is much more to honesty than just our interactions with individuals. Ethics is the term that covers this area of one's character. Do you pay 100% of the income tax you should? Do you request payments in cash so you don't have to pay taxes on them? If you do, you are not honest. You are not doing your share in paying for the services you use every day, and someone else, probably poorer than you, now has to pay more in order to cover the part you did not pay. Roads, schools, fire departments, police departments, health services, public welfare, military protection, and programs for the wellbeing of our fellow citizens all cost money.

I've heard people say, "I'm not going to pay my full share until others pay their full share."

That's another way of saying, "I'm dishonest and don't want to admit I'm selfish, so when every other citizen in the country becomes honest, I will join the group." As you see, it is a childish argument and emphasizes how selfish you are. Instead of being the last one to do what is right and honorable, be the first. Be a role model for others. Be the one your friends and relatives look to as an example of how an enlightened person operates.

We are all one family, one world, One Life. The person who is selfish and cares only about himself, or gives only of his excess to help others, still has much to learn. Only the one who is dedicated to the service of others can truly be enlightened.

Complete honesty and sterling ethics only develop when one has enough life experience to know that the law of karma is a fact. No one who is sane would walk up to the edge of the Grand Canyon and then take one more step. We know the law of gravity works because we have experience with it. The results of gravity always occur instantly. The results of karma sometimes occur instantly, but more often they play out over a long period of time, sometimes covering several lifetimes. Because of this, it takes an observant person to trace back again and again the causes for what we are experiencing today.

We often see how karma works in the lives of others before we recognize it in our own life. We don't have to make every mistake personally. If you want to take the long road to enlightenment, continue to believe life is unfair and that we suffer for no reason. Continue to complain about your situation and blame others for what happens to you. Or you can take a different approach and step back, observing and carefully noting the events in your own life and in others around you. If you observe carefully, without judgments and reactions, you will begin to get insight into how the law of karma works. Over time, our universe is exquisitely balanced. During the active period of life, imbalances occur, but everything is recorded to the tiniest degree. No thought, emotion, or action ever occurs without its result. It is your choice whether you consider that result a reward or a punishment.

Exaggeration is also a form of dishonesty. Children know when their parents are exaggerating. "I've told you a million times not to play in the street" is ignored because the child knows Dad is lying. It seems such a little thing, and yet nothing is little when it comes to the spiritual path. Ignore the little things at your own risk, but don't complain when you find you are not making progress. Be precise in communicating with others. The one who speaks seldom but always has something important to share when he speaks will get more attention than the person who talks non-stop and seldom has anything of importance to say. Those who talk do not know; those who know do not talk. Perhaps one of the worst things about lying is when people lie to themselves.

Do people actually do that?

All the time. Putting a spin on something, rationalizing the reason for doing it, or simply denying the obvious truth are things people do on a regular basis. We close our eyes and ears on purpose because we don't want to face the truth. It's the ego that doesn't want you to see things as they are. It will encourage you to pretend you are honest when you are not, that your motives are 100% unselfish when they are only 20% unselfish, and that you are making an honest effort when you obviously are not. It knows that once you see things just as they are, you will have clarity of vision. The end of lying is the beginning of seeing clearly, and seeing clearly spells doom for the ego.

Do you make illegal copies of CDs or DVDs for your friends?

I would like to consult with my attorney before answering that question.

If you do, you are not honest. You know it's illegal and unethical. You know you are stealing from the persons who created the material and who invested money in equipment and marketing to make it available to buy, yet you do it anyway. And you make a joke about it to hide the fact that discussing it makes you uncomfortable. If you think it's just a little thing and of no importance, it is not.

How you do anything is how you do everything.

THE LAW OF ATTRACTION

The law of attraction is a subset of the law of harmony, the ultimate law governing the universe. It has many applications on all levels of existence. In the lives of humans, it determines how others treat you, how the universe treats you, and the general "quality" of your life.

You have probably worked with people who have the attitude that they have to look out for themselves. No one else is going to because everyone is always trying to cheat them. Guess what? That person inevitably finds situations where he is mistreated and others take advantage of him.

Do you remember the smart aleck in grade school who walked up to you, slapped you on the back, and said, "How're you doin'?" He had just stuck a sign on your back that said "Kick Me," and other kids were more than willing to follow the directions.

I'm afraid I was that smart aleck.

We all have signs on our back. Some say "I don't deserve to be loved," or "I don't deserve prosperity." Another might say "Abuse me" or "I'm a victim." But guess what. You're the one who put those signs on your back, and everyone you encounter can read them. They might not be visible to the physical eye, but they are there nevertheless, and everyone responds to the subliminal messages you display.

Some people say repeatedly, "Nothing good ever happens to me." The universe responds, "Your wish is my command," and serves up one catastrophe after another. Why does the law of attraction work? It works because of energy fields. In electricity and chemistry, opposites attract. A positive ion repels another positive ion but attracts a negative ion. With the law of attraction, energy of a particular quality will attract more energy of that same quality. When you say to the universe, "Nothing good ever happens to me," you have created an affirmation, and each time you repeat it, even mentally, it becomes stronger. Your thoughts, which surround you at all times, automatically attract people who have similar thought-forms. You can make yourself ill by thinking you are ill. You attract misfortune when you're afraid of experiencing misfortune. The fear of failing attracts failure.

But obviously the opposite is also true.

Of course it is. We all have met people who are eternal optimists, and they invariably have good things happen to them. Even when a difficult situation appears, they look for something positive to come from it, the silver lining in the storm cloud. They recognize that every obstacle in the path of life is an opportunity to grow, to learn something new, and to gain experience that will be invaluable in the future.

If we are entirely unselfish, if we are loving and kind, if we help our fellow travelers in life, then our life will be easy, filled with affection and generosity, and we will never lack for anything we need in order to thrive. The person who is an instrument for peace may not be the wealthiest person in the world in terms of money, but he has wealth beyond measure.

There is one caveat about the law of attraction. Many "New Age" people have misunderstood it and misapplied it in their lives. They ignore the part about unselfishness and try to use it for enhancing their ego. "I want more money in my life, so I create an affirmation: I deserve more than I have right now and the universe will grant my request because I have a clear idea of what I want." Then this person waits for money to drop into his lap, or worse yet, gambles the little money he has, certain that the universe will respond to his affirmation and make him a lottery winner. The result is anger, frustration, and resentment. The solution—work harder, work smarter, exercise your intellect, do something that actually brings more money into your life if that is what you want. It is not the attaining of your goal that is important, but the journey you took to get there and the experience you gained along the way.

Once you learn how to manifest anything you set your sights on, this principle can be applied in a thousand different ways. You will never lose that experience, not even between lifetimes. People become "overnight successes" because they paid their dues long ago and learned the valuable lessons of how to attain their goals. It is never handed to someone without hard work on his part.

Chapter 15

THE COMPASSION OF THE
NIRMĀNAKĀYAS

Now bend thy head and listen well, O
Bodhisattva—Compassion speaks and
saith: "Can there be bliss when all that
lives must suffer? Shalt thou be saved
and hear the whole world cry?"

— *The Voice of the Silence*

THE PURPOSE OF THIS BOOK

Our purpose in writing this book is to provide some
practical hints for individuals who are at the point in their
spiritual evolution where they can make more rapid progress if they choose. As the reader will have learned from
previous chapters, this accelerated course is not easy. It
requires self-discipline, tenacity, and an unwavering de-

319

termination to reach the goal regardless of the effort required. Not everyone has had enough life experience to make this choice. Nevertheless, every person will at some point, even if not in this lifetime, achieve all that is required to pass beyond the human realm. The requirements never change. There are two choices before you. Either you can do nothing different, simply continuing as you have in the past, or you can make the effort required to figure out how life works. If you choose the latter course, pick one or two qualities of character to develop, and make it a habit to work on them every day. With persistent effort, you will see progress.

Do you have some suggestions for a daily spiritual practice?

Meditation and contemplation are almost always the basis of the student's spiritual practice. Early morning is best. Some students arise at 3:00 a.m. to meditate and then go back to sleep. This will not work for everyone, but it has been a common practice in monasteries for hundreds of years. Perhaps the monks know what they are doing.

Schedule a moment of silence three times during the day—as soon as you wake up, at midday, and before retiring at night. This may be only two minutes or a little longer if you wish, but consistency is important. In the morning, reflect on what you want to accomplish during the day. What character traits do you intend to work on? At the end of the day, you will see whether or not you made progress toward your goal. At noon, or whenever you have a break in the day, again spend a moment in quiet reflection. Close your eyes and let all your muscles relax. Feel the tension melt away as you reach upward mentally to contact your soul. Realize, if only for a moment, that the purpose of life is to gain experience. In the end, all the details will be forgotten, and only the essence of your life experiences will remain. Try to put everything in perspective. Before you go to sleep at night, review the events of the day. Did you achieve your intentions for that day? If not, what can you do tomorrow to improve that? Were you kind, respectful, and brotherly in your interactions with others?

The period between work and sleep is of prime importance. Maintain a quiet space for reading, writing, contemplation, or some other creative expression. If you're a musician, playing your instrument in the evening can be a form of meditation. Art is an important part of the spiritual practice for many people.

Be careful what you eat at the end of the day. If you come home tired from work, turn on the television, eat a heavy meal, and then go to bed, you will not be able to enter for several hours into that meditative realm that is essential, and the quality of your sleep will not be good. If you eat at all in the evening, make it a light meal. Some aspirants follow the guidelines of certain monasteries and do not eat after 2:00 p.m. This is not possible for everyone, but be aware of what works for the "experts," and try to adopt as many of their practices as you feel would be helpful to you.

Avoid alcohol entirely. You may be convinced that you need a drink to relax, but it deadens your brain. An alert mind, operating through a drug-free brain, is essential to the spiritual aspirant.

AFFIRMATIONS

Here are some affirmations you may want to use in your meditation:

- More radiant than the sun, purer than the snow, subtler than the ether is the Self, the spirit within my heart. I am that Self. That Self am I.

- I plunge myself into the pool of wisdom. From thence I come, bearing a knowledge of its mysteries for my fellow men.

- Lord, make me an instrument of your peace.
  Where there is hatred, let me sow love.
  Where there is injury, pardon.
  Where there is doubt, faith.
  Where there is despair, hope.
  Where there is darkness, light.
  Where there is sadness, joy.

  O Divine Master,
  Grant that I may not so much seek to be consoled,
      As to console;
  To be understood, as to understand;
  To be loved, as to love.
  For it is in giving that we receive.
  It is in pardoning that we are pardoned,
  And it is in dying that we are born to eternal life.

The first affirmation is from *The Masters and the Path*, by Charles W. Leadbeater. The second is from *Discipleship in the New Age, Volume One*, by Alice Bailey. The third is the well-known Prayer of St. Francis. It is not actually a prayer that was used in his time. In fact, no one knows who wrote it, but its first known use was in 1912. It was printed in French on a prayer card with an image of St. Francis and has been associated with his name ever since.

Of course, you may have other affirmations of your own.

Many people use the Lord's Prayer or other prayers. Whatever you use, repeat it each time with intention. If you simply repeat the words in parrot-like fashion, the effect will match the amount of mental effort you invested. Focus on the meaning behind the words and be clear about the intention of what you want to convey. Imagine you are reciting it to a group of students who are keen to grasp every word and feel the power that comes through you. This increased intention begins in your meditation and spreads to all areas of your life. Your words will be more powerful because of the thought and intention you put into them. It doesn't matter whether you say your affirmations aloud or silently. Try it both ways and notice how each is effective, but in different ways.

Many people find the Sanskrit word OM to be a powerful affirmation or mantra. When chanted with intention, it has a remarkable effect on everyone nearby. It should last the length of one full breath. At the beginning, the mouth is in the form of an O and the sound is very open. Then the lips slowly come together until the last part is entirely the sound of M.

Every aspect of your life must come under review if you propose to follow the spiritual path. It seems daunting at first when you stand at the foot of the mountain and gaze up at what appears to be insurmountable heights. You will never arrive if you don't take the first step, and then it is just a matter of one step after another. The only step that ever matters is the one you are taking right now. Then one day you will be surprised to find that you have reached the very summit of the peak which seemed impossible to scale.

The amount of progress a person can accomplish in a given lifetime is immense, but it will only happen with persistent effort on your part. Without that constant pressure from you, progress will be minimal, and in many cases almost negligible.

VEGETARIANISM

Is it necessary to be a vegetarian? I have friends who insist that no one can be very spiritual unless they are strictly vegetarian.

You can make great spiritual progress without being vegetarian. Follow your own instincts. If it feels right for you, then do it. If not, there's no need to worry. It is true, however, that most disciples who have achieved the highest levels of spirituality follow a vegetarian diet. This is because of two reasons. First, as you become more enlightened and more aware of your fellow creatures, you develop a great sensitivity to suffering. It naturally follows that you do not want to be the cause of the death of any animal, even if you hired someone else to kill it. Secondly, there comes a time when a pupil is ready to work intently on telepathic communication with his teachers and fellow pupils. In order to develop accurate vision on higher levels and perfect communication, the avoidance of animal flesh in the diet is essential. It eliminates one of the final ties to our old animal nature and opens up the final phases of existing entirely at the soul level.

FASTING

What about fasting? Is that something I should include in my spiritual practice?

How does fasting help you become more spiritual?

I don't know, maybe by becoming more disciplined.

Everything in esoteric studies and in personal spiritual development must be reasonable and logical. Always feel free to try something for a period of time as long as it is not unethical, but if you see no results and persist in practicing it, it becomes a superstition. A superstition is a belief that has no basis in fact. After you practice something for a reasonable period of time, assess the results. If the results are not in line with the effort, then put it aside for the time being.

Fasting does, in fact aid in spiritual growth, but only if you understand how and why. Many students view it as a type of asceticism. When carried to the extreme, it becomes a form of self-punishment worthy of a great martyr. When practiced in this manner, it is nothing more than an ego enhancer.

The reason for fasting is simple—when the physical body demands attention, you cannot be in a meditative state of mind. Many spiritual students, unknown to themselves, are being taught on the inner planes while the body is asleep. We sometimes get glimpses of these sessions in the form of vivid dreams or visions. If you have eaten a heavy meal or spicy food before going to sleep, the physical body is demanding attention in the form of digestion and sometimes indigestion. The body does not rest properly, and this prevents any possibility of learning during sleep. Alcohol paralyzes the brain to such an extent that even if you are taught something during sleep, the physical brain is unresponsive and unable to bring through any meaningful recollection.

What would be a proper fasting practice?

You should fast every day. What is the first meal you eat in the morning?

Breakfast.

Exactly—break fast. In many Latin-based languages, the word is the same. You have been fasting all night. But if you ate late at night, it wasn't much of a fast. The goal is to take in more nourishment early in the day. As mentioned above, some monks do not eat after 2:00 p.m., for example, and it may be helpful to follow their lead.

I'm afraid I would get very hungry if I did that, and I wouldn't be able to concentrate.

Do what works for you. Anything you eat later in the day should be easy to digest and unlikely to cause indigestion. Be aware of how your dietary practices affect your alertness and your well-being, both physical and mental. If you are mentally sluggish or your body is using all available energy sources, you will not be able to meditate well, and you will not remember night classes on the inner planes. You should avoid caffeine and refined sugar in the latter part of the day. Stimulants affect your receptiveness at night.

STEWARDSHIP

The person who is completely dedicated to service will always have what he needs. The universe provides for those dedicated individuals because they understand the concept of stewardship. They consider nothing to be their own personal property. Instead, they consider it a fiduciary responsibility to use everything for the highest and best purpose and in such a way that it is beneficial to all mankind.

You own nothing—not your house, your car, or even your body or the talents you have. Everything you have, even if you have "earned" it, is simply a part of your fiduciary responsibility. As an instrument of the universe, much more is required of you than of others.

GIVING

I've always struggled with giving to charity or for helping others. How much is enough?

It's not a question of how much you give, but your attitude toward giving. The sannyasin of old and the monk in the monastery gave up everything in the material world to enter a realm of solitary contemplation. The modern sannyasin and the modern warrior monk are expected to live in the world but not be attached to it. We can't do that without having some possessions. The goal is to travel light and be aware of our attitude toward possessions. Is your wealth used to enhance your ego, or in the service of mankind? Ask yourself the following questions:

- How important is it to me to obtain financial wealth in my life and how do I intend use it?
- How much of my time is spent attaining financial goals and how much attaining spiritual goals?
- When I give money to a homeless person, do I give it because I feel guilty that I have something he doesn't, because it makes me feel good when he says "thank you," or because I can send a blessing along with it, even if my gift is used to buy drugs or alcohol?
- If I lost everything I own through a financial catastrophe, what would be my reaction? How would I proceed to recover from it?
- What are my greatest assets in life?
- How much of my time is devoted to volunteer work?
- If I knew I were going to die soon, what would I think about losing all the material things I have worked so hard to accumulate?

COMPASSION

Those who have chosen to follow the spiritual path must always keep in mind the enormous variations in the levels of experience among our fellow travelers. Some are novices and struggle with even simple concepts. The learning curve is interesting. We spend hundreds of lives learning the basics of Life 101. Then there comes a lifetime where we are introduced to the teachings of the Ancient Wisdom, and something within us says, "That sounds true." This marks the beginning of a long and arduous journey. For several lifetimes we make a little progress and then come to a point where there are several options. There are no signposts to indicate which path is best for us, and no two individuals ever follow exactly the same path. The Spanish poet Antonio Machado wrote, "Caminante, no hay camino. El camino se hace al andar." Pilgrim, there is no path. You make the path as you go.

We are often sidetracked by mirages, otherwise known as ego, desire, and attachments. We substitute spiritual desires for material desires and higher forms of ego for lower ones. It is only later that we realize these too are obstacles which must be overcome. Glamor overtakes us again and again, and we fall into the trap of its appeal to our ego. But we overcome the obstacles one by one, and as we do, our vision becomes clear.

Currently, there is an enhanced energy being sent around the world in order to help fill some much-needed positions in the Spiritual Hierarchy. This system of forcing is not the normal procedure, but the time we live in is a critical one. It is our opportunity, should we choose, to make more rapid progress than normal. At the current time, those who make the grade will experience a tremendous spike in spiritual growth. Within a short time, cosmically speaking, this window of opportunity will close, and humanity will then have only the normal, slower path available.

THE TWO PORTALS

When an enlightened being reaches the level of consciousness which is the goal for our current group of souls, two portals appear before him. One leads to nirvāna and eternal rest. This is the right of those who have achieved such stupendous heights. The other portal leads to the path of renunciation. The enlightened one who enters here has renounced nirvāna and has chosen to remain behind until all his brothers are safe.

"Compassion speaks and saith: 'Can there be bliss when all that lives must suffer? Shalt thou be saved and hear the whole world cry?'" This path of renunciation is the path chosen by the Buddha and the Lord Christ. They have vowed not to enter the state of rest until all humanity has been given every possible chance to achieve the same state of enlightenment they have.

Not all who achieve that level of consciousness will choose the portal of renunciation. Those who do are called Nirmānakāyas. They have renounced the bliss of nirvāna in order to help others. It is an enormous sacrifice they make, and one for which we can be eternally grateful. We who have not yet reached the point where that decision looms before us can still decide whether we are only interested in achieving enlightenment for ourselves or whether we will use our time and energy to help those around us.

The stress that occurs in the lives of those who make a conscious effort toward self-transformation is huge. Anyone making the effort deserves our greatest respect. They often make mistakes, and some have egos as big as a house. Even so, they too are learning valuable lessons that help all of us. There is nothing wrong with observing the shortcomings of others. After all, if we pay attention, the mistakes of others can be a learning tool for us. Remember that they have the same goal you do—to achieve enlightenment. We all make serious mistakes from time to time. Let's not compound them by criticizing those who fail.

Be tolerant of your fellow travelers on the path. It's not an easy path to tread, and it is our responsibility to inspire and assist wherever we can, especially when our brothers fall. Be kind to yourself when you fail to live up to your highest potential. Each time you stumble, pick yourself up and move onward, never wavering in your determination to reach the goal. We all need all the help we can get.

SUMMING UP

We hope this treatise is helpful to those who have a deep and abiding love for their fellow human beings and are dedicated to helping those who travel with us on the path of spiritual evolution. It has been an honor and a pleasure to share some concepts we have learned with others. If it helps even one person achieve the goal, it will have been well worth the effort.

I've thought carefully about everything you have said. I don't understand it all yet, and there are some things I don't agree with, but I now have some tools I can use, and I intend to make some changes in my life. I hope in the future I will be able to make even better use of what you have taught me.

Where are you?

Here.

What time is it?

Now.

What is missing in your life?

Nothing.

All is well.

There is a peace which
passeth understanding;
it abides in the hearts of those
who live in the Eternal.

There is a power which
maketh all things new;
it lives and moves in those
who know the Self as one.

— Annie Besant

GLOSSARY

Sanskrit or Saṃskṛtam — संस्कृतम् — is a classical language in Asia, just as Greek and Latin are in Europe. Max Müller, a famous 19th century orientalist, called it the eldest sister of all known languages. Many words in European languages were derived from Sanskrit. Many of the words used in esoteric philosophy also come from Sanskrit. A number of people have tried to invent equivalent terms in English to express concepts already well developed in Sanskrit, but the results have generally been disappointing. Perhaps it is best simply to learn some key Sanskrit words. Most languages borrow heavily from other languages, especially those that have existed for many centuries and thus have a richness not found in younger languages.

In some older texts on the Ancient Wisdom, the transliteration is inconsistent. However, linguists have developed a standardized form of using combinations of Latin, or Roman, letters and diacritical marks to represent specific Sanskrit letters, which are written in the Devanāgarī script. This system is called the International Alphabet of Sanskrit Transliteration, or IAST. Hindi and some other Indian languages use the Devanāgarī script as well.

The following guide will help students approximate the proper pronunciation of Sanskrit words. Vowels in Devanāgarī are written as shown below only when they are at the beginning of a word. Otherwise they are indicated by diacritical marks in conjunction with other letters. Each consonant is generally followed by a vowel within a word. If two consonants are pronounced with no vowel between, a special compound letter indicates this. Sanskrit is quite scientific and fairly complicated in its structure and grammar. The very name Sanskrit means polished or perfected.

Special thanks to Vasuki Seshadri of Samskrita Bhāratī for his help with Sanskrit grammar and transliteration.

Transliteration	Devanāgarī	Pronounced as in
Vowels		
a	अ	organ
ā	आ	father
i	इ	lift
ī	ई	flee
u	उ	pull
ū	ऊ	pool
ṛ	ऋ	river (short trill)
ṝ	ॠ	reed (short trill)
ḷ	ऌ	(l with short trill)
ḹ	ॡ	(l with longer trill)
e	ए	grey
ai	ऐ	aisle
o	ओ	no
au	औ	how
Consonants		
k	क	karma
kh	ख	backhoe
g	ग	give
gh	घ	doghouse
c	च	chum

ch	छ	Chur**ch**ill
j	ज	**j**ar
jh	झ	hedge**h**og
ṭ	ट	**t**op
ṭh	ठ	ho**th**ouse
ḍ	ड	**d**ome
ḍh	ढ	roa**d h**og
t	त	**t**ip
th	थ	hi**t h**im
d	द	**d**im
dh	ध	re**d h**ot
p	प	**p**ull
ph	फ	loo**ph**ole
b	ब	**b**oy
bh	भ	clu**bh**ouse
ṅ	ङ	ha**ng**
ñ	ञ	be**n**ch
ṇ	ण	me**n**d
n	न	**n**one
m	म	**m**ore
y	य	**y**oung
r	र	**r**un
l	ल	**l**ove
v	व	**v**ery
ś	श	**sh**ip
ṣ	ष	**sh**ore
s	स	**s**ame
h	ह	**h**ave

Absolute Sat in Sanskrit, that about which nothing can be said. It has no qualities and thus cannot be described or measured. It is what was before anything existed, but even this is not correct. In a sense, it is the potential for existence. It is "be-ness" itself.

Adept (L.) One who has attained a certain mastery over the forces of nature by his understanding of how they work and through years of disciplined training. A master of the esoteric philosophy.

Advaita Vedānta अद्वैत वेदान्त A Vedānta sect that emphasizes the oneness or non-dualistic nature of life, as opposed to Dvaita Vedānta, which emphasizes dualism, self versus non-self. Advaita was taught by Shankaracharya (Śaṅkarācārya), the greatest of the Brahmin sages.

Ahura Mazda The personified deity of the Parsis. The word Ahura is similar to Ātma. The principle of Divine Light.

ājñā आज्ञा The "brow" chakra located in the center of the forehead. It is sometimes stimulated during meditation and can become useful in telepathy. It has a connection with the pituitary body and the remnants of an eye that functioned externally eons ago and still functions to some extent in some animals.

ākāśa आकाश Often but incorrectly identified as ether, it is the subtle spiritual essence which pervades all space. Ākāśa is the substance employed in kriyāśakti yoga. It is the substance which makes true telepathy and higher spiritual communication possible.

akashic records That aspect of ākāśa wherein a trained seer can see the past on all lower levels of consciousness—physical, etheric, astral-emotional and mental. The uninitiated clairvoyant sees only partially, and his interpretation is subject to personal prejudices and expectations.

alchemy The chemistry of nature. Modern chemistry owes its origins to the work of alchemists. It is popularly believed that the principle focus of alchemists was the transmutation of base metals into gold. True alchemists were metaphysicians and were the chemists, pharmacists, physicists and physicians of their time. The goal of the more advanced alchemists was the transformation of base human beings into spiritual beings, thus the symbolism of transforming lead into gold through refining is descriptive of this process. In the Dark Ages, alchemists were forced to work in secret. The penalty upon discovery was death at the hands of the Christian Church.

altruism (L.) The opposite of egoism. The quality which predisposes one to act for the benefit of others. Unselfishness as opposed to selfishness.

amanasa अमनस Mindless. A term used in *The Secret Doctrine* for early human races that could hardly be compared to modern humans. The element of mind was so little developed that they were more like the most intelligent animals of today.

amrita or **amṛtam** अमृतम् Ambrosia, the food or nectar of the gods. The elixir of life, that which conveys immortality. It is equivalent to the sacred soma juice of the Greater Mysteries. Sometimes written as amrit or the feminine form, amritā.

ānanda आनन्द Bliss or joy, a quality which has existence in more spiritual realms. It cannot exist at the level of emotions or that of the lower mind. Also the name of Gautama Buddha's favorite disciple.

Ancient Wisdom Bodhidharma of the Brahmins, the Kabbalah of the Jews, the Tao of the Chinese and the Prisca Theologia of the Christians. It is the core of every great religion. The teachings remain the same throughout the eons. Only the methods of teaching change, always adapted to suit the higher representatives of human spiritual achievement at the time.

angel   Deva, or shining one in Sanskrit. The angelic kingdom is one which evolves parallel to that of humans, but their members do not have dense physical bodies. Viewed in its entire range, it includes creatures lower than animals in consciousness, often called nature spirits, up to mighty individuals who are far higher than humans in consciousness. Some have passed through human evolution in previous cycles; others have yet to experience human existence. Some have forms, and some do not, but those who do are not at all similar to humans except as a general shape. Artists often depict them in human form because of their tendency to anthropomorphize. Angels do not have wings, but the flowing energy pattern in the area corresponding to human shoulders is such that it gives the appearance of wings. At the current time there is little true communication between angels and humans, but this will increase in future centuries.

antahkarana अन्तःकरण   The pathway or bridge between the higher mental and lower mental realms. It serves as the means of communication between the Higher Self and the lower self and is developed over a long period of time through meditation and spiritual practice. Only that portion of one's personal life which is noble, altruistic and divine can be transmitted via the antahkarana to the soul. On the other hand, by developing a stronger connection to the soul, it can inspire and direct the personality when the antahkarana is sufficiently developed.

arhat अर्हत्   One who has passed the fourth initiation and is on the verge of attaining adeptship. The fifth initiation, that of the Adept or Asekha, can often be passed in the same lifetime. In some books the terms Arhat and Asekha are used interchangeably.

arūpa अरूप Formless. Beings which exist only on levels higher than that of the lower mental realm are formless. Humans and many other spiritual beings have both a portion of their existence which has form and a portion which is formless. In humans, ātma, buddhi and higher manas are all formless, while the lower mental, astral-emotional and physical-etheric have a form which we call the personality or lower self.

asceticism A lifestyle characterized by abstinence from worldly pleasures, often as a means of obtaining spiritual advancement. When it becomes an obsession, it is a detriment to enlightenment instead of an aid. Carried to the extreme, it becomes a form of masochism and enhances the ego instead of eliminating it.

asekha असेख "He who has no more to learn." A Buddhist term for an Adept, one who has learned all that is necessary in the human kingdom.

astral The plane of manifestation which includes emotions. There are seven subplanes, with coarser emotions existing at the lower levels, and higher emotions, such as kindness and contentment at the higher levels. The enlightened individual will eliminate all but the highest emotions in his nature and will operate from the soul level instead of the personality level.

astral body Liṅga śariram in Sanskrit, it is the portion of the personality which exists in the astral-emotional realm. Trained clairvoyants can see the aura of the astral body and thus ascertain the emotional nature of an individual, both in general and at the current time.

astrology (Gr.) Just as modern chemistry and physics evolved from ancient alchemy, so did modern astronomy evolve from ancient astrology. The astrology practiced today is a poor residual of what was once a much more accurate science. Many modern astrologers use astrological calculations and charts as a starting point for clairvoyant observations, but unless they are trained by initiates, the results are still rudimentary. Astrology will resume its proper place in future centuries when there are more Adepts who can devote the necessary time and effort to bring it up to date.

atavism Fixation on the ego, or personality. Atavism focuses primarily on the importance of the individual and is egoistic as opposed to altruistic.

Atlantis (Gr.) A great continent which spanned the Atlantic and Pacific Oceans and was the home of a human population that may have included as many as two billion people. As they grew in intelligence, they became more evil and selfish in nature, blocking out nearly all that was spiritual. Over thousands of years, the entire continent was submerged, and millions of inhabitants were destroyed. Plato speaks of the last island, Poseidonis, which sank in 9,564 BC according to one of the Adepts.

ātma आत्म Universal Spirit, the Supreme Soul. The most spiritual aspect of our being.

ātma-buddhi-manas आत्म बुद्धि मनस् The Divine Triad, or Monad, it is Spirit and intuition operating through the highest aspect of mind. When the lower quaternary, the personality, has been completely mastered, only the divine nature, in the form of ātma-buddhi-manas, operates.

avatāra अवतार A divine incarnation. It generally refers to an individual who has progressed beyond the human realm of development, but who chooses to incarnate in order to fulfill a special mission on earth.

avīchi अवीचि The waveless state. The equivalent of hell, it can be the state of a person still living on earth, but more often that of those humans who, after death, are found to have developed no redeeming qualities during their lifetime. Fortunately, it is fairly uncommon.

baptism (Gr.) Ritual ablutions have been a part of religious rites for thousands of years, symbolizing a cleansing and renewal. It was practiced in the Chaldean and Assyro-Babylonian rituals as well as in the nocturnal ceremonies in the Egyptian pyramids.

bardo (Tib.) The intermediate period between two lives on earth, it includes kāma-loka and devachan.

be-ness A word invented to convey some comprehension of Sat, the Absolute. The Absolute is not being, since there is nothing in the realm of the Absolute which can exist. There is no polarity, which is essential to being. Be-ness at least suggests some sense of a potential existence.

Bhagavad Gītā भगवद्गीता Literally, The Lord's Song. It is one portion of the great epic poem of India, the Mahābhārata महाभारत. The Bhagavad Gītā is a dialogue between Krishna, the chariot driver, and Arjuna, his pupil, regarding esoteric principles of life. In the story, Arjuna represents the personality and Krishna the Higher Self in the battle about to begin between the Spiritual Man and earthly man.

bhakti yoga भक्ति योग The yoga of devotion to an ideal. The goal is to become one with the Beloved through efforts to be more like him. Many devout religious people are practicing bhakti yoga without realizing it. The greatest potential danger is the tendency to rely on authority figures rather than depending on oneself to determine what is true.

black magic All magic uses the same principle of kri-yāśakti, which involves the creation of a powerful thought form and bringing in of elemental energy to build the form in matter. The matter can remain strictly in the mental realm, or it can extend down into the astral-emotional and physical-etheric realms. Magic can be white, black or grey depending on the motives behind it. If it is purely motivated by the love of mankind, with no hint of selfishness, it is white magic. If it is motivated by personal gain and that gain negatively affects other persons, it is black magic. Every human practices a weak form of magic without realizing it. We create our circumstances in life by our thought forms and by the energy attracted to those forms. Most of these thoughts are partly selfish and partly altruistic, thus producing a sort of "grey" magic. As we gain enlightenment, the magic we engage in becomes more pure, eventually becoming white. The magic of an advanced being is far stronger than that of the average person.

bodhi बोधि Wisdom or enlightenment.

bodhidharma बोधिधर्म The Ancient Wisdom. Teachings of an esoteric nature which were scrupulously guarded from the profane and taught only to those who had proved themselves worthy through refining of the lower nature.

bodhisattva बोधिसत्त्व From bodhi (wisdom) and sattva (essence), it is the title applied to those who are on the threshold of becoming a Buddha, one who is enlightened and entitled to nirvāṇa.

Brahma or **Brahman** ब्रह्मन् Not to be confused with Brahmā, Brahma is the supreme principle of the universe from the essence of which all emanates, and into which all returns. It has no beginning or end and is all pervading, animating the highest spiritual beings and the lowliest atoms.

Brahmā ब्रह्मा The masculine creative component in the Indian trinity of Brahmā, Vishnu and Śiva. Brahmā periodically manifests from Brahma and then disappears again into a state of pralaya.

buddha बुद्ध Enlightened. A very high stage of spiritual development, marked by complete detachment from all that is temporary and finite, a supreme state of holiness which entitles one to eternal bliss if he so chooses.

buddhi बुद्धि The realm of consciousness in which intuition reigns. Buddhi is the vehicle of ātma. Man, at his highest level of human development, functions as a spiritual triad of ātma-buddhi-manas.

buddhi-manas बुद्धि मनस् In his lower nature, man functions through kāma-manas, the lower mind given impulse by desires and emotions. Upon reaching a certain state of enlightenment, he has gained mastery over personal desires and emotions and now functions as a truly spiritual human being, operating through his higher mind, given impulse by ātma and buddhi.

caduceus (Gr.) The Greeks adopted the symbol of the caduceus from the Egyptians. Metaphysically, it represents the descent of primordial matter into the terrestrial world, the One Reality becoming illusion. Physically, it represents the currents of life which animate the human form. The rod symbolizes the spinal column, and the two intertwining serpents represent the spiral trajectory taken by the kuṇḍalinī energy as it rises from its origin at the base of the spine to its destination in the head center.

Cathars A group of Christians whose beliefs contained many Gnostic elements. They lived primarily in southern France in the 12ᵗʰ and 13ᵗʰ centuries. They were predominantly vegetarian and were opposed to capital punishment. Because their beliefs were considered heretical by the Roman Church, they were severely persecuted by the Inquisition. In 1209, one hundred Cathar prisoners were blinded and mutilated by soldiers, then allowed to return as a warning to others. After an assault on the town of Béziers, Arnaud, the leader of the crusader army, wrote to Pope Innocent III, "Today your Holiness, twenty thousand heretics were put to the sword, regardless of rank, age, or sex." Many Catholics tried to protect the Cathars because they were kind and gentle neighbors, but many of them were killed as well because of their sympathy. Relentless assaults by the crusader armies finally exterminated the last remnants of this sect after killing tens of thousands of human beings for no other reason than their beliefs.

causal body   A term used sometimes in esoteric literature to indicate that portion of our human nature which exists at the higher levels of the mental realm. It is causal because it is the repository of the essence of each individual lifetime. Thus, it is the more permanent aspect of our humanness, that which carries over from one incarnation to the next. The causes, or karma, continue from one lifetime to the next through the intermediary of the causal body until all are finally resolved and there is no more need for experience in human form.

chakra or **chakram** or **cakra** चक्रं   A wheel or disc, it is an energy field, circular in nature. Most often, it refers to the seven major centers of energy in the etheric part of the physical body. As one gains in enlightenment, these centers gain more energy and appear to revolve, slowly at first and then with increasing velocity. To a seer, the chakras, together with a view of the person's aura, indicates the level of spiritual advancement of that individual.

chela or **cela** चेल In esoteric works it is generally used in reference to the pupil of a guru or spiritual teacher.

chit or **cit** चित् Abstract consciousness, although it is often used as a term for mind activity.

Chohan (Tib.) Lord or Master.

clairaudience (Fr.) The ability to hear at a distance. Some people are born with this ability and others attain it through spiritual training.

clairvoyance (Fr.) Second sight, or the ability to see things at a higher level than the physical, whether at a distance or in the immediate area. It also applies to the past, the current time, and the future. Common clairvoyants or psychics see almost entirely on the astral-emotional plane, and their visions are heavily influenced by their personal prejudices and expectations. Only an initiate trained by an Adept or one of his higher chelas is able to see on higher planes and interpret accurately that which is seen in the astral realms. This requires many years of purification—mentally, emotionally and physically—plus arduous training to learn to separate imagination from reality.

cross An ancient symbol. The vertical shaft represents the descent of Spirit into matter. The horizontal bar indicates the sense of separation felt by inhabitants in the lower realms and the possibility of overcoming that separation to join once again with our original Spiritual Source. To be crucified is to gain mastery over one's lower nature, thus opening the way to the return to Spirit.

crux ansata or **ankh** Egyptian symbol of life. It is in the form of a cross, but in place of the top of the vertical arm is a circle. Because of its association with the sun, it was most often crafted of gold, although highly polished copper was sometimes used.

Day and Night of Brahmā The day and night together compose a period of 4.3 trillion years according to esoteric sources. The day is a manvantara, a period of activity and manifestation. When this active phase draws to a close and nighttime descends, there occurs an equal period of repose, or pralaya, during which the worlds that were created vanish and all enters a resting phase. There is some mystery surrounding the length of time ascribed to these periods, but it is safe to say that they are of immense duration.

deva देव From the Sanskrit root div, to shine. The resplendent gods. Devas include all members of the angelic kingdom. Some are much more exalted than others, and those on the lowest levels are not necessarily good.

devachan देवचन् The realm of the gods, the shining ones. The term is most often used to describe the state of those who merit, through their karma, a stay in the "heaven world" before returning to a new incarnation. The period of time in devachan can vary from a few hours to several centuries, depending on the amount of energy accumulated which merits that experience.

Devanāgarī देवनागरी The language or alphabet of the gods. The characters of the Sanskrit language. They are also used in Hindi, Marathi and Nepali.

dharma धर्म The law or natural law. It is often rendered duty or even religion. It combines the precepts of harmony, justice, equity and virtue. In general it refers to that which is considered a proper mode of personal conduct in alignment with natural law.

Dharmakāya धर्मकाय See Nirmānakāya.

Dhyān Chohān (Tib.)   The "Lords of Light." The equivalent of Archangels in the Christian Church, they are Divine Intelligences in charge of supervising the Cosmos.

dhyāna ध्यान   Contemplation. One of the stages of meditation, it is a state of consciousness which transcends the plane of sensuous perception. It is equivalent to Chán in Chinese, Zen in Japanese, Seon in Korean, and Samten in Tibetan.

djinn or **jinn** (Arab.)   An elemental, or nature spirit. The word genie or genii is analogous to djinn.

dodecahedron (Gr.)   Plato claims in his work *Timaeus* that the universe is built on the geometrical figure of the dodecahedron, a sphere made of twelve regular pentagons.

drama   The emotional turmoil that is an addiction for many. As one progresses in spiritual development, the addiction to strong emotions and desires gradually falls away until almost none remains in the life of an initiate.

Dugpa (Tib.)   A member of a sect of Buddhist lamas. Before the era of Tsong-ka-pa in the 14th century, nearly all Tibetan lamas had embraced the adulterated tenets of the old Bon or Bön religion, whose practitioners were given to sorcery and black magic. After the purification instituted by Tsong-ka-pa, the lamas of the Gelugpa (yellow hat) sect were scrupulously pure in their practices, while the Dugpa (red hat) sect, continued to engage in drunkenness, immorality and sorcery. Today it is not possible to tell which is which simply by the color of the hat, since they do not always follow the old traditions.

dukkha दुक्ख Sorrow and pain. In the Four Noble Truths of Buddhism, dukkha is recognized as being omnipresent in the world. The desire to eliminate sorrow and pain is what moves humans forward on the spiritual path.

Dzyan (Tib.)   Equivalent to Sanskrit dhyāna and Japanese Zen. Wisdom, and more specifically, Divine Wisdom. The Book of Dzyan, which is the basis of The Secret Doctrine, is thus a book of wisdom or divine knowledge. It is only part of a series of texts known as Kiu-Te.

ego (L.)   Self, or self-identity. The self in the concept of self vs. not-self. In many esoteric books, ego or Ego is used to denote the Higher Self, the more permanent part of a human's existence. In this book it is used as a synonym for the personality or lower self, that with which the average person identifies when he thinks of himself.

egoism   Identification with the self, selfishness. Fixation on personal needs and desires as opposed to being attuned to the needs of others.

elementals   Spirits of the elements. They are associated with earth (gnomes), air (sylphs), fire (salamanders) and water (undines). When employed in the work of trained initiates, they can be used for great good, but they can also be used by black magicians to produce evil, and unwitting psychics often fall under the spell or glamor of these elementals, sometimes with disastrous results. They are recognized by almost every culture, and we find them under such names as peris, devas, djinns, genies, satyrs, elves, fairies, trolls, brownies, pixies, leprechauns, little people, goblins, banshees and spooks.

elementaries   Not to be confused with elementals, this term most often applies to the cast-off remnants of what were the astral and lower mental vehicles of an individual after moving beyond kāma-loka. These vehicles slowly disintegrate, just as the physical body does. They retain an imperfect memory of the individual who was once attached to them, and mediums frequently mistake them for deceased individuals. This is the reason "spirit" communications rarely have much substance to them. Elementaries are sometimes referred to as shells or shades.

Eleusinian Mysteries   Of the mystery schools in ancient times, this was considered one of the greatest. The origins of this school are believed to be from approximately 1500 BC. Secrecy was of utmost importance then as it is now. Eleusina is a town about 18 km from Athens.

eon or **aeon** (Gr.)   It originally meant "life" and later a "lifetime." Later still it was used to indicate an age, a very long period of time, an eternity. It is related to the Sanskrit word kalpa and the Hebrew word olam.

esoteric (Gr.)   Hidden, concealed, secret, teachings which are reserved for the inner group of pupils, the initiates.

Essenes   From the Hebrew Asa, a healer. A mysterious Jewish sect which lived near the Dead Sea. The Essenes followed many Buddhist ideas and practices. It is thought that they were the original Christians, or followers of Jesus. Members were considered part of a large family, and the use of the title "brother" in the early Christian Church comes from the Essenes.

eternity   This word is used to mean many different things. One usage is to indicate infinity, or the fact that there is no beginning or end to the process we call life. It also can refer to realms of existence where time has no meaning. Certainly there are phases of the life process that last for extremely long periods of time. Both the term eon and eternity can be used to indicate these periods. Thus, we see references to something that endures for "seven eternities."

ether   The term has been used in many different ways, but primarily indicates a pervading network or medium of fine, subtle matter. In this book it is used specifically to denote the four higher subplanes of the physical realm. They cannot be detected by the average person, but many people who are sensitive can feel, see or hear vibrations on these levels. It is the substance through which telepathy, while in a physical body, is possible. Etheric is the adjective for that which pertains to this realm of existence.

evolution   The continual growth which occurs according to a Divine Plan. Although various experiments and changes occur during the evolutionary process, the overall methods and final goal are known from the beginning. Evolution occurs not just in physical forms, but more importantly, in enlightenment or the expansion of consciousness. The ever-changing physical bodies are simply vehicles that permit growth in consciousness to occur.

fakir (Arab.)   In India, an Islamic ascetic, somewhat equivalent to a yogi. In general it means someone who has developed one or more siddhis through certain practices.

fire   In esoteric terms, it denotes the One Life. The sun is the outward symbol of living fire. Fire and electricity, in their various forms, are responsible for life as we know it.

fohat (Tib.)   The male or active potency of Śakti, the female reproductive power in nature. It is the essence of cosmic electricity. Fohat is the universal propelling Vital Force.

Ganesh or **Ganesha** गणेश   The son of Śiva, Ganesh is of human form with the head of an elephant, and is considered the God of Wisdom. He is the same as the Egyptian Thoth-Hermes and Anubis.

Gaṅgā गङ्गा The Ganges, a most sacred river in India. It is considered good karma to die on the banks of the river at Varanasi.

Gāyatrī गायत्री Also called Sāvitrī सावित्री, it is a sacred mantra in veneration of the sun as representative of the Solar Logos. One phrase can be translated as, "We meditate upon the Divine Light of that adorable Sun of Spiritual Consciousness. May it stimulate our power of spiritual perception." It is often chanted each morning and evening.

glamor or **glamour** A state of illusion or māyā which is the bane of the spiritual disciple. Being subject to glamor is similar to being under a spell or enchantment. The state of glamor exists entirely on the astral plane and is the lure which entraps human egos. In Greek mythology it is represented by the song of the sirens. The illusion is a result of the combination of human emotions over hundreds of thousands of years. It requires great effort to rise above this realm of glamor and illusion. No one can see clearly until he rids himself of ego and glamor.

Gnosis (Gr.) Knowledge. A school of esoteric religious philosophy which existed prior to the advent of the Christian era and continued for the first few centuries of that era. Gnostics were forced underground when the authority-based Christian Church gained power and decided to eradicate all schools of religious philosophy it considered heretical. It is the equivalent of gupta vidyā. The knowledge was only imparted to initiates of the Sacred Mysteries.

Gnostics (Gr.) The practitioners of Gnosticism who flourished during the first three centuries of the Christian era. Prominent among them were Simon Magus and Valentinus.

guṇa गुण A quality or attribute. Triguṇa त्रिगुण is a term that includes three specific qualities: rajas (creation or activity), sattva (goodness or essence), and tamas (inertia or decay).

gupta vidyā गुप्त विद्या Esoteric or secret science. Knowledge of a spiritual nature which is imparted only to those who have undergone a purification process and are entitled by their efforts to be taught the Secret Doctrine.

guru गुरु A spiritual teacher.

hatha yoga हठ योग A school of yoga based on poses or postures (āsanas) and breathing exercises (prāṇā-yāma). Swatmarama, a Hindu sage of the 15th century, is considered the founder of hatha yoga, a preparation for higher forms of yoga, including rāja yoga. Hatha is a Sanskrit term which means persistence or forced.

Hermes Trismegistus (Gr.) Trismegistus means thrice great. A mythical Egyptian personage after whom the Hermetic philosophy is named. The same as the Egyptian god Thoth. Hermes was considered the God of Wisdom in ancient Greece.

hierophant From the Greek hierophantes, one who explains sacred things, the chief of the initiates. In Attica, it was the chief priest of the Eleusinian Mysteries. The title is applied to the highest Adepts, those who teach the Mysteries to their pupils.

Higher Self The term generally is applied to the Divine Triad—ātma-buddhi-manas—but it sometimes refers only to ātma. The Higher Self is so called to differentiate from the lower self or personality, composed of the physical body, astral-emotional vehicle, and lower mental vehicle.

Holy of Holies The inner sanctum of many temples from antiquity forward. It was a feature of Assyrian, Egyptian and Hindu temples. Only the highest priests and initiates were normally permitted entry.

Horus (Egypt.)   The last in the line of divine kings in Egypt, he was said to be the son of Osiris and Isis. He was especially revered in the form of an infant at the time of the winter solstice.

hylozoism   The doctrine, especially among certain Greek philosophers, that all matter contains life. According to one teacher, "All forms are composed of many forms, and all forms—aggregate or single in nature—are the expression of an indwelling or ensouling life. The fusion of life with living substance produces another aspect of expression: that of consciousness."

Hypatia   A Neo-Platonist, she lived in Alexandria in the 5th century of the Christian era and was famous for her occult knowledge. The Christian Church considered her dangerous because of her renown, and she was murdered by followers of Theophilos, Bishop of Alexandria, and his nephew Cyril. With her death ended the Neo-Platonic School.

illuminati (Lat.)   Initiated Adepts, those who are "enlightened."

initiate   In ancient times, the term denoted those who had passed certain steps in the process of advancement under the tutelage of the Hierophants and high priests of the temples. Today initiation is conferred by the Hierarchy. Because it is the soul that is initiated and not the personality, it is possible to have passed some of the lower initiations with no recollection in the physical brain. They may also have been passed in a previous lifetime.

involution   The act of enfolding or entangling. Involvement. Although the word evolution covers the entire process of the descent of Spirit into matter and its eventual return to the Source, the process is sometimes divided into two phases, with involution describing the increasing densification and "entanglement" during the descent, and evolution reserved for describing the return journey.

Isis   Issa, or Isis, was the Egyptian virgin-mother goddess, the personification of nature. She is the female reflection of Osiris and is often depicted as the mother of Horus. The legend of a virgin-mother is found in the stories of many world teachers.

jāgrat जाग्रत्   The waking state. Generally considered a normal state of consciousness.

jīva जीव   Life force. That which vivifies a form and which, when it is withdrawn, results in death. Jīva is the universal principle, and prāṇa is the personal equivalent.

jñāna yoga ज्ञान योग   Jñāna yoga teaches that there are four means to gain enlightenment or escape the cycle of birth and death based on knowledge—viveka (discernment), vairagya (non-attachment), shatsampatti (development of six virtues to control the lower nature) and mumukshutva (an intense longing for liberation).

Kabbalah or **Kabala**   The esoteric wisdom of the Hebrew rabbis of the middle ages, derived from more ancient teachings concerning cosmogony and theology which were derived at the time of the captivity of the Jews in Babylon. All teachings of an esoteric nature are termed Kabbalistic.

Kālī काली   From kāla, which means black. A term for Parvati, the consort of Śiva, and synonymous with darkness and wickedness. Kālī is considered the goddess of time and change.

kali yuga कलियुग   The age of vice or darkness. Different sources ascribe different time periods to the various ages. It is said in some to last 432,000 years. It began, according to one source, at midnight on February 18, 3102 BC and the first cycle ended about 1897.

kalpa कल्प A major period of time in cosmic evolution, it represents a Day and Night of Brahmā or one thousand mahāyugas. According to some sources, it lasts 4.32 billion years, although this figure has esoteric significance and does not necessarily equate to the current length of an earth year.

kāma काम Desire in its baser forms such as lust, greed, envy, gluttony and inordinate pride. It is often associated with Māra, the tempter, who tries to strengthen our animal nature.

kāma-loka कामलोक A state of being after death where the coarsest of human emotions and desires must be resolved. It can last from a few minutes in the case of very pure individuals to several decades for those who did not subdue their baser desires while still alive. It is the Hades of the ancient Greeks and the Amenti of the Egyptians, the land of silent shadows.

kāma-manas काममनस् The lower level of mind given impetus by the emotions. Most humans operate in the realm of kāma-manas, but the Adepts and higher initiates operate through Buddhi-manas, in which case emotion is never a motivating factor.

karma कर्म Action. Metaphysically, the term refers to the law of cause and effect and is not a system of rewards and punishment, as often thought. It is the natural law which unerringly guides all sentient creatures along the path of spiritual evolution. Those actions which are selfish in nature and contrary to natural law cause pain and suffering, while those in alignment with it result in indescribable bliss. It cannot be eradicated by an outside source, thus contradicting the idea of vicarious atonement. The karma generated during a lifetime carries over through the intermediary of the causal body until it is finally resolved through proper actions in a future lifetime.

karma yoga कर्म योग The yoga of action, of being fully present in the now in every action performed. It often includes acts of charity and physical help for others. It is the Right Action of the Buddhists.

Krishna or **Kṛṣṇa** कृष्ण A highly revered divine incarnation of Vishnu, Krishna is the most popular of Hindu gods. The story of his conception, birth and childhood are similar to the conception, birth and childhood of Jesus in the New Testament.

kriyāśakti क्रियाशक्ति The power of thought in action, one of the seven forces of nature. The creative power or siddhi of an Adept, it is the ability to perform true magic.

kuṇḍalinī śakti कुण्डलिनी शक्ति The serpent power, it lies coiled at the base of the spine and is the life force which makes a body a living form. The awakening of kuṇḍalinī power through meditation and breathing exercises can result in seership for those who are spiritually ready, but can result in insanity or death if awakened prematurely.

kuṇḍalinī yoga कुण्डलिनी योग The practices used to awaken the kuṇḍalinī energy. This form of yoga should only be done under the guidance of a highly advanced spiritual guru who is himself a seer. Much of what is called kuṇḍalinī yoga in hatha yoga classes is not true kuṇḍalinī yoga.

lama (Tib.) Properly used, it is a title that applies only to the priests of the highest levels in Tibetan Buddhism. Unfortunately, many "lamas" in Tibet today are little more than fortune tellers of a distinctly inferior grade.

laya लय That point where substance becomes homogeneous and is unable to differentiate. See pralaya.

laya yoga लय योग A school of yoga that focuses on the chakras. Kuṇḍalinī yoga is a form of laya yoga.

Lemuria A term first used by biologists, but adopted by esotericists as the name of a continent which preceded Atlantis. Its inhabitants, referred to as Lemurians, were still descending into physical matter in the earlier stages of its development, and only later acquired completely physical bodies, began developing the use of mind and intellect, and invented languages for communication. Prior to that point, telepathy was the means used for communicating ideas.

Lévi, Eliphas A well-known Kabbalist, his Christian name was Alphonse Louis Constant. He was an Abbé, a type of clergyman in the French Catholic Church, and was a member of the Brothers of Light, an esoteric fraternity. He wrote five books that are well known: *Dogme et rituel de la haute magie* (1856), *Histoire de la magie* (1860), *La clef des grands mystères* (1861), *Legendes et symbols* (1862) and *La science des esprits* (1865). The Catholic Church defrocked him when he became famous as a Kabbalist.

Lha (Tib.) Highly evolved beings. Thus, Lhasa is the abode of Lha.

liṅga śarīram लिङ्ग शरीरम् The astral-emotional vehicle used during a person's physical incarnation. After death, it disintegrates over time, and a new one is built for the next incarnation, just as a new physical body is created.

liṅgam लिङ्गंम् A symbol of the male polarity of the creative force.

Logos (Gr.) The "Word" or "Verbum" as used in the Bible in its metaphysical sense, or "Vāch" in Sanskrit.

It indicates the creative power used to create planets and solar systems and refers to the members of the Spiritual Hierarchy in charge of them.

loka लोक A realm or circumscribed place. The term is used to indicate different realms of consciousness, for example—kāma-loka. The Latin word locus, from which we derive location in English and lugar in Spanish, comes from this Sanskrit word.

lotus *Nelumbo nucifera* is a sacred flower in Egypt and India. It symbolizes our quest for enlightenment. Starting in the dark depths of mud in the bottom of a murky body of water, the seed sends forth a stalk as high as necessary to break through the surface and bloom in order to receive the rays from the sun which shine down upon it. Esoterically, our solar system is depicted as a twelve-petalled lotus.

lower quaternary The personality, composed of the physical body, life force in the form of prāṇa, the astral-emotional vehicle, and the lower mental vehicle. It is the lower reflection of the Spiritual Triad, ātma-buddhi-manas.

Lucifer (L.) The light-bearer, often applied to Venus in its role of the morning star. Previous to the works of John Milton, it was never used as a name for the devil. It is unfortunate that his misuse of the term demeaned what was previously a beautiful symbol.

maga मग The priests of the sun mentioned in Vishnu Purana. They later became the magi of Chaldea and Babylonia.

magi (L.) The root of our word magician, they were the priests of the Fire God. The legend of the three magi who visited the Christ child comes from the idea that they were highly advanced men in metaphysical knowledge, including astrology.

magic The use of natural forces in a creative act, either for the benefit of mankind in white magic, or for selfish reasons without regard to its effect on others, black magic. The safest course of action is not to try to develop these powers, but to work instead on your own character development. As one grows in understanding, powers will be acquired as they become necessary in working with the Spiritual Hierarchy.

magician   The term has come to mean one who uses devices, illusion and sleight of hand to imitate what can actually be accomplished by a true magician. The real magician never uses his powers to amaze or impress people.

Mahābhārata महाभारत   The great war. An epic Hindu poem which includes both the Ramayana and the Bhagavad Gītā.

Mahāchohan (Tib.)   The head of a spiritual brotherhood of Adepts. Specifically, the chief of the trans-Himalayan brotherhood.

Mahātma महात्म   "Great soul." A highly advanced Adept. Mahātmas are enlightened beings who have gained mastery over the lower realms and who have knowledge and powers far beyond that of average humanity.

Maitreya Buddha मैत्रेय बुद्ध   A high ranking member of the Spiritual Hierarchy. Maitreya is the World Teacher who, together with several Adepts, is responsible for disseminating new teachings as humanity reaches new levels of consciousness. He holds the rank of a Bodhisattva.

manas मनस्   Mind, the faculty which distinguishes man from animals. The word man comes from manas. All beings at or above the level of human consciousness are able to use a form of mind to accomplish desires or wishes. Kāma-manas is use of the mind to realize personal, selfish desires. Buddhi-manas is use of the higher aspect of mind for the good of all, with no regard for personal desires.

mantra मन्त्र   A chant, or prayer, an affirmation capable of creating transformation. The creation of Sanskrit mantras is both an art and a science. Some mantras are extremely powerful, such as the Gāyatrī.

Mantra Shāstra मन्त्र शास्त्र   The Brahmanical texts which contain information on creating mantras.

manvantara मन्वन्तर   Literally, the period of time between two Manus. It is a period of active manifestation, followed by pralaya, a rest period. When a new period of activity commences, a new Manu is in charge. Fourteen Manus and their respective manvantaras make a kalpa, an eon, or a Day and Night of Brahma. The current Manu is Vaivasvata Manu.

Māra मार   The demon who tried to seduce Gautama Buddha by tempting him with visions of beautiful women. He is the embodiment of forces which try to keep us ensnared as long as possible in the underworld, enticing us by means of our earthly desires through use of enchantment or glamor so we are unable to see clearly.

māyā माया   Illusion. It is the universal power which makes possible phenomenal existence. Only the Absolute is real. All else is illusion or māyā, but this illusion gives us the chance to gain experience.

māyāvirūpa मायाविरूप   From māyā (illusion) and rūpa (form or body). A temporary body or vehicle created by advanced beings in order to communicate with someone unable to communicate with them at their own higher level of consciousness. It is used only as long as necessary to accomplish the objective. Since the form must be held together by force of the will, it disintegrates immediately when the force is removed. It may be a complete human form or only part of a form.

metamorphosis   The successive use of different grades of forms to make possible the growth of consciousness, which is the purpose of life. The concept is embodied in the Kabbalist maxim "A stone becomes a plant, a plant an animal, an animal a man, a man a spirit, and a spirit a god."

metempsychosis (Gr.)   This term was previously used for what is now called reincarnation. For a time in the 19th century, the term reincarnation referred only to cases where the soul used the same astral and lower mental vehicles of the previous lifetime to create a new personality. This situation is rare and generally applies only in the death of a young child or one who never progressed mentally beyond the stage of childhood. This can only happen when the reincarnation is almost immediate, and it occurs because the person never reached the age of accountability, which normally occurs around seven or eight years old. In normal reincarnation, both the astral and lower mental vehicles are newly created, just as the physical body is. Today the terms metempsychosis and reincarnation are used interchangeably, making some texts of the 19th century somewhat confusing.

moksha or **mokṣa** मोक्ष   To release or let go. The end of the cycle of reincarnation.

monad (Gr.)   One, or unity. In esoteric texts it is often used to denote the Divine Triad, ātma-buddhi-manas, or the Duad, ātma-buddhi. The Monad is for an Adept what the soul is for a human being. It is that part of our being which inspires us to reach ever higher in our quest for greater enlightenment.

mudrā मुद्रा   A system of mystical symbols made with the hands. They are in imitation of ancient Sanskrit letters having magical powers. They were later misused by Tantrikas for purposes of black magic.

mukti मुक्ति To release or let go. The practice of non-attachment. It results in liberation from the lower realms, and one who practices it is a candidate for moksha, freedom from the cycle of death and rebirth.

mūlaprakṛti मूलप्रकृति The Parabrahmic root, the abstract feminine principle or undifferentiated matter. The very earliest phases of a new manvantara.

mumukṣutva मुमुक्षुत्व Intense desire for liberation from the cycle of death and rebirth. One of the four means to salvation of jnāna yoga.

Mysteries Concepts often taught by theatrical and other means to select students regarding the origin of the universe, the nature of human spirit, the fall into matter, and the plan of redemption through the purifying power of spiritual practices. The Sacred Mysteries were enacted in the ancient temples by the initiated Hierophants. The same methods are still used for instruction of neophytes, but not in the physical realm. Instead, they take place on the higher levels of the mental plane, the realm of the soul.

nāga नाग A serpent. Nāga is often a symbol of wisdom.

nature spirit See elementals.

Neo-Platonism An eclectic school of philosophy founded by Ammonius Saccas in Alexandria in the early Christian era. Its aim was to reconcile the teachings of Plato and Aristotle with esoteric oriental philosphy. Based on pure spiritual philosophy, metaphysics and mysticism, it was an effort to bring higher understanding to a world steeped in superstition and blind faith. The death of Hypatia at the hands of Christian fanatics ended the Neoplatonic movement.

Nirmāṇakāya निर्माणकाय When one reaches the highest level of enlightenment proposed for our current humanity, he has become a Buddha and is entitled to take the Dharmakāya vesture, entering a state of eternal bliss if he so chooses. If he does, he is separated forever from the world of form and suffering. If he chooses the Nirmānakāya vesture, he embarks on a mission of self-sacrifice to help his fellow men in their own struggle for enlightenment. It involves a supreme act of compassion.

nirvāṇa निर्वाण The realm of those Buddhas who chose the Dharmakāya vesture, a state of indescribable bliss unmarred by pain or suffering of any kind.

nous (Gr.) A term used by Plato for the Higher Self or soul. In the more common usage, it is simply mind or intellect. See also psyche.

Obeah A sect of sorcerers in Africa and parts of the Caribbean. Their practices are a low form of magic, a remnant of Atlantean times.

occult sciences The study of the hidden side of nature in all realms—physical, astral, mental and spiritual. It includes Hermetic philosophy, Kabbalah, yoga, esoteric Buddhist teachings, and the esoteric traditions of the Brahmins. For ages these teachings have remained hidden from the outside world. Only in recent times has the veil been slightly lifted.

od (Gr.) A term used during the mid-nineteenth century to describe a force which can be manipulated. It is involved in magnetism, chemical activity, electricity, heat and light. It is sometimes referred to as "odic" or "odylic" force. The term is seldom encountered today.

Om or **Aum** ॐ or ओम् The Sacred Word in India. It is at the same time an invocation, a benediction, an affirmation and a promise. The symbol ॐ is called praṇava.

Orpheus   A great teacher in Greek mythology. Some esoteric texts suggest he was Arjuna, the son of Indra and disciple of Kṛṣṇa. The very name Orpheus means "tawny," someone with a dark skin. He was considered the founder of the Orphic Mysteries.

Osiris   The greatest god of ancient Egypt, he was the son of Geb, symbol of celestial fire, and of Nut, symbol of primordial matter and infinite space. He is the same as Ahura Mazda of the Parsis. According to one legend, he was born at Mount Sinai and was murdered by his brother Set, or Typhon, at the age of twenty-eight. The four principal aspects of Osiris are light (spirit), mind (intellect), lunar light (psychic nature) and physical form. He thus represents the dual nature of man, a combination of spiritual and material. The legend says that three days after he was buried he rose again and ascended into heaven.

pagan   Originally, the term meant a country-dweller, just as the word heathen was applied to someone living on the heaths. Many pagans possessed astral sight and worshipped the indwelling life in all forms—mineral, plant, animal and human. As the Christian Church gained power, they were declared idolaters, and an effort was made to crush their traditional beliefs, absorbing pagans into the Church by creating Christian festivals to replace existing pagan festivals. We see this specifically in the Christmas and Easter celebrations.

Pāli   A classical language of India which preceded the more refined Sanskrit. The early Buddhist scriptures were written in Pāli.

Parabrahm or **Parabrahman** परब्रह्मन् "Beyond Brahm." The Absolute, that about which nothing can be said.

Pāramitā पारमिता Variously listed as either six or ten virtues whose cultivation leads to enlightenment, according to Buddhist philosophy. The longer list includes generosity, morality, renunciation, wisdom, diligent effort, patience, honesty, determination, loving-kindness, and equanimity.

Patañjali पतञ्जलि   The founder of rāja yoga, or yoga philosophy. All other schools of yoga are derived from his yoga sutras. Some orientalists say he lived about 200 BC, but esotericists claim he lived about 500 years earlier.

personality   That which most humans identify as the self. It is composed of the physical vehicle, astral-emotional vehicle and the vehicle of the lower mental realm. For the average individual, no part of the personality reincarnates, all vehicles being newly created for each incarnation. It is the primary reason we do not remember previous lifetimes, since the soul ignores the details of the life of the personality. Nor would it help to remember details of previous lives, as we would resume former resentments and negative thinking. A new set of vehicles gives us a chance to make a new start, weighed down only by the karma of previous lifetimes, which cannot be discarded.

phenomenon (Gr.)   In mysticism, the term generally refers to something which appears because of unseen causes. Once we understand the cause and result relationship, it is called science. Until then, it seems to be magic, or a "miracle." Nothing can ever occur that contradicts the laws of nature. Those who know how to work with them can produce phenomena that seem miraculous to the uninitiated.

pisācha or **piśāca** पिशाच   Goblin, or spook. Pisāchas are the shells or elementaries of deceased individuals who have passed through kāma-loka. When animated through the power of mediums or nature spirits, these shells can exhibit many characteristics of the person, but the connection with the Higher Self has been withdrawn, and it is for this reason they seem more like actors than living individuals.

Pistis Sophia An important Gnostic text from as early as the second century AD. It was re-discovered in 1773.

pitṛis पितृ Spiritual ancestors of mankind.

plane As used in esoteric texts, it denotes a specific range of consciousness. Each plane includes vibrations of a particular nature, but with many variations in characteristics. Each plane has seven subplanes. The lower three of the physical realm are our well-known divisions of solid, liquid and gas, and the four higher contain matter of an etheric nature. Just as we see some overlap between adjoining physical subplanes, so is there some overlap on all levels, between planes as well as subplanes. As we grow in consciousness, we become more aware of the extent of these planes.

Planetary Spirits or **Planetary Logoi** The spiritual rulers or governors of planets. Just as our own earth has a Spiritual Hierarchy affiliated with it, so does every other planet on which evolution is taking place. Relatively few planets have physical evolution occurring on them as we know it, but many planets have evolutionary schemes on other levels of consciousness. The Planetary Spirits correspond to the Christian Archangels. All have passed long ago a stage equivalent to our own human evolution. Our earth is far too young to have produced any Planetary Spirits from its own humanity. Thus, our Planetary Logos, Sanāt Kumāra, and his assistants came to us from other evolutionary systems. The Lord of the World, which is one of the titles of our Planetary Logos, is the closest we have to a "personal god," though he does not fulfill many of the qualifications generally ascribed to such a being. Most conceptions of a personal god are an amalgamation of traits of the Absolute, various members of the Spiritual Hierarchy, and even of elementals.

Plato Approximately 424 BC – 348 BC. An initiate of the Ancient Mysteries, he is considered one of the greatest Greek philosophers. He was a student of Socrates and the teacher of Aristotle.

Popol Vuh The sacred books of the Quiché (K'iche) in Guatemala. During the Spanish occupation of Central America, nearly all Mayan records were destroyed, but the legends had also been passed down by oral tradition. In 1558 a native wrote them down in Quiché transliterated in Latin characters. According to the creation story in part one, animals were created first and then men. The first race of humans was made of earth and mud, but they dissolved. The second race was made of wood but had neither souls nor minds. It also includes the story of a great flood that covered the earth.

Porphyry One of the greatest of the Neo-Platonist philosophers, he followed the precepts of rāja yoga. He was born in Tyre about 234 AD and died about 305 AD. "Do not defile the divinity," he said, "with the vain imaginings of men; you will not injure that which is forever blessed, but you will blind yourself to the perception of the greatest and most vital truths." (*Ad Marcellam*) "If we would be free from the assaults of evil spirits, we must keep ourselves clear of those things over which evil spirits have power, for they attack not the pure soul, which has no affinity with them." (*De abstinentia ab esu animalium*) The Church Fathers railed against Porphyry and his views, which they considered heretical. Not only did he preach purity of life but lived it as well, so they perhaps thought it best to leave him alone.

Poseidonis (Gr.)   The last remnant of the once great continent of Atlantis, it sank in 9,564 BC according to esoteric sources.

prakriti or **prakṛti** प्रकृति   Nature, or matter, in contrast to puruṣa, Spirit. Together, puruṣa and prakṛti form the earliest phase of every manvantara. They are "two primeval aspects of the One Unknown Deity," according to *The Secret Doctrine.*

pralaya प्रलय   A period of inactivity or obscuration, whether planetary or cosmic. It is the opposite of a manvantara. As a manvantara corresponds to a person's waking period of activity, so pralaya corresponds to the period of rest and sleep at night.

prāṇa प्राण   The life principle, or breath of life, that which imparts "life" to a form. It is a manifestation of fohat on a more individual level. It is comparable to the Chinese qi or chi.

praṇava प्रणव   The name of the symbol used for Om ॐ.

prāṇāyāma प्राणायाम   Yoga breathing exercises. They are much more powerful than one might think, and they should be practiced only under the supervision of a competent teacher.

psyche   The lower mind, and more specifically, kāma-manas, as opposed to nous, or buddhi-manas.

psychic   Pertaining to astral clairvoyance and mediumship. Psychic phenomena are of the astral-emotional realm. Those who are trained in techniques of perceiving vibrations on higher planes of consciousness while still in the physical are often called seers.

psychology   The science of the human mind and personality. It has made great strides in the past century. Esoteric studies have always emphasized the need to understand human psychology, and through this understanding to gain mastery over the lower nature. This allows the Higher Self to use the personality as an instrument for helping the spiritual evolution of the world. This is an aspect that will gain more momentum in exoteric psychology in the coming decades.

psychometry (Gr.) A form of extra-sensory perception which uses contact with a physical object and its energy field to see things that have affected the object.

pūjā पूजा Worship of, or offerings to, a divine being or revered person. Adoration.

puruṣa पुरुष The Spirit which pervades the universe. The primordial spiritual aspect of first manifestation, as opposed to prakṛti. The "Spiritual Self."

Pythagoras A famous Greek philosopher, he was born at Samos, a Greek island in the Aegean Sea, around 570 BC. He traveled extensively, and his teachings carry the imprint of his vast experience with various cultures. He studied with Brahmins in India and learned astrology and astronomy in Chaldea and Egypt. He eventually settled at Crotona, a Greek colony in southern Italy, where he established a group known as the Pythagorean Brotherhood, a secret society devoted to the study of mathematics. Both Rosicrucianism and Freemasonry claim origins in the Pythagorean Brotherhood. Pythagoras was one of the leading experts in geometry of his time. He is responsible for the word philosopher, composed of two Greek words meaning lover of wisdom. Not only was he proficient in physical sciences, but in occult sciences as well. He taught reincarnation and studied the mathematical properties of music. He died about 495 BC.

rabbi (Heb.) Originally, a master or teacher of the Sacred Mysteries. Later, every male member of the tribe of Levi was considered a rabbi.

rāja राज A prince or king. Mahārāja महाराज denotes one of great standing.

rāja yoga राज योग The system of developing contact with the soul and of seership through the practice of meditation and thought control, as taught by Patañjali in the yoga sūtras.

rajas रजस् One of the three guṇas. It is responsible for action, energy and preservation.

reincarnation Originally, it had a more limited meaning (see metempsychosis), but today means the creation of a series of personalities which have a life experience in the physical world. The essence only of each lifetime is retained by the Higher Self and is the basis, along with all residual karma, for the next incarnation. The successive putting on of flesh by the soul was a universal belief among many ancient cultures.

Rig Veda or **Ṛg Veda** ऋग्वेद A collection of the ancient sacred Vedic Sanskrit hymns. It is primary among the four Vedas.

ring-pass-not A curious term which means a defined field of action, not just physically, but on higher planes as well. The human body, including its aura, is the ring-pass-not for an individual during incarnation, and the corresponding ovoid field of energy is the ring-pass-not when out of incarnation or absent from the sleeping physical body. The ring-pass-not for a solar system includes not only the physical central sun and its planets, but also the extended field of vibrations on higher planes of consciousness.

rūpa रूप Body or form, the opposite of arūpa. It includes not just physical forms, but also those on the astral and lower mental levels of being.

salamander The Rosicrucian name for the elementals of fire. The name in Sanskrit is very similar, salamandala सलमण्डल.

salvation Attainment of the maximum level of consciousness expected of humanity. One who is saved is liberated from the cycle of death and rebirth and will reincarnate only if he chooses to return to help his fellow men.

sannyāsī or **samnyāsin** संन्यासिन् One who has renounced everything worldly and dedicated himself to meditation and contemplation. In previous times, he would have retreated in solitude to the jungle or a mountain top, but the modern sannyāsin is expected to be "in the world but not of the world."

samādhi समाधि A state of absolute bliss. Porphyry spoke of it as, "sublime ecstasy, in which state divine things and the mysteries of Nature are revealed to us." It is the goal of rāja yoga, and its attainment is the mark of one who has conquered the lower nature.

Sanāt Kumāra सनात् कुमार The principal of the seven Kumāras, regents of our planet and one of the titles of the Lord of the World, our Planetary Logos.

saṅgha or **saṃgha** सङ्घ A community or association of Buddhist monks or nuns. It can also mean a group of lay followers who meet for meditation or spiritual teachings.

Śaṅkarācārya शङ्कराचार्य A great religious reformer in India. He was born in 788 AD and is regarded as an incarnation of Śiva by Adwaitees.

Sanskrit or **Saṃskṛtam** संस्कृतम् A classical language of India, originally used only by initiated Brahmins. It was a mystery language because of the secrecy surrounding it.

Santería (Sp.)   A system of beliefs brought to the New World by slaves imported to work the sugar plantations in the Caribbean. Their practices include entering a trance condition to communicate with dead ancestors and deities, animal sacrifice, and ceremonial trance-inducing drumming.

Sat सत्   The ineffable word. The Absolute, that about which nothing can be said. It is incomprehensible, indefinable, indescribable, inconceivable and indivisible. Be-ness is a term coined to suggest its *potential* for being, but even this is not accurate.

sattva सत्त्व   The essence, or innate nature, of something. It is the most rarified of the three guṇas.

Secret Doctrine   The name generally given to ancient esoteric writings. The Ancient Wisdom.

seer   One who sees through a spiritual inner vision in realms higher than the astral and lower mental planes. This ability comes at the cost of several lifetimes of concerted effort and is in contradistinction to lower psychism, or astral clairvoyance.

Self   With a capital S, it denotes the Higher Self, or soul, whose existence is on the higher levels of the mental plane. With a lowercase s, it is the lower self, the personality, composed of a physical, an astral-emotional, and a lower mental vehicle.

Senzar   The secret sacerdotal language known only to initiated Adepts of the world. The Stanzas of Dzyan were written in Senzar.

Shaddai or **El Shaddai** (Heb.)   A name of the Supreme Hebrew Deity. It is found in the books of Genesis, Exodus, Numbers, Ruth and Job, and is usually translated God Almighty.

shade or **shell**   Both are terms for the astral remains of a deceased person who has moved on in the afterlife experience. Shells and shades have a slight difference in components, but both denote the cast-off vehicles which fade out and disintegrate over a period of time. They are the same as pisāchas.

shakti or **śakti** शक्ति The dynamic feminine creative forces which move through the entire universe. See also kuṇḍalinī śakti.

shatsampatti षट्संपत्ति The development of six virtues in jñāna yoga, consisting of: sama (control of the mind), dama (control of the senses), uparati (renunciation of activities that are not duties), titiksha (forbearance), śraddhā (faith), and samadhāna (perfect concentration).

siddhi सिद्धि A power or special skill developed by one who engages in certain yoga practices. The true yogi never displays his powers in order to impress or entertain others.

sin Any action which is contrary to the natural flow of spiritual evolution, but it also takes into account one's present level of consciousness. Thus, for the more enlightened individual, there are more actions considered sinful than for one who has less experience in the human kingdom. "From him to whom much has been given, much is required."

skandha स्कन्ध Literally, a "bundle" or group of five desires for: form, sensation, perception, mental processes, and consciousness. After death, once all astral-mental energy is discharged in kāma-loka and all higher mental energy in devachan, these desires re-assert themselves and cause an individual to re-incarnate. They should not be confused with the karma that is taken up again at the beginning of a new incarnation.

śloka श्लोक A classical Sanskrit meter formed of thirty-two syllables, either in four lines of eight or two lines of sixteen syllables.

Solomon's Seal or **Star of David**   The ancient symbol of double interlaced triangles is also used in India, where it is the "Sign of Vishnu." The upward pointing triangle signifies Spirit and divine fire, while the downward pointing triangle signifies matter, the female principle. The interlaced triangles are an apt symbol of involution and evolution, the path of the Prodigal Son.

soma सोम   A name for the moon. Also a drink made from the sacred soma plant and used in temples for trance purposes.

sophia (Gr.)   Wisdom, Universal Mind, the female Logos of the Gnostics.

soul   Nephesh of the Bible. In esoteric writings it is generally used as a synonym for the Higher Self or human soul. It is the individual spiritual self which encourages and entices the personality to grow in consciousness and wisdom until it has reached the level of the soul. At this time the soul ceases to exist, having accomplished its goal, and further spiritual development is under the guidance of the Monad.

Spirit   The term has been used in so many contexts that it is bewildering to the student. In this book its use is reserved for that which is closer to the Absolute as opposed to farther away. It is that which is ever higher in nature and toward which we aspire to attain.

spiritual   That which guides one toward a greater degree of enlightenment or consciousness. That which is attuned to the natural law of the evolution of spirit.

Spiritual Hierarchy   The brotherhood of advanced beings who oversee the evolution of our physical forms and consciousness. It includes higher initiates, Adepts, Chohans, Mahāchohans, Manus, Bodhisattvas, Buddhas, the Planetary Logos, and Archangels, among others.

spiritual triad See ātma-buddhi-manas.

Spiritualism In philosophy, it means that which is more spiritual as opposed to materialistic in nature. In the United States and Great Britain, the term has unfortunately come to mean communion with the spirits of the dead through mediumship. It is the necromancy of old and is best left alone, for it helps neither the living nor the dead. It can interfere with and delay a person's normal after-death process.

sthūla śarīra स्थूल शरीर The material physical body.

Sufism A mystical sect in Persia (modern day Iran). It claims to have the esoteric doctrine of true Islam and teaches respect and tolerance for all religions. There are four stages of initiation for Sufis, the fourth leading to a state of ecstasy or samādhi.

Sūryadeva सूर्यदेव The sun, worshipped as a god, the Solar Deity of the Vedas. The Son of Aditi (space), who is the mother of the gods, and is the husband of Sarijnā, spiritual consciousness. The physical sun we see is only a fraction of and incomprehensible symbol of the Solar Logos, the spiritual regent of our solar system.

sushupti or **suṣupti** सुषुप्ति Deep, dreamless sleep. Unconsciousness.

superstition A practice or belief which is not based on logical reason. Often, the belief is based on traditional thought or authoritative religious dogma. Students of New Age philosophy are just as prone to superstition as those who adopt more traditional beliefs.

sūtra सूत्र In Sanskrit it means a thread or filament, anything on which items can be strung. In philosophy it means a collection of aphorisms or teachings in the form of a manual.

svapna स्वप्न   Semi-consciousness. The state of consciousness during dreaming or when hypnotized.

svāstika स्वास्तिक   An ancient symbol of a fiery four-armed cross, it is found in numerous places in India and in esoteric organizations. When rotating counter-clockwise, it is symbolic of involution, and when rotating clockwise, of evolution. It is unfortunate that Hitler chose it as a symbol for his repressive and murderous regime; it was not previously used in that manner.

symbolism   The expression of an idea or concept in graphic form. Ancient writings did not have individual letters, but rather ideograms or pictographs, with one symbol representing a word or entire phrase. Chinese and other Asian languages descended from these ancient languages which used symbols in this manner.

talisman   From the Arabic word tilsam, "magic image," it is an object of stone, metal or wood imbued with specific energy by someone versed in esoteric knowledge for a specific purpose, often for protection or healing. Its greatest power, however, exists because of the faith of its possessor, which magnifies many times the original energy conveyed to it by its maker.

tamas तमस्   Darkness, ignorance, inertia, death. It is one of the three guṇas. A tamasic life is one marked by indolence, excuses, lack of ambition and complaining. It implies ignorance of the workings of the law of karma.

taṇhā (Pāli)   The thirst for life, or desire for sentient existence. Equivalent to skandha. The Buddha identifies taṇhā as the primary cause of pain and suffering.

Tantra तन्त्र   Mystical practices which work specifically with the female creative potency or śakti. In its lower forms, it becomes black magic involving sexual rites. The original Tantra practices were developed in medieval India and were spiritual in nature.

Tao The philosophy of the Chinese sage Lao-Tzu. The Chinese word means the Way or the Path. It is a metaphysical philosophy, one of the main objects being to become the Path. Many of the principles of the Taoist religion were later incorporated in Confucianism, Chán and Zen Buddhism, in which it is the natural order of the universe and the primordial essence of Nature. Tao also includes recognition of The Absolute.

Tathāgata तथागत A name for the Nirmāṇakāyas, often used as a reverential title for the Lord Buddha. Gautama Buddha often used the term when referring to himself. It means both one who has gone and one who has come, an appropriate term for one who, when faced with the choice of entering into eternal bliss or returning to help his fellow travelers, chose the latter course of action.

tattva तत्त्व Essence, or true state. It is generally used in referring to the essential nature of various deities or ideals.

tau See crux ansata.

thaumaturgy The working of wonders or "miracles." Another word for magic. "Divine work" in Greek.

theodicy The divine right or privilege of an omniscient, omnipresent, omnipotent and loving god to inflict pain and suffering on apparently innocent persons. The term is also used in the sense of being an apologist for Divinity.

Theosophy From the Greek theosophia, "Divine Wisdom." The basis of all world religions and philosophies. In practice, Theosophy is pure, divine ethics.

Titans (Gr.) In Greek mythology, they were giants of divine origin who made war against the gods and were overthrown by a race of younger gods. They represent early humans who were not yet completely physical in form.

trinity There are a number of trinities in ancient religions, including Brahmā-Vishnu-Śiva, and Osiris-Isis-Horus. These were trinities of father-mother-son. Athanasius, the Church Father who defined the Christian trinity as dogma, changed it slightly to Father-Son-Holy Ghost, but the Holy Ghost has a distinctly feminine aspect, and in Gnostic writings, Jesus addresses the Holy Ghost as his mother.

Tulku (Tibetan) In Tibetan Buddhism, this term applies to advanced spiritual leaders, lamas, who are able to determine the manner and circumstances of their next incarnation, which occurs very soon after death. The Dalai Lama and Panchen Lama are the two best known examples of this phenomenon, but there are approximately two thousand individuals to whom this applies.

turya तुर्य Super-consciousness. The consciousness experienced during deep meditation.

Universal Mind Intellect, or mind, exists on more than just the mental plane of consciousness. As we rise in consciousness, our existence is less and less individualized and becomes more of a group phenomenon.

Upanishads उपनिषद् A collection of sacred scriptures of Brahmanism. It is from the Upanishads, echoes of the primeval Wisdom Religion, that the Vedānta philosophy was developed. The number of accepted treatises comprising the Upanishads is about 150, treating such matters as the origins of the universe, the Absolute, the primeval and current relationship of Spirit and matter, universality of mind, and the nature of the human soul.

vāch वाच् The mystic personification of speech, the "Word" in the Gospel of St. John. In one sense it is the creative force, and in another the "power of the Holy Ghost" or "tongues of fire" that inspired the prophets.

vairāgya वैराग्य Indifference to pleasure or pain. Equanimity. It is an essential quality for spiritual growth and includes both non-reaction and non-attachment.

Vedas वेद The body of sacred texts in Hinduism

Vedānta वेदान्त The esoteric wisdom of the Upanishads. Vedānta was developed through the efforts of generations of sages into a philosophy which interprets the secret teachings contained in the Upanishads.

vidyā विद्या Knowledge, and more specifically, the occult sciences, gupta vidyā, or hidden knowledge.

Vishnu विष्णु The second person of the Hindu Trinity, from the Sanskrit root vish, to pervade. In the Rig Veda, Vishnu is not one of the higher gods, but in later scriptures he is accorded a higher status as the Preserver.

viveka विवेक Discernment. The ability to distinguish between what is real and what is unreal, between what is helpful to the aspirant and that which is not.

white magic See magic.

Will The first of all powers. In esoteric philosophy, Will is that which creates and governs the manifested universes during a manvantara, sometimes referred to as Divine Will. It is the property of all spiritual beings and manifests more strongly as they are freed from matter. Paracelsus taught that "determined will is the beginning of all magical operations." Sexual desire is its lowest form of manifestation, while a much higher manifestation of Will created solar systems and universes.

wisdom   The ability to extrapolate new concepts from current knowledge and, more specifically, to apply that knowledge in ways which elevate consciousness. Wisdom is the intelligent use of knowledge in furthering the plan of evolution.

Wisdom Religion   The core of all world religions and philosophies which yearn for truth. It is upon this Wisdom Religion that Theosophy is based.

wizard   A wise man. An adept in practical esoteric knowledge.

yoga योग   A school of philosophy founded by Patañjali, although even his treatise is based on earlier writings. The meditation practices of rāja yoga lead to contact with the soul, control of the mind, and the eventual development of seership.

yoni योनि   A symbol of the female polarity of the creative force.

yuga युग   An epoch, or era consisting of four ages, termed satya yuga, treta yuga, dvapara yuga and kali yuga.

Zarathustra or **Zoroaster**   The great teacher and lawgiver, the founder of the Zoroastrian religion, that of the Parsis in India. Zoroaster was not one individual, but a series of great teachers, as many as thirteen according to some sources. Many of their sacred texts were destroyed by Alexander the Great.

Zen   A school of Buddhism which originated in China in the 6th century AD. It spread first to Vietnam, then to Korea and Japan. Zen focuses on attaining enlightenment through meditation and through the practical application of spiritual knowledge.

Zend Avesta   The general name for the sacred scriptures of the Parsis or Zoroastrians. Zend means a commentary or explanation, and vesta means the law.

BIBLIOGRAPHY

A Brahmin. *Some Thoughts on the Gita.* Talent, OR: Eastern School Press, 1983.

Algeo, John. *Theosophy: An Introductory Study Course.* 4th ed. Wheaton, IL: The Theosophical Society in America, 2007.

Arnold, Sir Edwin. *The Light of Asia.* Philadelphia: Henry Altemus Company, 1899.

Autobiography of Alfred Percy Sinnett. London: Theosophical History Centre, 1986.

Bailey, Alice A. *A Treatise on Cosmic Fire.* New York: Lucis Publishing Company, 1962.

-------. *A Treatise on White Magic.* New York: Lucis Publishing Company, 1934.

-------. *Discipleship in the New Age, Volume One.* New York: Lucis Publishing Company, 1944.

-------. *Discipleship in the New Age, Volume Two.* New York: Lucis Publishing Company, 1955.

-------. *Esoteric Astrology.* New York: Lucis Publishing Company, 1951.

-------. *From Intellect to Intuition.* New York: Lucis Publishing Company, 1932.

-------. *Glamour: A World Problem.* New York: Lucis Publishing Company, 1950.

-------. *Initiation, Human and Solar.* New York: Lucis Publishing Company, 1951.

-------. *Reappearance of the Christ.* New York: Lucis Publishing Company, 1948.

-------. *Telepathy.* New York: Lucis Publishing Company, 1950.

-------. *The Externalisation of the Hierarchy.* New York: Lucis Publishing Company, 1957.

-------. *The Light of the Soul.* New York: Lucis Publishing Company, 1955.

-------. *The Soul and Its Mechanism.* New York: Lucis Publishing Company, 1965.

Barborka, Geoffrey A. *The Divine Plan: Written in the Form of a Commentary on H.P. Blavatsky's Secret Doctrine.* 2nd revised. ed. Adyar, Chennai, India: The Theosophical Publishing House, 1964.

-------. *The Mahatmas and their Letters.* Adyar, Chennai, India: The Theosophical Publishing House, 1973.

-------. *The Story of Human Evolution.* Adyar, Chennai, India: The Theosophical Publishing House, 1980.

Besant, Annie. *A Study in Consciousness.* Adyar, Chennai, India: The Theosophical Publishing House, 1938.

-------. *Thought Power: Its Control and Culture.* Wheaton, IL: The Theosophical Publishing House, 1995.

Besant, Annie and Charles Webster Leadbeater. *Man: Whence, How and Whither.* Adyar, Chennai, India: The Theosophical Publishing House, 1913.

-------. *Thought Forms.* Adyar, Chennai, India: The Theosophical Publishing House, 1901.

Blavatsky, Helena Petrovna. *The Key to Theosophy.* London: The Theosophy Company Ltd, 1889.

-------. *The Secret Doctrine: Volumes I and II—A Facsimile of the Original Edition of 1888.* Los Angeles: The Theosophy Company, 1964.

-------. *Theosophical Glossary.* Los Angeles: The Theosophy Company, 1973.

-------. *Transactions of the Blavatsky Lodge: Discussions on the Stanzas of the First Volume of The Secret Doctrine.* Pasadena, CA: Theosophical University Press, 1946.

Bulwer-Lytton, Edward. *Zanoni.* London: George Routledge & Sons, 1901.

Codd, Clara M. *Meditation: It's Practice and Results.* Adyar, Chennai, India: The Theosophical Publishing House, 1952.

Collins, Mabel. *The Idyll of the White Lotus.* New York: The Metaphysical Publishing Co., 1900.

Cranston, Sylvia. *HPB: The Extraordinary Life and Influence of Helena Blavatsky, Founder of the Modern Theosophical Movement.* New York: G.P. Putnam's Sons, 1993.

Das, Bhagavan. *The Science of the Emotions.* 3rd ed. Adyar, Chennai, India: Theosophical Publishing House, 1924.

Eek, Sven. *Damodar and the Pioneers of the Theosophical Movement.* Adyar, Madras, India: The Theosophical Publishing House, 1978.

Farthing, G.A. *After Death Consciousness and Processes.* San Diego, CA: Point Loma Publications, 1993.

Five Years of Theosophy: Mystical, Philosophical, Theosophical, Historical and Scientific Essays Selected from "The Theosophist." London: Reeves and Turner, 1885.

Gawain, Shakti. *Creative Visualization: Use the Power of Your Imagination to Create What You Want in Life.* Novato, CA: New World Library, 1995.

Guirdham, Arthur. *The Cathars and Reincarnation: The Record of a Past Life in Thirteenth-Century France.* Wellingborough, Northamptonshire, England: Turnstone Press Limited, 1970.

H.P. Blavatsky to the American Conventions. Pasadena, CA: Theosophical University Press, 1979.

Haich, Elisabeth. *Sexual Energy and Yoga.* New York: Aurora Press, 1982.

Hall, Manly P. *The Secret Teachings of All Ages: An Encyclopedic Outline of Masonic, Hermetic, Qabbalistic and Rosicrucian Symbolical Philosophy.* Los Angeles: The Philosophical Research Society, 1975.

-------. *Twelve World Teachers: A Summary of Their Lives and Teachings.* 3rd ed. revised. Los Angeles: Philosophical Research Society, 1973.

Hanson, Virginia. *Masters and Men: The Human Story in the Mahatma Letters: A Fictionalized Account.* Wheaton, IL: The Theosophical Publishing House, 1980.

Harrison, Vernon. *H.P. Blavatsky and the SPR: An Examination of the Hodgson Report of 1885.* Pasadena, California: Theosophical University Press, 1997.

Hints on Esoteric Theosophy. Varanasi, India: Theosophical Publishing Society, 1909.

Hodson, Geoffrey. *Reincarnation: Fact or Fallacy?* Wheaton, IL: The Theosophical Publishing House, 1967.

-------. *The Brotherhood of Angels and of Men.* London: The Theosophical Publishing House, 1927.

-------. *The Yogic Ascent to Spiritual Heights.* Manila: Stellar Books, 1991.

Incidents in the Life of Madame Blavatsky: Compiled from Information Supplied by Her Relatives and Friends, Alfred P. Sinnett, Editor. London: George Redway, 1886.

Jayakar, Pupul. *Krishnamurti.* New York: Harper and Row, 1986.

Leadbeater, Charles Webster. *Dreams.* 4th ed. Adyar, Chennai, India: The Theosophical Publishing House, 1918.

-------. *Man Visible and Invisible.* Adyar, Chennai, India: The Theosophical Publishing House, 1925.

-------. *The Astral Plane.* Adyar, Chennai, India: The Theosophical Publishing House, 1933.

-------. *The Chakras.* Adyar, Chennai, India: The Theosophical Publishing House, 1927.

-------. *The Hidden Side of Things.* Adyar, Chennai, India: The Theosophical Publishing House, 1913.

-------. *The Masters and the Path.* Chicago: The Theosophical Press, 1925.

-------. *The Monad and Other Essays upon the Higher Consciousness.* Adyar, Chennai, India: The Theosophical Publishing House, 1920.

Letters from the Masters of Wisdom, First Series. 3rd ed. (Transcribed and compiled by C. Jinarajadasa). Adyar, Chennai, India: The Theosophical Publishing House, 1945.

Letters from the Masters of the Wisdom, Second Series. (C. Jinarajadasa, editor). Chicago: The Theosophical Press, 1926.

Lévi, Eliphas. *Dogme et Rituel de la Haute Magie.* (two volumes). Paris: Editions Niclaus, 1947.

Light on the Path. (written down by M.C.) Philadelphia: David McKay Company, 1885.

Lutyens, Lady Emily. *Candles in the Sun: The Story of a Spiritual Ferment.* Philadelphia: J.B. Lippincott Company, 1957.

Māvalankar, Dāmodar K. *The Service of Humanity.* Santa Barbara, CA: Concord Grove Press, 1985.

Mills, Joy. *Reflections on an Ageless Wisdom.* Wheaton, IL: The Theosophical Publishing House, 2010.

Morehouse, David. *Remote Viewing: The Complete User's Manual for Coordinate Remote Viewing.* Boulder, CO: Sounds True, 2011.

Pagels, Elaine. *The Gnostic Gospels.* New York: Random House, 1979.

Ponder on This: A Compilation. New York: Lucis Publishing Company, 1971.

Psychiatry and Mysticism. Stanley R. Dean, editor. Chicago: Nelson-Hall, 1975.

Ruiz, Don Miguel and Don José Ruiz. *The Fifth Agreement: A Toltec Wisdom Book.* San Rafael, CA: Amber-Allen Publishing, Inc., 2010.

Sinnett, Alfred P. *Esoteric Buddhism.* (revised). London: The Theosophical Publishing House Ltd, 1972.

-------. *The Occult World, 9th edition.* London: Theosophical Publishing House London Ltd, 1969.

Stevenson, Ian. *Twenty Cases Suggestive of Reincarnation.* New York: American Society for Psychical Research, 1966.

Taimni, I.K. *Gāyatrī: The Daily Religious Practice of the Hindus.* Adyar, Chennai, India: The Theosophical Publishing House, 1978.

-------. *The Science of Yoga: The Yoga-Sūtras of Patanjali in Sanskrit with Transliteration in Roman, Translation and Commentary in English.* Adyar, Chennai, India: The Theosophical Publishing House, 1961.

The Bhagavad Gita: Introduced & Translated by Eknath Easwaran. 2nd ed. Tomales, CA: Nilgiri Press, 2007.

The Mahatma Letters to A.P. Sinnett from the Mahatmas M. & K.H. Transcribed and Compiled by A.T. Barker, arranged and edited by Vicente Hao Chin, Jr. Adyar, Chennai, India: The Theosophical Publishing House, 1998.

The Voice of the Silence. (translated and annotated by H.P. Blavatsky). Wheaton, IL: The Theosophical Publishing House, 1992.

Tolle, Eckhart. *A New Earth: Awakening to Your Life's Purpose.* New York: The Penguin Group, 2005.

-------. *The Power of Now: A Guide to Spiritual Enlightenment.* Novato, CA: New World Library, 1997.

Wood, Ernest. *The Occult Training of the Hindus.* 2nd ed. Adyar, Chennai, India: Ganesh & Company, 1952.

Yogi Ramacharaka. *The Spirit of the Upanishads.* Chicago: The Yogi Publication Society, 1907.

INDEX

eating, 321, 326
Ecclesiastes, 62
ego. See personal ego
Einstein, Albert, 30, 241
electricity, 209
emotions
  compound, 252, 258
  control of, 64, 250–52
  dissipation after death, 64
  God and, 121–22
  grief and sadness, 266–68
  joy *versus* happiness, 269–70
  kāma-manas and, 42
  as level of consciousness, 49
  love and happiness, 261-63, 265–67
  meditations and, 200–201
  power of, 248–50
  pride, 286
  thoughts and, 145–46, 246–47
  vibrational frequencies of, 216
  worry, 281–87
"end justifies the means," 311
energy
  after death, 64
  field, 129
  flowing from thought, 189, 193
  law of attraction and, 316
enjoyment, 76
enlightenment
  as expanded conscious-ness, 39–45
  as goal, 29

as not final, 306–7
  religious teachings and, 206
eternal life, 218–19
eternal progression, 47
etheric plane/realm/state, 108
ethics, 311–14
ethnic groups, 152–53
Eve, 110, 304
evil, 106, 117–21
evolution
  of consciousness, 16–19
  early human, 109–117, 303–8
  Kaballah on, 14
  of mind, 74–75
  physical, 16–19
  of plants, 9–11
exaggeration, 313
existence, planes or states of, 30
experience
  absorbed by Higher Self, 66
  gained in many forms, 73–74
  human, 21–32
  of prodigal son, 3–7
  reality and, 247–48
  remaining after lifetime, 58

failure, 74, 91, 293
fairness, 131–32
faith, 35–38
families, 148, 166
fasting, 325–27
"final judgment," 67
forms, 16, 43, 51

freedom, 125
free will, 15–16, 110
future
    as not existing, 185–88
    science of, 108

Garden of Eden, 110, 267
Gautama Buddha, 29
gender, 303–4
Genesis, 101, 110
genius, 60
giving, 327–28
Gnosticism, 206
God
    concept of, 105–7, 115–16,
        119–21
    emotion and, 121–22
    evil, suffering and, 106
    nature of, 105–125
    personal, 122–24
gong, 212
gravity, 312
Great Architect, 155–56
Greek mythology, 25
grief, 266–67
group karma, 147–54
groups, belonging to, 13–14

habit, worry as, 283
happiness
    joy *versus,* 269–70
    as temporary, 25–26
hatha yoga, 206
heart chakra, 281
higher mind, 43, 203
Higher Self. See *also* soul

alignment with, 41, 217–18
clairvoyance and, 181
experience absorbed by, 66
messages from, 84
as sexless, 295–96
as soul, 57
struggle with personality,
    49–50, 94, 291–92
homosexuality, 300–2
honesty, 26–28, 308–310
human beings
    advanced beings as, 80–81
    animal nature and, 15–16,
        296
    constitution of, 26, 31, **32,
        33**
    dual nature of, 123
    early development of, 109–
        117, 303–8
    goal as, 73–81
    guided by Spiritual Hier-
        archy, 112
    life cycle of, 159–71
    spiritual growth of, 79
    spiritually advanced, 78, 80
human kingdom, 47
human life cycles
    first twenty-five years, 161–
        64
    second twenty-five years,
        164–66
    seven-year cycles, 170–71
    third twenty-five years,
        166–70
humor, 90
hypnosis, 214

393

Lévi, Eliphas, 35, 292
life review, 179
lightning, 208
Light of the Soul, The (Bailey),
  189
lion, 246,298
Logos (Word), 102, 190
Lord of the World, 120
Lord's Prayer, 323
"lose one's soul," 66–67
love, 221, 261–63, 265–67
lower mind, 190
lower nature, 123

Machado, Antonio, 329
magic toy, 21–24, 240
Mahāchohans, 120
Mahātmas, 82–86. See *also*
  Adepts; Spiritual Hierarchy
manas (mind), 30, 43, 145,
  203
Manus, 120
Masters and the Path, The
  (Leadbeater), 322
material world, 49
Matrix, The (film), 108
matter, 28–29, 31, **32**
māyā (illusion), 184
medication, 288
meditation
  advanced beings and, 80
  effects of, 200–201
  enlightenment and, 206
  goal of, 189, 216
  "monkey mind" in, 193
  practice of, 197, 221–22
  preparation for, 200

samādhi and, 229–30
schedule for, 320–21
as spiritual practice, 198–
  203
as state of being, 200
mediumship, 181, 256
memory
  of past lives, 173
  as unreliable, 175–78, 180–
    81
mental plane/realm/state,
  191
mesmerism, 214
messages from Adepts, 83, 87
migrations, 7–8
mind. See *also* manas
  control over, 145–46
  as evolving, 74
  existing at all levels, 190
  realm of higher, 43–44
mindfulness, 286
mineral kingdom, 8–9
Minority Report, The (film),
  108
monad, 47, 120, 154
monarchies, 109
monastic life, 78–79
"monkey mind," 193, 202–4
Mother Teresa, 207
motivation
  in actions, 245
  of advanced humans, 78
  purity of, 146–47
  spiritual path and, 89
  suffering as, 295
music, 212
mystics, 78–79

meditation
affirmations, 322–24
basis for, 320–21
center of the universe
    exercise, 222
consistency in, 202
everyone can read my
    thoughts practice, 234–
    35, 307–8
fasting, 325–27
giving, 327–28
journal in, 224–25
nature walk, 225–27
quiet time in, 320
spiritual journal, 224–25
stewardship, 327
tree connection exercise,
    223–24
ultra-slow motion, 227–28
vegetarianism, 324–25
visualization, 228–34
spiritual practices, 198–99
spiritual science, 98, 305
starfish, 276–81
states of being, devachan as,
    71
stewardship, 101, 327
"still, small voice," 87
study, as spiritual practice,
    198–99
suffering, 106, 295
Sufism, 206
sun, 121
super-consciousness, 215–16
sushupti (unconsciousness),
    213
svapna (semi-consciousness),
213–14

Tantra, 209
teaching, 164–66
teachings, 244
telepathy, 307
*The Mahatma Letters to A. P
    Sinnett* , 97
theodicy, 106
third eye, 108
Thoreau, Henry David, 91
thought-forms, 140, 144, 316
thoughts
    concrete and abstract, 190
    control of, 192–93, 228–29
    as creative force, 102–3,
        189–90
    as energy pattern, 193
    everyone can read my, 234–
        35, 307–8
    frequency and strength of,
        193–94
    law of attraction and, 316
    "monkey mind," 202–4
    power of, 246–47
    result of, 128–29
Timaeus (Plato), 113
time, as single point, 182
transformation, 8, 14–15, 37
tree connection exercise, 223–
    24
trials on spiritual path, 293
truth, 35–39

ultra-slow motion, 227–28
unconsciousness, 213
underworld, 25

CPSIA information can be obtained at www.ICGtesting.com
Printed in the USA
BVOW02*1013010813

326999BV00001B/1/P